Birder's guide to

TEXAS

Second Edition

Gulf Publishing Company
A Member of the Rowman & Littlefield Publishing Group
Lanham • New York • Oxford

Birder's guide to

TEXAS

Second Edition

- Packed with maps and detailed directions
- More than 250 locations statewide
- 606 species

Edward A. Kutac

Birder's Guide to Texas, 2nd Edition

This book was originally published in 1982 as *Texas Birds: Where They Are and How to Find Them.*

Gulf Publishing Company
A Member of the Rowman & Littlefield Publishing Group
4720 Boston Way
Lanham, Maryland 20706

Distributed by NATIONAL BOOK NETWORK

Library of Congress Cataloging-in-Publication Data

Kutac, Edward A.
    Birder's guide to Texas / Edward A. Kutac ; illustrations by
Judy Teague. — 2nd ed.
       p. cm.
    Includes bibliographical references and index.
    ISBN 0-88415-551-X (alk. paper)
    1. Birdwatching—Texas—Guidebooks. 2. Texas—
Guidebooks. I. Title.
  QL684.T4K875   1998
  598'.07'234764—dc21   97-42011
                                             CIP

Region maps by David T. Price, Paige Stevens Holsapple, and Senta Eva Rivera.

To the women in my life—

Albina, my mother, for being everything a mother
should be and more.

Amy, my wife, for 50 wonderful years;
I am hoping for 50 more.

Mary, Anne, and Lucy Kay, my daughters,
who have made fatherhood a great
adventure and totally stimulating
experience.

Contents

Colorado Bend State Park, 104. Kerrville, 106. Kerrville-Schreiner State Park, 108. Lost Maples State Natural Area, 109. Uvalde, 111. Garner State Park, 111. Junction, 114. South Llano River State Park and Walter Buck WMA, 114. Seminole Canyon State Historical Park, 116.

Hagerman NWR, 120. Eisenhower State Park, 124. Heard Natural Science Museum and Wildlife Sanctuary, 124. Dallas, 126. Cedar Hill State Park, 136. Elm Fork Nature Preserve, Carrollton, 136. Lake Tawakoni, 137. Cooper, 140. Cooper Lake State Park, 140. Fort Worth, 142. Arlington and Eastern Tarrant County, 151. Dinosaur Valley State Park, 154. Waco, 156. Meridian State Park, 167. Mexia, 168. Alcoa Lake, 170. Bryan–College Station, 171. Lake Somerville, 173. Lake Somerville State Park, 174. Bastrop and Buescher State Parks, 174. Lake Bastrop, 175. Palmetto State Park, 176. McKinney Falls State Park, 177.

Northeast Texas, 181. Atlanta State Park, 184. Caddo Lake State Park and WMA, 185. Daingerfield State Park, 186. Lake Bob Sandlin State Park, 186. Nacogdoches, 188. Huntsville, 193. Huntsville State Park, 193. Lake Livingston, 198. Lake Livingston State Park, 199. W. G. Jones State Forest, 200. Martin Dies, Jr. State Park, 201. Big Thicket National Preserve, 203. Roy E. Larsen Sandyland Sanctuary, 208. John K. Kirby State Forest, 208. Village Creek State Park, 208.

Beaumont, 212. Sabine Pass Battleground State Historical Park, 212. McFaddin and Texas Point NWRs, 216. Sea Rim State Park, 218. Anahuac NWR, 220.

Acknowledgments

As always, a book of this kind is impossible without a lot of assistance. Every person who has contributed to the regional checklists of Texas birds (particularly the compilers) and all Christmas Count participants have made a direct contribution. The many friends who have traveled around the state with me (they know who they are), local birders who have led or accompanied field trips I have participated in, the Texas Ornithological Society members who have hosted and helped with the 54 meetings in 46 different Texas locations I have attended, and the authors mentioned in the Selected References have all enhanced my Texas bird experiences and kept my interest and curiosity level high through the years. The birders are greater than the birds.

Responses to requests for updated information from the National Park Service, United States Fish and Wildlife Service, United States Forest Service, U.S. Army Corps of Engineers, Texas Parks and Wildlife Department, Texas Department of Highways and Public Transportation, Colorado River Municipal Water District, Lower Colorado River Authority, Titus County Fresh Water Supply District No. 1, and Houston Audubon Society have been prompt and courteous.

I am very grateful to the following individuals for their direct contribution to this edition: Dr. Keith A. Arnold, Ray Berry, Lorie D. Black, David Brotherton, Fred Collins, Rosalie Cutrer, Victor Czaja, David Dauphin, Jennifer DeLeon, Brush Freeman, Jim Gallagher, Dr. William Graber III, Richard Grant, John W. Hall, David Haukos, Carl Haynie, Dick Heller, Gayle Jackson, John Kelly, Gregory W. Lasley, Carol Levine, Mark Lockwood, Melvin G. Maxwell, Dorothy Metzler, Martha Micks, Dr. Ralph R. Moldenhauer, June Osborne, Paul C. Palmer, Dr. Dwight Peake, Terry A. Rossignol, Steve R. Runnels, Rod Rylander, Hart R. Schwarz, Willie Sekula, Charles Sexton, Kenneth D. Seyffert, Pat Simmons, Cliff Stogner, Dr. Delbert G. Tarter, Sue Wiedenfeld, Matt White, Frances Williams, J. M. Williams, David Wolf, and Barry R. Zimmer. Persons who contributed indirectly by providing input in prior printings are as follows: Peggy Acord, Thomas R. Albert, Alma Barrera, Sharon Bartels, Ronald G. Bisbee, Gene W. Blacklock, Margaret Broday, Kelly Bryan, Domenick R. Ciccone, Russell Clapper, Charles Clark, Robert C. Coggeshall, Sue M. Corson, Charles Crabtree, Maurice and Esther Crawford, Richard Cudworth, Wesley Cureton, David D. Donatchik, Dr. Charles Dean Fisher, Tony Gallucci, Karl W. Haller, Vernon H. Hayes, Kelly Himmel, Joe Ideker, Barry A. Jones, Edgar B. Kincaid, Jr., Donald McDonald, Deanna Metcalf, James Middleton, Ernest and Kay Mueller, Derek A. Muschalek, Margaret Parker, Royce Pendergast, Charles Potter, Thomas Prusa, Midge Randolph, Barbara Ribble, David Riskind, Wayne Shifflett, Jessie May Smith, Judy Teague, Dan Watson, Clarence C. Wiedenfeld, and Kevin J. Zimmer. Needless to say, I made the final decisions and therefore take responsibility for any errors or omissions.

I would be remiss if I did not extend my gratitude to Lucy Kay Jalbert for rescuing me when I bogged down with various computer programs and procedures. Special thanks are due Gregory W. Lasley, who read the entire manuscript and made many valuable suggestions. Also, he has kept me current with the list of birds accepted by the Texas Bird Records Committee in his capacity as secretary of the committee. In my opinion, Greg is currently the most knowledgeable student of the Texas avifauna.

Thanks are also due the entire staff at Gulf Publishing Company for their usual counsel and assistance.

Finally, thanks to my wife, Amy, for her understanding and support for over one-half of a century.

Foreword

The state of Texas is like a country within a country, an area so vast that it can boast the largest avifauna of any of the 50 states, exceeding by a wide margin even California. East meets West, faunally, in mid-state, and formerly those bird-watchers who lived near the center line—Fort Worth, Dallas, Waco, Austin, San Antonio and Brownsville—had to carry into the field both my eastern *Field Guide* and the western *Field Guide.* This changed when the Texas Fish and Game Commission prevailed upon me to put things into one book, just for Texas. Indeed, to this day, Texas is the only state with its own *Peterson Field Guide.*

It was inevitable that still another kind of guide was needed, a directory, or sort of *Baedeker,* which would tell the birder where to look for birds and what species to expect. The field observer of today is mobile, and in an area as large as Texas it saves time to know the key places or "hot-spots." Olin Sewall Pettingill's *Bird Finding West of the Mississippi,* first published in 1953, filled the niche for a number of years, but inasmuch as only a limited number of pages could be devoted to any one of the 22 states west of the Mississippi, local guide books soon proliferated. At least four such regional directories were produced for various sections of Texas by Lane, Kutac, and others.

This book by Ed Kutac is the first to cover the entire state in one volume in a comprehensive way. The author, who has been president of the Texas Ornithological Society and intimately involved with other bird-oriented groups in the state, is familiar with virtually all of the sites described in these pages.

Nearly 800 miles from top to bottom or from east to west and covering some 267,000 square miles, Texas can claim diversity by virtue of size alone, and even more significant than the size in determining its rich avifauna is the state's location on the continent. East meets West, biologically, along the 100th meridian, and North meets South, especially along the Rio Grande, where birds from the northern plains meet Mexican types. Altitudes range from sea level along the Gulf to 8,000 feet in the Trans-Pecos; rainfall varies from a wet 50-plus inches on the Louisiana border to less than 10 inches in the extreme west.

Truly, Texas is the state above all others that offers the most lively birding, a factor that is now luring binocular-toting tourists from the rest of the United States, especially during spring migration when massive "fall outs" of migrants along the Gulf Coast must be seen to be believed. The varied avifauna of Texas has attracted so many people from out-of-state that several travel agencies have found it profitable to schedule special tours for birders.

Some birders enjoy group companionship or competition with their friends; others prefer to be on their own or with their spouses. It is for both of these groups of bird-watchers that this book has been prepared.

Roger Tory Peterson

About the Author

E dward A. Kutac is a native Texan with a keen interest in his state's natural history, in particular its birds, plants, and geology. He is a past president of the Texas Ornithological Society and the Travis Audubon Society and a past treasurer of The Nature Conservancy (Texas Chapter). He has taught bird identification classes since 1977 for many groups, including students at Austin Community College and Amarillo College. Kutac is the co-author of *Birds and Other Wildlife of South Central Texas.*

Introduction

This book is to provide visitors and newcomers to Texas a list of places for finding birds in the state. All of the larger cities (each with several locations), all National Parks, all National Recreation Areas, all National Wildlife Refuges, numerous State Parks, and many other spots are included.

The current Rare Bird Alert numbers in Texas are as follows:

Texas and Upper Texas Coast	(713) 964-5867
Abilene	(915) 691-8981
Austin	(512) 926-8751
Corpus Christi	(512) 265-0377
Lubbock	(806) 797-6690
North Texas (Dallas, Fort Worth, McKinney)	(817) 237-3209
Northeast Texas	(903) 234-2473
Rio Grande Valley	(956) 969-2731
San Antonio	(210) 308-6788

New birding locations in this third edition are Alcoa Lake; Arlington and Eastern Tarrant County (5 locations); Balcones Canyonlands National Wildlife Refuge; Baytown Nature Center; Big Bend Ranch State Park; Bryan–College Station (3 locations); Candy Cain Abshier Wildlife Management Area; Cedar Hill State Park; Chaparral Wildlife Management Area; Colorado Bend State Park; Cooper (2 locations); Junction (2 locations); Laredo (2 locations); Port Lavaca (5 locations); and Uvalde (2 locations). In addition, 25 other birding places have been added and 12 have been deleted. Altogether, about 290 bird locations are included.

Birds have increasingly become a means of encouraging tourism in Texas by governmental agencies and local organizations such as chambers of commerce. The Great Texas Birding Trail mentioned in the introduction to Chapter 7 is an example, plus birding festivals that have occurred in recent years, such as the Eagle Fest, Emory, January; Whooping Crane/Winter Bird Fest, Port Aransas, February; Cranefest, Big Spring, February; Attwater's Prairie-Chicken Festival, Eagle Lake, March; Southern Brazoria County Migration Celebration, Lake Jackson, April; Texas Tropics Nature Festival, McAllen, April; Bluebird Festival, Wills Point, April; Hummer/Bird Celebration, Rockport/Fulton, September; and Rio Grande Valley Birding Festival, Harlingen, November.

In 1997 the first annual Great Texas Birding Classic, sponsored by Texas Parks and Wildlife Department, Partners in Flight, and Texas Audubon Society, was held with 27 teams of up to 4 birders each competing to see which team could record the most bird species in 3 days along the Texas Gulf Coast during the week beginning April 20th. The winning team found 298 species; the composite total for all teams was 357 different species. Grand prize was $50,000 for avian habitat conservation projects designated by the winners.

Habitat and Diversity

Texans are known to boast about how everything in Texas is bigger and better than anywhere else. In the case of birds, the boasting is justified. Texas has more bird species recorded within its borders than any other state. Appendix 1 in this book lists 606 species that have been accepted by the Texas Bird Records Committee of the Texas Ornithological Society, along with another 13 species on the presumptive list. There are several reasons for this large diversity.

Texas is big—after Alaska, the largest state—with 267,000 square miles: 821 miles from Texarkana in the northeast corner to El Paso in the far west, 908 miles from Texline in the extreme northwest to Brownsville at the southern tip. In between are mountains, desert, pine and hardwood forests, prairies, numerous man-made lakes and farm ponds, extensive farm and ranch lands, the 367-mile coastline of the Gulf of Mexico, barrier islands, estuaries, and the subtropical Lower Rio Grande Valley. Average rainfall varies from 8 inches per year at El Paso to more than 50 inches on the eastern border. The land surface in Texas rises from sea level on the coast northwestward to more than 4,000 feet in the northern Panhandle. In the Trans-Pecos there are at least 20 peaks of more than 7,000 feet. Average frost-free days vary from 178 at Dalhart to 341 at Brownsville.

The location of the state in the middle of the North American continent means most migrants of the Mississippi, Central, and Rocky Mountain Flyways pass through some part of the state in spring and fall. In spring many trans-Gulf migrants make landfall along the coast. Add to this number the oceanic birds found in the Gulf, along with strays blown in by Gulf storms (hurricanes), and an impressive total is achieved.

For the purposes of this book, Texas is divided into eight regions: Llano Estacado, Trans-Pecos, Rolling Plains, Edwards Plateau, Central Texas, Pineywoods, Gulf Coast, and South Texas. Some of the regions are divided on the basis of their geology, some on their vegetation, and some are arbitrary and convenient. In some cases the boundary between regions is sharply defined and can be easily recognized, while in others the transition is indistinct and may be many miles wide.

I have personally visited and looked for birds in about 80% of the 290 or so locations listed in this book. Of course, Texas is too big for anyone to visit all areas in all seasons; therefore, my experience has been augmented by that of the collaborators named in the Acknowledgments. Local checklists and Christmas Count data have been used extensively to determine abundance, nesting, and other information.

Birds that commonly nest in all eight regions are Turkey Vulture, Killdeer, Mourning Dove, Yellow-billed Cuckoo, Common Nighthawk, Scissor-tailed Flycatcher, Tufted Titmouse, Northern Mockingbird, Eastern Meadowlark, Red-winged Blackbird, Brown-headed Cowbird, Northern Cardinal, Painted Bunting, Blue Grosbeak, Lark Sparrow, Rock Dove, European Starling,

and House Sparrow. It is noteworthy that the last three are introduced birds. Nesting species common in all but one area are
Green Heron (uncommon in the Llano Estacado), Northern Bobwhite, Carolina Chickadee, Chimney Swift (not in the Trans-
Pecos), Great-tailed Grackle, and Bewick's Wren (not in the
Pineywoods). These 24 species will be minimized in the location
accounts, since all are easily found.

The same can be said for wintering birds. A total of 377
species were found on the 77 Christmas Counts conducted
throughout the state in December 1995, and January 1996. Sev-
enty-six species were found in all 8 regions as defined for this
work, and 87 species were recorded in only one region. My esti-
mate of the most widespread of the 76 species is as follows: Pied-
billed Grebe, Great Blue Heron, Mallard, Northern Harrier, Red-
tailed Hawk, American Kestrel, American Coot, Killdeer, Rock
Dove, Mourning Dove, Belted Kingfisher, Ruby-crowned
Kinglet, American Robin, Northern Mockingbird, Loggerhead
Shrike, Orange-crowned Warbler, Yellow-rumped Warbler,
Northern Cardinal, Field Sparrow, Savannah Sparrow, Song
Sparrow, White-crowned Sparrow, Dark-eyed Junco, Red-winged
Blackbird, Brown-headed Cowbird, and House Sparrow.

What does all this mean? It means that if one wants to see most
of the birds in Texas, a lot of travel is required. It will be necessary to climb some mountains, tromp through some marshes, take
a few boat trips into the Gulf of Mexico, and otherwise cover the
wide variety of habitats in the state during different seasons.

National, state, county, and city parks, National Wildlife
Refuges, and other preserves protect many unique areas of the
state, many of which are described in the appropriate sections;
however, only about 2.6% of the land in the state is publicly
owned or managed. Approximately 27% of this public acreage is
in the Trans-Pecos region. Latest figures available show that
Texas Parks and Wildlife Department and the U.S. Department of
Interior own or manage about 60% of the publicly-owned land in

Texas. If many forms of wildlife are to survive, the understanding and cooperation of private landowners is imperative.

It is assumed the reader knows something about bird identification, or "birding" as the hobby or sport of looking for birds has come to be known, and wants to know some places in Texas where certain birds can be found. If learning to identify Texas birds is what is desired, the reader is referred to *A Field Guide to the Birds of Texas* by Roger Tory Peterson, *Birds of North America: A Guide to Field Identification* by Robbins et al., and/or the National Geographic Society's *Field Guide to the Birds of North America*. At least one of these is indispensable in the field; all three are better. In addition, all serious Texas bird students should have in their libraries the two-volume *The Bird Life of Texas* by Oberholser and Kincaid, an encyclopedic treatment of the avifauna of the state. There are also many other fine guides and books that can be obtained, depending on one's interest and financial resources.

Electronics

Available technology has always played a part in the study and enjoyment of birds. Development of guns to collect birds, modern field guides, light collection and refraction advancements in optics, mist nets to study bird movements, vast improvements in transport time, and speed of communications all serve to aid in the study of birds and to transform bird watching into the sport or hobby of birding.

Today, we are in an electronic age with the Internet and electronic mail (e-mail). Schools, professional ornithologists, ornithological organizations, bird organizations, and bird enthusiasts have developed home pages dedicated to all forms of bird information. Volumes of data from every part of the world are instantly accessible to anyone with a computer, modem, and Internet service provider.

The Internet can provide information on planning trips, learning about specific birds, the location of rare birds, or likely any other information one could want. One home page, dedicated to Hummingbirds, provides an example of the gap being bridged between professionals and non-professionals. The page contains individual species maps listing sightings of Hummingbirds as they migrate north in spring and south in fall. The visual image of migration progression is simply astounding and is provided by individual birders communicating their sightings to one central resource using the new computer resources of the Internet.

E-mail, devised originally in 1972 and the most popular feature of the World Wide Web, provides almost immediate linkage to birders of all abilities who have Internet access. Birders can send personal communications to individuals, or they can subscribe to e-mail list servers. E-mail list servers distribute individual contributions, queries, answers, rare bird sightings, technical articles, or personal musings to large numbers of list subscribers with the push of a button. The sender types one message, then sends it to the master e-mail address for the list server. The server then resends the original message to everyone who has subscribed to that particular list. Another example of what is possible is when a rare bird is found at a location on the Gulf Coast. The finder quickly types it up on a personal portable computer, hooks the computer to his cellular phone, and transmits an e-mail message to the "Texas Audubon" list server, instantly sharing the rare bird with over 400 e-mail recipients. Should the finder have a digital camera, it would be possible to document the find with the Texas Bird Records Committee on the spot, transferring an electronic image to the committee's e-mail address.

Internet access and e-mail capability provide an endless source of entertainment for persons interested in birds. The World Wide Web, e-mail, list servers, and home pages will provide a positive influence on the world of birding and will become a requirement for birders of the twenty-first century.

Nomenclature

Bird names used herein follow the *Check-list of North American Birds, Sixth Edition,* 1983, American Ornithologists' Union, as amended through the Forty-first Supplement, 1997. The Committee on Nomenclature and Classification of the American Ornithologists' Union, the compiler of the checklist, updates the list from time to time when research determines the need for such changes. Species are "lumped" (combined with other species formerly considered separate) and "split" (a species divided into two or more previously considered one). Names are changed to achieve international uniformity and for other reasons.

This list is the most widely accepted authority for scientific and English names and is used in the vast majority of field guides, checklists, publications, etc. It would be helpful if the A.O.U. committee would issue supplements at known five-year intervals and a new checklist every 25 years. If nomenclature change time is known, the publication of guides and checklists could be timed to help prevent releasing a publication with names that become obsolete soon after printing.

Local Checklists

In doing a work of this kind, a fact that quickly becomes apparent is the wide diversity of opinion as to the makeup of a bird checklist. For what it is worth I recommend the following: (1) The main body of a checklist should only list recent records, e.g., birds recorded in the last 10 or 15 years. Historical records should be listed separately. (2) Abundance symbols should indicate probability of finding rather than population numbers. Presently, what is common in one checklist can mean something entirely different in another. For example, I think *Abundant* should mean a bird that is widespread and easy to find regardless of the degree of observer competence; *Common,* not so widespread but relatively easy to find; *Uncommon,* present but limited in occurrence or requires experience or a higher degree of competence; *Rare,* occurs with a degree of regularity but not expected; *Accidental,* has been recorded but is not expected, etc. (3) A checklist for an area, such as a one-hour drive from a central location, is much preferred over one based on a political boundary, such as a park or a county. (4) A symbol, such as an asterisk (*) should be used for nesting species. (5) Some checklists try to convey too much information with many symbols for every type situation—simpler is better.

Checklists with bar charts should be the goal of all checklist preparers. For those checklists where data is not sufficient for bar charts, the symbols used can also be standardized, e.g., PR—Permanent Resident; SR—Summer Resident; WR—Winter Resident; SM—Spring Migrant; FM—Fall Migrant; X—Accidental. I think terms like Casual, Sporadic, etc., are appropriate for annotated checklists and field guides, but Accidental can mean all these things on a checklist.

In short, checklists should be easy to use and understand.

Additional Notes

No one should assume that the locations included herein are all the places to look for birds in Texas or that the ones mentioned are even the best places. All habitats are presented, and most of the best public places are included. Some species are most easily found from public roads or on private property, both of which have been minimized here. For example, Barn Swallows are found nesting under highway culverts and bridges in nearly all regions. Information about roads, trails, and access is that known at the time of publication and should be taken as a general guide. Over time, with habitat modification for urbanization, industrialization, agriculture, and increased preservation through new parks and refuge additions, etc., some changes are inevitable. Some species are aided by these changes and prosper; some suffer and decline. This fluctuation is one of the interesting aspects of bird study.

Also, no attempt has been made to list every bird, whether common or rare, for any particular location, but rather a sampling of what might be expected or has been found in the past.

Edward A. Kutac

Regions of Texas

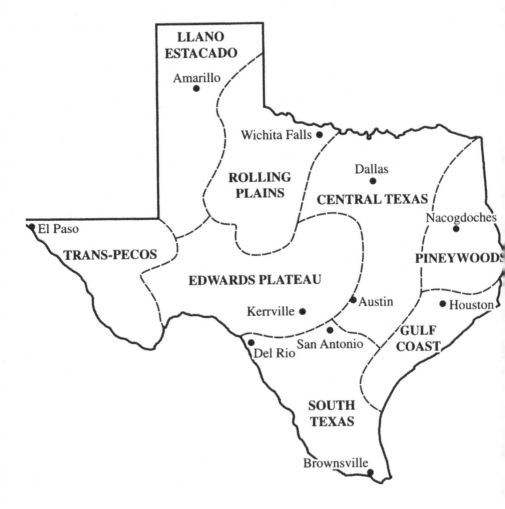

1

Llano Estacado

The Llano Estacado region, also known as the Southern High Plains or Staked Plains, is the northwest part of the state and covers about 12% of Texas. The region, thought by the average traveler passing through to be a flat, featureless plain, actually rises in elevation about 2,000 feet from south to north and from east to west. The area contains about 20,000 shallow depressions,

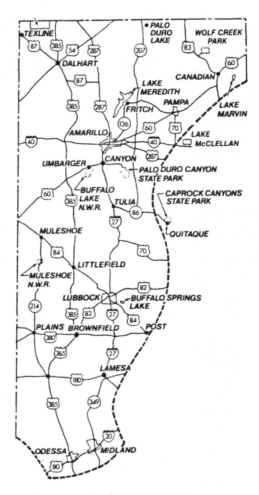

LLANO ESTACADO

known as playas. The boundary on the east is the Caprock Escarpment, a dramatic elevational change from the Rolling Plains. It extends irregularly south to north from near Big Spring to east of Lubbock and Amarillo, then northeastward to the northeast corner of the Panhandle. The Mescalero Escarpment on the southwest marks the boundary between the Llano Estacado and the Trans-Pecos. There is no topographic division between the Llano

Estacado and the Edwards Plateau, but in this book the division is arbitrarily located just south of Odessa and Midland.

The region marks the southern end of the Great Plains that extend north into Canada. Just east of the Caprock Escarpment and west of the Rolling Plains is an area with deeply dissected canyons that could be considered a subregion of either the Llano Estacado or the Rolling Plains. The steep slopes, thin soil, and sheltered canyons support redberry and Rocky Mountain junipers and many brush species not common either east or west. Palo Duro Canyon State Park, Caprock Canyons State Park, and the "Canadian Breaks," the area adjacent to the Canadian River, are representative of this subregion. For convenience this area is included with the Llano Estacado in this book.

Formerly short-grass prairies, the Llano Estacado is now extensively devoted to farming, much of it irrigated from deep wells. The playas, depressions with no outlet to the sea, collect rainwater, which is very important to wildlife, especially wintering waterfowl. Some are large and almost permanent. The few drainages and stream crossings have cottonwoods, soapberry, and hackberries as the dominant woody plants. The soils are derived mostly from Tertiary outwash deposits from the Rocky Mountains of New Mexico.

Nesting birds include Lesser Prairie-Chicken, Long-billed Curlew, Ferruginous Hawk, Scaled Quail, Mississippi Kite, Swainson's Hawk, American Avocet, Burrowing Owl, Horned Lark, and Western Meadowlark.

Lesser Prairie-Chicken are found in the sandhills of Cochran, Hockley, Terry and Yoakum counties near the New Mexico border, and in Lipscomb, Hemphill, and Wheeler counties near the Oklahoma border. All are on private property. Pronghorn (antelope) are found in the Panhandle north and west of Amarillo, as well as in the sandhills.

There are many feedlots in the Llano Estacado. Ring-necked Pheasant year round, Brewer's Blackbird in winter, and other birds are often found at or near the feedlots.

BURROWING OWLS

AMARILLO

Amarillo, population 168,000, is centrally located for bird seeking in the Texas Panhandle, as the upper part of the Llano Estacado is known. Ranching predominates north of Amarillo, while farming is more common between Amarillo and Lubbock.

The principal birding locations of the area are Palo Duro Canyon State Park, 20 miles south; Caprock Canyons State Park, 95 miles south; Buffalo Lake National Wildlife Refuge, 23 miles southwest; Lake Meredith National Recreation Area, 38 miles north; and Rita Blanca National Grassland, 120 miles northwest of Amarillo.

It is not necessary to go very far to find nesting Mississippi Kites. They can usually be found in summer at nearly every golf-course and wooded park in Amarillo, particularly in Thompson Municipal Park, which contains 583 acres. The park is north of downtown at 24th Street and US 87-287, and is a very reliable

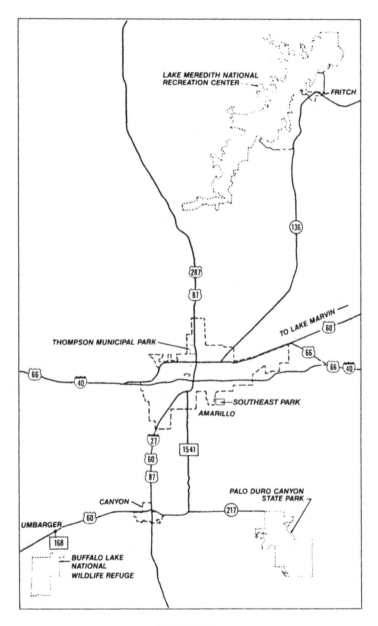

AMARILLO

spot. In winter look for waterfowl on the lakes. American Robin also nest in the park. Southeast Park, 337 acres, located at the intersection of 46th Street and Osage, is another good winter waterfowl location. The small wooded area north of the lake should be checked for migrating passerines.

In addition to the principal areas mentioned, there are a few smaller Panhandle sites that can be well worth a visit.

Lake Marvin, part of the Black Kettle National Grassland, is only about 10 miles west of the Oklahoma state line. From Amarillo drive northeast 97 miles on US 60 to Canadian, then 2 miles north on US 60-83, then east 12 miles on FM 2266. The lake was constructed for soil conservation, flood control, recreation, and the promotion of wildlife. The park is administered by Black Kettle National Grasslands, Route 1, Box 55-B, Cheyenne, OK, 73628, (405) 497-2143. Facilities such as cabins and restrooms are available for camping, picnicking, and fishing. There is an entrance fee. Many Eastern species are near their western nesting limit in Texas, including Wood Duck, Least Tern, Barred Owl, Great Crested Flycatcher, Carolina Wren, Field Sparrow, Baltimore Oriole, and American Goldfinch. Lake Marvin has been a reliable winter location for American Tree and Harris' Sparrows along with numerous waterfowl, most abundantly Canada Goose. Eurasian Wigeon and Tundra Swan have been found in recent years. Lesser Prairie-Chicken are also present in the surrounding area, but, again, most are found on private land. During April, the "booming" of the males can lead to the places where the chickens carry on their mating rituals.

Lake McClellan Recreation Area, located about 60 miles east of Amarillo, is also part of the Black Kettle National Grasslands (address above). The purpose of the lake is the same as Lake Marvin. Camping, picnicking, restrooms, open shelters, fishing, and a small store are available. There is an entrance fee. From Amarillo drive east on I-40 for 60 miles to FM 2477 (Exit 128), then go north 3 miles to the park entrance. The park is below the Caprock

Escarpment. Eastern and western species meet here: Red-bellied and Golden-fronted Woodpeckers, Bullock's and Baltimore Orioles, Downy, Hairy, and Ladder-backed Woodpeckers, Eastern and Western Kingbirds, Great Crested and Ash-throated Flycatchers, Eastern and Western Meadowlarks. House Wren and Warbling Vireo are common nesting species. In winter, the small lake attracts Bald Eagle as well as most of the typical waterfowl of the Panhandle. Rarities for this part of Texas include Tricolored Heron and Carolina Wren.

Wolf Creek Park, operated by Ochiltree County, southeast of Perryton, has produced some interesting birds. Perryton is about 120 miles northeast of Amarillo. To reach Wolf Creek Park drive south from Perryton on US 83 about 13 miles, then east on the county road about 5 miles to the park entrance. Lake Fryer, in the middle of the park, was built for the same purposes as Lake Marvin. Facilities are available for camping, picnicking, swimming, and fishing, and there are restrooms and a grocery store. There is an entrance fee. The heavily wooded valley along Wolf Creek contrasts sharply with the typical High Plains habitat surrounding it. Nesting species include Mississippi Kite, Carolina Chickadee, Northern Rough-winged Swallow, and House Wren. In winter American Tree and Harris' Sparrows may be found. On at least one occasion a Common Redpoll was found feeding with a flock of American Goldfinches.

Palo Duro Lake, 2,413 surface acres, is owned and operated by the Palo Duro River Authority. Created by a dam on Palo Duro Creek, the lake will supply water to five cities. The office is located about 10 miles north of Spearman on FM 760 in Hansford County. Visitors should check with the office about road conditions, which depend on the lake level.

The area has the northernmost nesting area for Double-crested Cormorant in Texas. In addition to the cormorants, nesting species include Great Blue Heron, Yellow-billed Cuckoo, Red-headed and Ladder-backed Woodpeckers, Western and Eastern Kingbirds, and

Orchard and Bullock's Orioles. The areas along the streams feeding the lake, as well as the area below the dam, offer ample opportunities for arboreal birds. Winter records include Common Merganser, Bald Eagle, Red Crossbill, sparrows, etc.

There are picnic tables and shelters, camping areas, and restrooms.

Lakes and Playas

Canada, Snow and Ross' Geese, along with Northern Pintail, Mallard, and American Wigeon, winter in the Panhandle in great numbers. Any lake or playa with sufficient water can be good, but two locations that have been especially productive in recent years are the playa one mile east of Etter on FM 281 and Rita Blanca Lake, immediately south of Dalhart. Etter is on US 287 about 12 miles north of Dumas.

Large numbers of migrating shorebirds, including Wilson's Phalarope, Long-billed Dowitcher, Long-billed Curlew, etc., congregate near lakes and playas in spring and fall. In summer American Avocet and Black-necked Stilt nest. Yellow-headed Blackbird migrate through in large numbers and can be found in summer in the southwest portion of the Panhandle.

PALO DURO CANYON STATE PARK

Palo Duro Canyon State Park, 16,402 acres, is located 12 miles east of Canyon on SH 217. The park preserves a small portion of Palo Duro Canyon, a dramatic western extension of the Caprock Escarpment. The elevation drops approximately 800 feet in the mile or so from the park entrance to Prairie Dog Town Fork of the Red River. Four geological periods representing about 280 million years are exposed in the canyon walls: Permian, Triassic, Tertiary, and Quaternary. To the non-geologist, the walls are a brilliant display of color layers of varying thickness: brick-red, gray, purple, yellow, orange, and tan.

There are restrooms with hot showers, a gift shop with snack bar and restaurant, picnicking, camping, laundry tubs, horseback riding, hiking trails, an excellent interpretative center, and an amphitheater. The musical extravaganza "TEXAS" is presented in the amphitheater nightly (except Sunday) from late June through August. The spectacle depicts the history and culture of the High Plains.

The vegetation of the park is mostly mesquite, junipers, and various shrubs, but large cottonwoods, hackberries, and soapberries are found along the Prairie Dog Town Fork. A hike along this stream can be an excellent way to find the birds of the park.

Nesting birds in the park are Mississippi Kite, Wild Turkey, Scaled Quail, Golden-fronted Woodpecker, Ash-throated Flycatcher, Blue Jay, Western Scrub-Jay, Bushtit, Canyon and Rock Wrens, Painted Bunting, Bullock's Oriole, and Rufous-crowned Sparrow.

This is where I found my first Northern Shrike, which can usually be expected in limited numbers in winter in the area, if not in the park. Other wintering birds are Northern Flicker, Mountain Bluebird, Townsend's Solitaire, Golden-crowned Kinglet, Pine Siskin, American Tree Sparrow, and Golden Eagle. Also, be on the alert for Evening Grosbeak, and White-breasted and Red-breasted Nuthatches.

A bird checklist for the park is available at headquarters. The address is RR 2, Box 285, Canyon, TX 79015, (806) 488-2227.

LAKE MEREDITH

Lake Meredith is on the Canadian River approximately 35 miles north of Amarillo on SH 136. Its purpose is to supply water to several Panhandle municipalities. The lake is created by Sanford Dam, near the town of Sanford, about nine miles west of Borger. At conservation pool level, the lake has 16,505 surface acres and a shoreline of 100 miles. The recreation area consists of 44,977 acres.

Though included in this book as part of the Llano Estacado, the Canadian River basin, also known as the Canadian Breaks, is geologically and vegetationally a subregion of the Rolling Plains. Through time the river has carved a wide valley approximately 200 feet below the High Plains.

The National Park Service administers the Lake Meredith National Recreational Area. The area is divided into eight units with camping, picnicking, boating, fishing, cycling, hunting, and water-skiing. The facilities in some units are primitive.

The Alibates Flint Quarries National Monument is near the southeast shore of the lake, the site of prehistoric Indian flint quarries for more than 12,000 years. The flint areas can be visited only on guided tours, presently 10 am and 2 pm during the summer months, or by prearrangement during the rest of the year. From archeological evidence, it is known that tools and weapons from alibates flint were widely used by Indians all over the Great Plains and the Southwest.

Common permanent resident birds include Mallard, Wild Turkey (Plum Creek), American Coot, Northern Flicker, Horned Lark, Rock Wren, House Finch, and Rufous-crowned Sparrow. Less common are Golden Eagle and Curve-billed Thrasher.

Common summer residents are Mississippi Kite (Bonita), Red-headed Woodpecker, and Cassin's Sparrow. Less common are Blue-winged and Cinnamon Teals, American Kestrel, Burrowing Owl, Ash-throated Flycatcher, Hairy Woodpecker (McBride Canyon), Carolina Chickadee (McBride Canyon), and Painted Bunting. Look for Indigo Bunting in the salt cedars near the river. Eastern Meadowlark is found in the river valley; Western Meadowlark away from the river in the uplands. Common Moorhen and Virginia and King Rails can be found in the marsh at Sanford Dam.

Regular migrant shorebirds are Snowy and Semipalmated Plovers, Long-billed Curlew, Stilt, Baird's, Least, Semipalmated, Western, Upland, and Spotted Sandpipers, Long-billed Dowitcher, Wilson's Phalarope, Greater and Lesser Yellowlegs, and Common Snipe.

Near Alibates at the upper end of the lake, Canada Goose, Gadwall, American Wigeon, Northern Shoveler, Green-winged Teal, Redhead, Lesser Scaup, Common Goldeneye, Bufflehead, and Common Merganser winter, some species in substantial numbers.

In addition to the previous species, winter residents are Golden Eagle, Mountain and Eastern Bluebirds, Townsend's Solitaire, and American Tree Sparrow. More difficult to find are Rough-legged Hawk, Prairie Falcon, and Northern Shrike. Bald Eagle are frequently seen over the lake in winter. They roost in the Bonita area where 30 to 40 birds can sometimes be found at one time.

Pronghorn (antelope) can be found in the grasslands surrounding the lake, and occasionally a coyote comes loping along.

A bird checklist (1982) is available at the Lake Meredith Recreation Area office. The address is P.O. Box 1460, Fritch, TX 79036, (806) 857-3151.

BUFFALO LAKE NATIONAL WILDLIFE REFUGE

Buffalo Lake National Wildlife Refuge, 7,664 acres, is located on Tierra Blanca Creek approximately 28 miles southwest of Amarillo. To reach the refuge, drive southwest from Canyon on US 60 for 12 miles to Umbarger. Turn south on FM 168, then go 1.5 miles to the refuge entrance.

Picnicking, camping, and restrooms are available. Many areas of the refuge are open to hiking. There is a 4.7 mile auto tour road.

Formerly Buffalo Lake had about 1,100 surface acres, but the lake is now dry except after very heavy rain, as Tierra Blanca Creek is no longer a flowing stream. At the upper end of the old lake an earthen embankment (known as Stewart Dike) is the site of a moist-soil management area that consists of 5 eight-acre units. The objective of the moist-soil units is to provide habitat for wetland-dependent species including waterfowl, shorebirds, and wading birds. Moist-soil management involves timing for wetland flooding or drawdown to create the moist-soil conditions that promote the germination, growth, and seed production of wetland plants. The units are connected to a well for flooding and designed for rapid gravity drawdown for management purposes. When rainfall is sufficient to provide water behind Stewart Dike in the fall, winter and spring waterfowl can be abundant.

Nesting species of the woodlands and extensive grasslands around the lake include Swainson's Hawk, American Kestrel, Wild Turkey, Ring-necked Pheasant, Ladder-backed Woodpecker, Western and Eastern Kingbirds, Blue Grosbeak, Lark and Grasshopper Sparrows, and Bullock's and Orchard Orioles.

Winter residents are Golden and Bald Eagles, Long-eared Owl (I have seen them here on several occasions), American Tree Sparrow, and occasionally Northern Shrike and Prairie Falcon.

The Cottonwood Canyon Birding Trail and other canyons at the refuge can be some of the better locations in the area for migrating Orange-crowned, Nashville, Yellow, Yellow-rumped, American Redstart, Northern Waterthrush, Common Yellowthroat, MacGillivray's, and Wilson's Warblers, and other passerines. There are 38 warblers on the checklist. There is a large Black-tailed Prairie Dog town on the east side of FM 168, two miles south of the FM 1714 intersection, where Burrowing Owls are present spring, summer, and fall, and Ferruginous Hawks winter.

The refuge is surrounded by farmlands where McCown's, Chestnut-collared, and Lapland Longspurs may be found in winter. With good luck, there may be a Smith's Longspur also.

A bird checklist (1991) is available at headquarters. Refuge hours are 8 am to 10 pm. The address is Refuge Manager, P. O. Box 179, Umbarger, TX 79091-0179, (806) 499-3382.

RITA BLANCA NATIONAL GRASSLAND

The Rita Blanca National Grassland, 77,463 acres in Texas and 15,860 acres in Oklahoma, is located in the extreme northwest corner of the Panhandle. The grassland is managed to promote the development of grassland agriculture, outdoor recreation, forage, water, and wildlife through multiple-use and sustained yield principles. Hunting is permitted on certain sections in season.

The grassland in Texas consists of about 38 separate units, with the largest unit located about 8 miles east of Texline at the junction of FM 296 and FM 1879. This unit contains the Thompson Grove Recreation Site, where picnic tables and restrooms are provided. This wooded site is cool in summer and is an oasis for a variety of arboreal birds.

Common nesting birds of the grassland include Long-billed Curlew, Lark Bunting, Ring-necked Pheasant, Ferruginous and Swainson's Hawks, Horned Lark, Cassin's and Lark Sparrows,

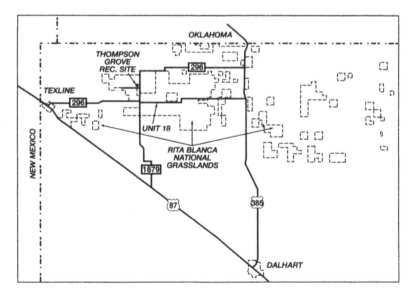

RITA BLANCA NATIONAL GRASSLAND

and Bullock's Oriole. Cassin's Kingbird may also occur in summer. Other species to watch for are Mountain Plover (have nested), Black-billed Magpie (extremely rare), Canyon Towhee, and Common and Chihuahuan Ravens. The Black-tailed Prairie Dog towns are good places for Burrowing Owl and Ferruginous Hawk. Pronghorn and coyote are common residents.

Unit 18 has several groves of Russian olive trees with dense undergrowth. To reach the entrance (Gate 18 on the north side of the road) drive about 4 miles east on the county road from the intersection of FM 296 and FM 1879. A high clearance vehicle may be needed. Winter birds recorded include Long-eared Owl and American Tree Sparrow. It is necessary to drive through several gates to bird all the groves. Always close all gates immediately after passing through, not just when leaving. No littering please. The county road is excellent for wintering raptors including Golden Eagle, Rough-legged and Ferruginous Hawks, Merlin, and Prairie Falcon.

Playas and/or stock ponds on or near the grassland are host to shorebirds in spring and fall migration.

MOUNTAIN PLOVERS

The office for the grassland is the Kiowa and Rita Blanca National Grasslands, 714 Main Street, Clayton, NM 88415, (505) 374-9652. The Kiowa National Grassland is near Mills and Clayton, New Mexico, west of Texline, TX.

CAPROCK CANYONS STATE PARK

Caprock Canyons State Park, 15,160 acres, is located almost equidistantly between Amarillo and Lubbock just east of the Caprock Escarpment. To reach the park from Amarillo, drive south on I-27 for 49 miles to Tulia, southeast on SH 86 for 51 miles to Quitaque, then north on FM 1065 about 3 miles to the park. To get to Quitaque from Lubbock, drive east on US 62-82 for 27 miles to Ralls, then north on SH 207 for 52 miles to FM 145. Go east 17 miles to Quitaque.

The park is at the southern end of Palo Duro Canyon with rugged canyonlands and wide, dry, stream beds. Mesquite is the dominant woody plant in the uplands, while cottonwoods are found along the watercourses. The flora and fauna are similar to that described earlier for Palo Duro Canyon State Park, except for

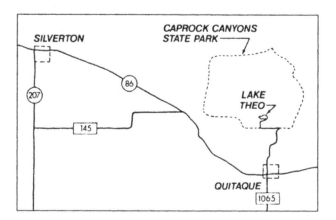

CAPROCK CANYONS STATE PARK

100-acre Lake Theo, where waterfowl and shorebirds can be found in fall, winter, and spring.

The park has hiking trails, equestrian trails, camping, restrooms with hot showers, picnicking, a boat ramp, and fishing.

Permanent resident birds include Canyon Towhee, Bewick's, Rock, and Canyon Wrens, Western Scrub-Jay, Golden-fronted Woodpecker, Rufous-crowned Sparrow, Bushtit, and Verdin. In summer look for Mississippi Kite, Painted Bunting, and Swainson's Hawk. At night listen for Common Poorwill. Watch for Golden Eagle which nest locally.

On Lake Theo, practically all waterfowl found in West Texas make an appearance in fall, winter, and spring. Some common species are Canada Goose, Northern Pintail, and Lesser Scaup. Rare waterfowl recorded include Red-throated Loon, Red-necked Grebe, Greater Scaup, Surf Scoter, and Least Bittern. Osprey and Forster's and Black Terns are regular migrants.

Mountain Bluebird, Townsend's Solitaire, and many sparrow species, including Brewer's Sparrow, winter in the park.

Aoudad sheep, first introduced into Palo Duro Canyon State Park from North Africa in 1957, have been successful in adapting to the environment east of the Caprock. Many can be found in Caprock Canyons State Park, with groups of 40 to 50 sighted regularly in all areas of the park. Other mammals include mule deer and porcupine.

A bird checklist is available at headquarters. The address is P.O. Box 204, Quitaque, TX 79255, (806) 455-1492.

LUBBOCK

Lubbock, population 193,000, is located in the heart of the Llano Estacado, and while the plains seem endless and devoid of birds, there are actually many excellent opportunities for birding in the area. In addition to the specific locations detailed in this section, it is beneficial to check the many playas along the high-

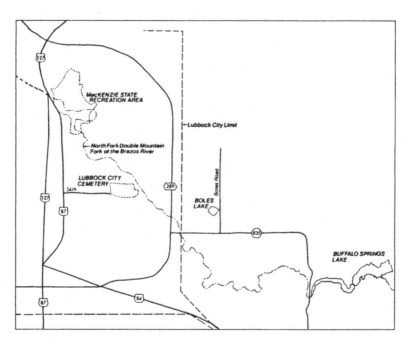

LUBBOCK

way for waterfowl and shorebirds. Ring-necked Pheasant, which are permanent residents, are often found along the roadsides and near feedlots. In winter, Ferruginous and Rough-legged Hawks are seen on utility poles, and Mountain Bluebird can be abundant.

RARE BIRD ALERT, (806) 797-6690.

West of Lubbock, near the New Mexico state line, Lesser Prairie-Chicken are permanent residents in the sand hills country (south Cochran, western Hockley, northern and central Yoakum, and western Terry counties). During March and early April, listen for the "booming" of the males, a part of their courtship behavior. All the land is private property; permission to enter must be obtained. Two good roads on which to look for the chickens are FM 1780 between Whiteface and Seagraves, and SH 214 between Lehman and Denver City. When the chickens are not booming, finding them is a matter of pure luck (but possible).

LESSER PRAIRIE-CHICKEN

Mackenzie State Recreation Area

Mackenzie State Recreation Area, 542 acres, is owned by the State of Texas but operated by the City of Lubbock. It is located in the northeast section of Lubbock on the North Fork Double Mountain Fork of the Brazos River at the intersection of I-27 and 4th Street. The park has the most extensive Black-tailed Prairie Dog town on public property in the state, along with a sizable resident population of Burrowing Owl. Mississippi Kite nest here and are present May through August. Playgrounds, a swimming pool, and picnicking facilities are available.

Lubbock City Cemetery

From downtown, drive east on 34th Street to Martin Luther King Boulevard, then left to the entrance of the Lubbock City Cemetery, which has land birds not easily found elsewhere in the area. The plains are naturally treeless (except along water courses) so the many ornamental plantings at the cemetery are a magnet for migrating land birds and winter residents. One year a Bohemian Waxwing spent the winter at the cemetery.

Two other areas that are popular in-town bird spots are Maxey Park (Quaker Avenue between 24th and 30th Streets), and Clapp Park (University Avenue and 45th Street).

A checklist, Birds of the Texas South Plains (1994), is available from the Llano Estacado Audubon Society, P.O. Box 6066, Lubbock, TX 79493, for 50 cents plus a stamped, addressed envelope.

Buffalo Springs Lake

To reach Buffalo Springs Lake, a recreation area, drive 4.5 miles east of Loop 289 on FM 835 to the entrance of the lake. There is an entrance fee. Canada Goose, numerous ducks and sometimes Western Grebe winter on the lake. Twenty waterfowl species have been recorded on recent Christmas Counts. Below the dam, the shallow ponds, marshes, and thickets should be checked for Sora, Virginia Rail, Marsh and Winter Wrens, and Fox and Swamp Sparrows. Canyon Towhee, Rock Wren, Verdin, and Rufous-crowned Sparrow are present on the dry slopes. This is one of the favored local areas during spring migration.

On the way to Buffalo Springs Lake, a stop at Boles Lake is sometimes good for the unexpected. To reach Boles Lake from FM 835, turn north on Boles Road about one mile east of Loop 289. The lake, on the west side of Boles Road about one-half mile north of FM 835, is a playa used for treating sewage water for irrigation. Waterfowl, shorebirds, and marsh birds are present in migration and in winter. Many rare waterfowl and shorebirds have been found here, including Whimbrel, Marbled Godwit, White-rumped Sandpiper, Dunlin, Sanderling, and Ross' Goose. Black-necked Stilt, American Avocet, and Eared Grebe have nested here.

MULESHOE NATIONAL WILDLIFE REFUGE

Muleshoe National Wildlife Refuge has 5,809 acres of shortgrass prairie, typical of the Llano Estacado before farming and ranching began less than 100 years ago. Established in 1935 to provide resting and wintering areas for Sandhill Crane and waterfowl, the refuge is the oldest national wildlife refuge in Texas.

From the city of Muleshoe, drive south on SH 214 for 20 miles to the refuge entrance on the right (west). From Lubbock, drive northwest on US 84 for 38 miles to Littlefield, west 19 miles on FM 54, 4 miles west on FM 37, then north on SH 214 about 5 miles to the refuge entrance on the left.

There are three playa lakes in which the water level varies with the amount of rainfall. In wet years there are approximately 500 surface acres of water, but in some years they are practically dry.

The wintering Sandhill Crane are the main attraction. On recent Christmas Counts, the number of cranes at the refuge has been between 10,000 and 30,000, likely the largest winter concentration of these birds in Texas. The all-time peak of 250,000 cranes was reached in February, 1981. From late September through March, the cranes use the refuge for roosting at night and resting during the day. The largest concentrations are present either at dawn or dusk, when they leave for or return from feeding areas. The cranes are also frequently seen feeding in nearby fields during the day.

SANDHILL CRANES

Permanent residents include Northern Bobwhite, Scaled Quail, Barn Owl, Great Horned Owl, Loggerhead Shrike, Horned Lark, Curve-billed Thrasher, and Canyon Towhee. The latter three are often found near the headquarters building.

Other nesting birds, which usually go south in winter, include American Avocet, Snowy Plover, Common Nighthawk and Cassin's and Grasshopper Sparrows.

Ferruginous and Rough-legged Hawks, Northern Harrier, Bald and Golden Eagles, Prairie Falcon, and Long-eared and Short-eared Owls may be seen during fall, winter, and spring. Look for migrating waterfowl from August to December when peak numbers are reached. Northern Pintail are more common, followed by American Wigeon, Mallard, Green-winged Teal, and Ruddy Duck. A few Canada Geese winter when water is available.

Some birds found on Christmas Counts include Common Merganser, Oldsquaw, Gray Flycatcher, Bushtit, Mountain Chickadee, Townsend's Solitaire, and LeConte's, American Tree and Sage Sparrows. Other birds that may be found in winter are Green-tailed Towhee, Dark-eyed (Gray-headed) Junco, and Brewer's Sparrows. McCown's, Chestnut-collared, and Lapland Longspurs winter in the grasslands. Black-tailed Prairie Dog are also found on the refuge.

Lesser Prairie-Chicken are rare in summer, fall, and winter.

A bird checklist with 282 species is available at headquarters. The refuge address is Refuge Manager, Muleshoe National Wildlife Refuge, P.O. Box 549, Muleshoe, TX 79347, (806) 946-3341.

MIDLAND

Midland, population 95,000, is in the heart of the Permian Basin, one of the nation's most productive petroleum reservoirs. It is located at the southern end of the Llano Estacado with the Edwards Plateau just south and the Trans-Pecos only a few miles west. Although some birds thrive in the arid land that surrounds

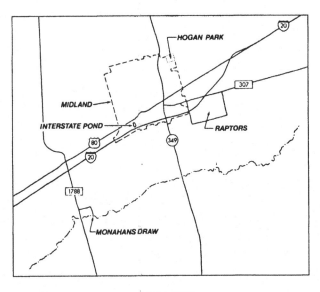

MIDLAND

the city and over 350 species of birds have been recorded in the county, in drought years birds may be hard to find. Then, gardens in the city, stock tanks on ranches, and "woodlands" along the draws become magnets for birds.

(All directions are from the intersection of I-20 and SH 349, on the south edge of Midland.)

West Midland County

From SH 349, drive west on I-20 about 9.5 miles to Exit 126 (FM 1788), just west of the Midland Regional Airport. Drive north on FM 1788 4 miles to the Center for Energy and Economic Diversification (CEED). Drive in and park in any of the parking areas. On the west side of the building is a pond where ducks may be found during the winter months. Wood Duck, Cinnamon Teal, Canvasback, and Bufflehead are often present, as well as the more common species. As you leave the parking area, stop and view the field to the south. The low area just ahead is frequently covered with water. This is an excellent spot for McCown's and Chestnut-collared Longspurs, which are present from late December until early April. The birds circle above the area and drop briefly to the water's edge to drink. A spotting scope is a great help in getting a good look. A Golden Eagle sometimes sits on the windmill tower to the southeast. Other winter species include Horned Lark, Eastern and Western Meadowlarks, Ferruginous and Red-tailed Hawks, and Prairie Falcon. Swainson's Hawk, Scissor-tailed Flycatcher and skylarking Cassin's Sparrow are present in summer. A few shorebirds may be seen in season, including Long-billed Curlew in winter and Black-necked Stilt in summer. Chihuahuan Raven are present all year.

The large dam to the west of FM 1788 encloses a reservoir for the city water supply. The area is locked and closed to the public.

Return to FM 1788 and go south across I-20. On the left is the Texas Instruments facility, and between the building and FM 1788 is another pond. It is necessary to look at the pond from the road, as the park is a private recreation area for TI employees. In midwinter this is an excellent location to see Hooded Merganser and Common Goldeneye. Other waterfowl appear all season long. It is famous among Midland birders for having once hosted an immature White Ibis.

Return to the south access road of I-20 and go east one mile to County Road 1270. About three miles south on this road is Monahans Draw. Treated, odorless sewage effluent from Odessa flows into the draw. The draw is choked with cattails and has no open water, but Virginia Rail are year-round residents, and Sora are abundant from August through April. An occasional King Rail or American Bittern may be glimpsed. Just after crossing the draw, turn east on County Road 170, which crosses the draw several times. Stop at each crossing to look and listen for Marsh Wren and Swamp Sparrow in winter. The mesquite thickets, patches of sunflowers, and open fields provide a variety of habitats, where common resident species such as Ladder-backed Woodpecker, Cactus

Wren, Curve-billed Thrasher, Verdin, and Pyrrhuloxia may be found. At the gate across the road, turn around and return to I-20.

Hogan Park

From SH 349 drive east on I-20 two miles to exit 136 (Garden City), then drive north on FM 715 (Fairgrounds Road). At 2.7 miles stop by the TU electric substation. The ground around the facility is riddled with Black-tailed Prairie Dog burrows, and they are much in evidence. Burrowing Owl may be standing on their mounds, or just barely sticking their heads above ground. The owls are present all year long, but are uncommon in winter. Continue north on FM 715 past Ranchland Hills Country Club and turn left (west) on Wadley Road. The entrance to Hogan Park is about one-half mile on the right.

Entering Hogan Park, stop and look to the west at a large water tower. In winter, Prairie Falcon frequently perch on the tower just below the overhang. Drive past the Sibley Learning Center and Midland Woman's Club buildings to the sign reading "Sibley Nature Trail." Park, go through the gate and walk the half-mile trail. Resident birds include Verdin, Cactus Wren, Pyrrhuloxia, Curve-billed Thrasher, and Ladder-backed Woodpecker. Summer birds include Mississippi Kite, Black-chinned Hummingbird, Scissor-tailed Flycatcher, Western Kingbird, Ash-throated Flycatcher, Bullock's Oriole, Blue Grosbeak, Lesser Goldfinch, Lark and Cassin's Sparrows. In winter, fourteen species of sparrows may be present, as well as Green-tailed, Spotted, and Canyon Towhees, American Goldfinch, Pine Siskin, and the ever-present House Finch. Sage Thrasher and Harris' Hawk are frequent winter visitors. The small pond and the cattails around it host Swamp Sparrow, Marsh Wren, and Sora in winter. During migration, Yellow-headed Blackbird brighten the landscape, and the trees and shrubs around the ponds are visited by neotropical migrants. Burrowing Owl are found in many places in Hogan Park; one summer a pair excavated a burrow under a picnic table and successfully fledged young.

City of Midland

In the city there are three spots worthy of checking: Wadley Barron Park and the two cemeteries. From the junction of US 349 and I-20, go north on US 349 (Big Spring Street) about four miles and turn west on Cuthbert Street. Waldley Barron Park is at the junction of Cuthbert and North A Street. The attraction here is a small pond at which American Wigeon winter by the hundreds. Occasionally some surprising visitors appear, such as Osprey, Purple Gallinule, Forster's Tern, and Double-crested Cormorant. It is best to view the pond from the west side. Return to A Street, continue north one block, turn right on Nobles, and then left on Pecos to Fairview Cemetery, about four blocks from Wadley Barron Park. In winter a variety of woodpeckers are found; Lewis' and Acorn Woodpeckers have been recorded. Some winters there are Mountain Bluebirds. If birds are not present it may mean a Sharp-shinned Hawk or Merlin is in the area. In this case, try Resthaven Cemetery. From the entrance to Fairview go east to SH 349 (Big Spring Street), then drive north on Big Spring past Loop 250. Resthaven Cemetery is on the right. In summer look for Mississippi Kite overhead. During migration check the many oak trees for warblers. In winter look for Ruby-crowned and Golden-crowned Kinglets, Red-naped and Yellow-bellied Sapsuckers, Townsend's Solitaire, Yellow-rumped and Orange-crowned Warblers, Pine Siskin and American Goldfinch. On at least one occasion a flock of Red Crossbill spent the winter at Resthaven.

A Short Winter Drive For Raptors

From Exit 138 on I-20, drive north one mile to FM 307 (Cloverdale Road), turn right (east) and drive three miles, then right (south) on County Road 1140. Go two miles, turn right (west) on County Road 120, then three miles to FM 715 (north) and return to I-20. There are several alfalfa fields in this area where Long-billed Curlew and Sandhill Crane forage. Check the tops of all utility poles on the route and keep one eye on the sky above, for raptors find the alfalfa fields a prime hunting area. Ferruginous, Red-tailed, Rough-legged (rare), American Kestrel, Merlin, and Prairie Falcon are all possible. Beware of dark morph buteos—most of them are Red-tails and a few are Ferruginous, so don't jump to the conclusion that any dark hawk is a Rough-legged.

The Midland Naturalists, Inc. have a field trip every Saturday morning throughout the year to a local birding area. Many of these areas are private property, so it is necessary to go with the group to enter. Visitors are welcome on these trips, which usually take less than four hours. To participate, call the Sibley Environmental Center at (915) 684-6827 for directions and time. "A Field Check List, Birds of Midland County," is available from the Midland Naturalists, c/o Frances Williams, 1407 East County Road 130, Midland, TX 79706, for $1 (this includes mailing costs).

2
Trans-Pecos

The Trans-Pecos is approximately 11% of Texas and is generally thought of as the section of the state west of the Pecos River. However, in this book the Monahans Sand Hills, east of the river, are included in the Trans-Pecos, while the Stockton Plateau to the west of the river is placed with the Edwards Plateau.

The eastern boundary of the Trans-Pecos is roughly a north-to-south line from the New Mexico state line just north of Kermit southeastward between Monahans and Odessa to near

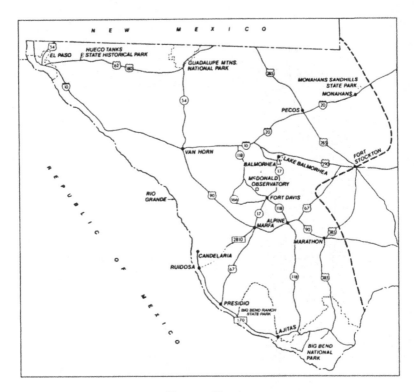

TRANS-PECOS

McCamey. The boundary line continues to the west, north of Fort Stockton, to the eastern edge of the Davis Mountains, and then turns southeast to the Rio Grande.

The area is the northern portion of the Chihuahuan Desert, which extends far south into Mexico between the Sierra Madre Oriental and the Sierra Madre Occidental. There are several distinct mountain ranges in the region with peaks ranging from 5,000 to 8,751 feet elevation above sea level. The Howard Bolson and Salt Flats, with no outlet to the sea, are just west of the Guadalupe Mountains. The elevation of the desert is from 1,800 to 4,000 feet.

Rainfall varies from 8 to 12 inches per year, with up to 20-plus inches in the higher elevations.

The geology is complex. The Chisos and Davis Mountains are of igneous origin, whereas the Guadalupes are composed of sedimentary rocks and are block-faulted. The other mountain ranges in the Trans-Pecos are not included in this book as they are all privately owned and not readily accessible to the general public. See the El Paso section for a brief treatment of the Franklin Mountains.

The vegetation in the lower elevations of the Chihuahuan Desert is desert scrub, creosote, mesquite, and tarbush. Surrounding the mountains are desert grasslands. Well-developed montane woodlands contain a mixture of Mexican and Rocky Mountain vegetation, predominately oaks, junipers, firs, and pines. Douglas fir and aspen can be found on some of the peaks.

More bird species will be found near water or where there are trees. If there are both, it is usually an excellent spot for birding.

The Trans-Pecos has more nesting bird species that do not nest in another region than any other in Texas. White-throated Swift, Crissal Thrasher, Violet-green Swallow, Black-chinned Sparrow, Phainopepla, Black-headed Grosbeak, Western Wood-Pewee, Cassin's Kingbird, Hepatic Tanager, Peregrine Falcon, Gambel's Quail, Band-tailed Pigeon, Broad-tailed and Blue-throated Hummingbirds, Cordilleran Flycatcher, Western Bluebird, Spotted Towhee, Whip-poor-will, Steller's Jay, Mountain Chickadee, Pygmy Nuthatch, Western Tanager, Hutton's Vireo, Virginia's Warbler, Pine Siskin, and Flammulated Owl are among the nesting species of the region. Species with perhaps a more restricted nesting area are Montezuma Quail, Lucifer Hummingbird, Lucy's, Colima, and Grace's Warblers, Mexican Jay, Hermit Thrush, Dark-eyed (Gray-headed) Junco, and Painted Redstart.

Species not unique to but that nest throughout the region include Scaled Quail, Greater Roadrunner, Black-chinned Hummingbird, Western Scrub-Jay, Cactus and Rock Wrens, Curve-billed Thrasher, Pyrrhuloxia, and Black-throated Sparrow.

ALPINE

Alpine, population 5,600, the home of Sul Ross State University and the Museum of the Big Bend, is the hub for birding in the Trans-Pecos. Big Bend National Park is 78 miles south, the Davis Mountains are 26 miles northwest, and El Paso is 220 miles west. Each highway from Alpine has its bird attractions.

Look for wintering hawks along US 67 northeast to Fort Stockton and US 90 east to Marathon. Red-tailed, Ferruginous, Rough-legged, and Harris' Hawks, Golden Eagle, Merlin and Prairie Falcon are all regulars, and with great luck, a Northern Goshawk may be seen, but it is extremely rare anywhere in Texas.

In winter the roadsides should be checked for Prairie Falcon, Grasshopper, Brewer's, Clay-colored, and Chipping Sparrows,

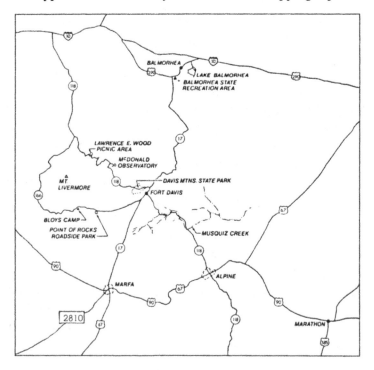

DAVIS MOUNTAINS AND ALPINE

Dark-eyed Junco, Lark Bunting, and McCown's and Chestnut-collared Longspurs. After summer rains commence, Cassin's Sparrow are very visible. North of Alpine, in the first low ridge of mountains check the brushy draws for the rare but regular Baird's Sparrow in fall and winter, while Montezuma Quail are found year-round. Along Musquiz Creek, approximately 20 miles from Alpine at the rest area, summer birds include Bushtit, Cassin's Kingbird, Vermilion Flycatcher, Black Phoebe, Warbling Vireo, Painted Bunting, and Blue Grosbeak. This location is excellent for observing migrants in spring and fall.

At Paisano Pass, about 13 miles west of Alpine on US 90 toward Marfa, Cliff and Violet-green Swallows and White-throated Swift can be seen overhead. In the oaks look for Cassin's and Western Kingbirds, Black-headed Grosbeak, House Finch, and Western Bluebird. Watch the power lines for Chihuahuan Raven and Swainson's Hawk, both of which nest along this highway. During migration watch for Cave Swallow.

In the highlands on SH 118 south toward Big Bend National Park, the rest areas should be checked for Phainopepla, Bushtit, Crissal Thrasher, Western Bluebird, and the very light Fuertes race of the Red-tailed Hawk, which lacks the "belly band" often used to identify Red-taileds.

BIG BEND NATIONAL PARK

Big Bend National Park is one of the "must" birding places in Texas. The park, 800,000-plus acres, is huge, about 50 miles north to south, 60 miles east to west. A complete mountain range, the Chisos, is within the park boundaries. The mountains are surrounded by grasslands, which in turn are surrounded by the Chihuahuan Desert.

To reach the park, drive south from Marathon on US 385 (85 miles) to park headquarters. Or, from Alpine, drive south on SH 118 (117 miles) to park headquarters.

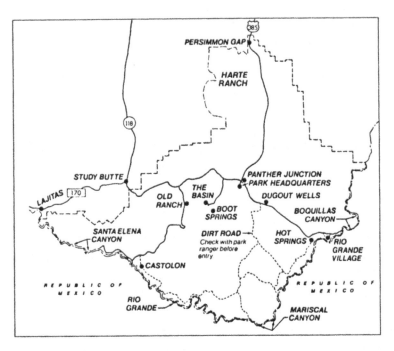

BIG BEND NATIONAL PARK

A wide variety of accommodations is available in the park. For non-campers there is a modern lodge, a dining room, and stone cottages. Advance reservations are strongly recommended, (915) 477-2291. There are large campgrounds in the Basin, at Rio Grande Village, and in Cottonwood Campground, at Castolon. RV hookups are offered at Rio Grande Village RV Park only. Groceries are available near all campgrounds. In addition, there are service stations at Panther Junction and Rio Grande Village. Float trips on the Rio Grande through Santa Elena, Mariscal, and Boquillas canyons may be arranged individually with Ranger approval. Finally, there are 32 hiking trails totaling more than 150 miles. These are listed in the *Hiker's Guide,* published by the Big Bend Natural History Association and available at park headquarters. Also, see *Hiking and Backpacking Trails of Texas* by Mildred J. Little (Lone Star Books) for more information.

Big Bend is a naturalist's paradise of geologic formations, fossils, plants, mammals, birds, reptiles, amphibians, and fish. Many are unique to the area. A stop at headquarters where exhibits, maps, pamphlets, books, and checklists are available is highly recommended. The desk at headquarters should be checked for recent notable bird sightings.

Big Bend National Park is one of a handful of spots in Texas where bird seekers from outside Texas can be encountered nearly every day of the year. Most are willing to share what they have found.

For the visitor with limited time, the first "must" areas to visit are Rio Grande Village, the Basin, Boot Springs, Santa Elena Canyon, and those few places in the desert where there is water, such as Old Ranch and Dugout Wells. The park is so large it will take several visits in different seasons before adequate attention can be given to the different habitats.

A hike to Boot Springs, elevation 6,300 feet, between mid-April and September will take the bird seeker to the nesting area of the Colima Warbler, the park's most famous bird. Big Bend is the only place in the United States where it can be found. The Colima Warbler is not always easy to find, but patience will usually be rewarded. Most are found in Boot Canyon, but they can also be seen along the trail near the Pinnacles between the Basin and Boot Springs, and between Laguna Meadow and Boot Springs. Painted Redstart are occasional nesters at Boot Springs.

Other nesting birds to watch for on a spring or summer mountain hike are Hutton's Vireo, Acorn Woodpecker, Mexican Jay, Common Raven, Zone-tailed Hawk, White-breasted Nuthatch, White-throated Swift, Bushtit, and Broad-tailed and Blue-throated Hummingbirds. Laguna Meadow and the Basin are good spots for Black-chinned Sparrow. Flammulated Owl and Whip-poor-will call in Boot Canyon at night, and at dawn and dusk Band-tailed Pigeon is sometimes present in large numbers. Gray Vireo is reported to nest in Blue Creek Canyon, Oak Canyon and other canyons in the Chisos. I have seen Gray Vireo in Campground

Canyon, a very steep canyon near the Basin campground. Black-capped Vireo has been recorded in Blue Creek Canyon in summer. The Pinnacles area on the Boot Springs Trail is a good place to watch for Zone-tailed Hawk, White-throated Swift, and an occasional Golden Eagle or Peregrine Falcon.

For the nonhiker, there are excellent birding possibilities in all seasons in the Basin, elevation 5,400 feet, from the sewage ponds up to the Juniper Flat and Boulder Meadow area. Nesting birds in those areas and along the Window Trail include Lucifer and

ACORN WOODPECKER

Black-chinned Hummingbirds, Crissal Thrasher, Violet-green Swallow, White-winged Dove, Elf Owl, Ash-throated Flycatcher, Black-chinned Sparrow, Scott's Oriole, Pyrrhuloxia, Varied Bunting, and Canyon Towhee.

Cottonwood Campground, located at Castolon near the Rio Grande on the road to Santa Elena Canyon, is another birding location where an easy short walk can produce lots of good birds. Hooded and Bullock's Orioles, as well as Summer Tanager nest here. Records here include Zone-tailed and Gray Hawks, Tropical Kingbird, and Ruddy Ground-Dove. Lucy's Warbler have been recorded in spring.

In summer the century plant blossoms provide food and moisture for a wide variety of creatures—insects, birds, mammals—and should be especially watched for hummingbirds. Scott's Oriole is often seen feeding on century plants. The Lucifer Hummingbird, which can be found in the Basin, seems to prefer the arroyos of the grasslands. A walk on the Grapevine Hills Trail, located about ten miles north of park headquarters on a gravel road, is a good Lucifer Hummingbird location. In late summer (late August and early September) western hummingbirds migrate through the park. Rufous Hummingbird is common and Broad-tailed, Broad-billed, Costa's, and Calliope Hummingbirds have been recorded. Mexican Jay is easily found above the cottages on the trail to Juniper Flat. Cactus Wren call all around the parking lot in the Basin, Phainopepla are sometimes on the power lines, and Black-chinned Sparrow should be looked for in the grass and shrubs near the Boot Springs-Window Trail trailhead.

A complete change in bird life occurs at Rio Grande Village, elevation 1,850 feet, on the river at the eastern end of the park. Here Vermilion Flycatcher, Orchard and Hooded Orioles, Lesser Nighthawk, Elf Owl, Yellow-billed Cuckoo, Verdin, Common Yellowthroat, Summer Tanager, Painted and Varied Buntings, and Bell's Vireo are all common nesters. More Vermilion Flycatcher are here than any other single spot I know of in Texas. Cottontail, Greater Roadrunner, and Inca and White-winged Doves walk around the campground like pets. Turkey Vultures will help you eat your lunch. There is a nature trail through a marshy swamp and several ponds, each of which should be checked for birds. Rio Grande Village is an excellent place to be in late April and early May for spring migration.

The most visible bird in the desert is the Black-throated Sparrow. A stop at Old Ranch, Dugout Wells, or any of the other springs in the desert will usually add Scott's Oriole, Pyrrhuloxia, Curve-billed Thrasher, Blue Grosbeak, Ash-throated Flycatcher, and Black-tailed Gnatcatcher. In winter, watch for Green-tailed Towhee. The Varied Bunting is often found at Old Ranch, and occasionally Gray Vireo. Sitting quietly on a bench at Old Ranch and waiting for the birds to come to water is a favorite way for photographers to get pictures of the birds of Big Bend. In the desert nearby, check for Sage Thrasher in winter and early spring.

The park checklist has 50 warbler species—5 nest, 2 are winter residents, and 43 are migrants or accidentals. Regular migrant western species include Townsend's, Grace's, MacGillivray's, and Hermit (rare) Warblers. Being on the alert for the unexpected is one of the attractions of Big Bend, such as finding Ruddy Ground-Dove (Rio Grande Village), White-eared Hummingbird (mountains), Elegant Trogon (Window Trail or mountains), Tufted Flycatcher (Rio Grande Village), Aztec Thrush (Boot Canyon), Slate-throated Redstart (Boot Canyon), Rufous-capped Warbler (Campground Canyon and Santa Elena Canyon), and Black-vented Oriole (Rio Grande Village).

Roland Wauer, former Chief Naturalist of Big Bend National Park, has written a book that all serious bird seekers should obtain: *A Field Guide to Birds of the Big Bend,* Second Edition. It is available at park headquarters, or your local bookstore.

A seasonal bird checklist (1994) is available at headquarters that lists 388 species plus 59 hypothetical species. Eleven of the hypotheticals have not been documented in Texas. The park address is Superintendent, Big Bend National Park, TX 79834, (915) 477-2251.

BIG BEND RANCH STATE PARK

Big Bend Ranch State Park, 287,000 acres, is located just west of Big Bend National Park. Take RR 170 (River Road) from SH 118 just north of the west entrance to Big Bend National Park through Terlingua to The Barton Warnock Environmental Educational Center located just east of Lajitas. Stop at the center, where there is a self-guided botanical garden with Chihuahuan Desert plants, sales area, and an information area.

The park offers opportunities for hiking, birding, nature study, and photography. RR 170 follows closely the southern boundary of the area near the Rio Grande for about 50 miles. Between the

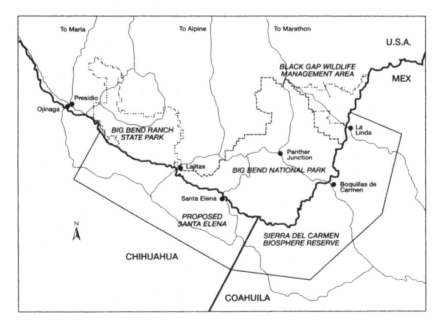

BIG BEND RANCH STATE PARK

road and the river there are three areas (Colorado Canyon, Madera [Monilla] Canyon, and Grassy Banks River Access) where there is primitive camping, picnicking, fishing, and swimming. The interior is accessible only by tour bus or hiking. Primitive camping is also available along hiking trails in the interior. Only experienced hikers in good physical condition should venture into the backcountry. Lodging is available at La Sauceda, the ranch headquarters, and at the nearby Sauceda Lodge. Reservations for lodging and meals must be made in advance. Trail maps are available at The Barton Warnock Environmental Education Center and at Fort Leaton State Historical Park at the western boundary of the park. Bus tours to the interior are offered the first and third Saturdays of the month. For reservations call (512) 389-8900.

Nesting species include Mallard/Mexican Duck hybrids, Black Vulture, Zone-tailed Hawk, Golden Eagle, Elf Owl, Lesser Nighthawk, White-throated Swift, Western Wood-Pewee, Black Phoebe, Black-tailed Gnatcatcher, Crissel Thrasher, Varied Bunting, and Scott's Oriole.

Many waterfowl species winter on the river. Migrants include warblers in the spring and fall and hummingbirds in August and early September.

The area differs from Big Bend National Park in that there are more springs with associated woodland sites and there are more tinajas (natural tanks), plus the springs, waterfalls and associated woodlands found along the Fresno Creek drainage do not have a counterpart in the National Park.

The geology, with over 500 million years of earth's history, is one of the area's top attractions. To quote from the brochure:

"The geology section is prominent by virtue of folded and upturned rock layers, volcanic domes and desert basins that tell of long-gone mountains and ancient sea beds, upwelling molten rocks and a rifting crust, dissected into the steep-walled canyons of today by the Rio Grande and its side channels."

Perhaps the most famous geological feature is the Solitario, an impressive collapsed volcanic dome located in the northeast section of the park.

The address of The Barton Warnock Environmental Education Center is HC 70, Box 375, Terlingua, TX 79852, (915) 424-3327.

Along RR 170 through the Natural Area a stop at the high overlook in the canyons in summer should turn up Violet-green Swallow and White-throated Swift flying in the updrafts. Cliff Swallow is also present, and Cave Swallow has been found in migration. Canyon Wren can be heard singing their distinctive song. At least one pair of Zone-tailed Hawk nest along this canyon, and a little time spent checking the numerous Turkey Vulture overhead will sometimes result in a good look at the hawk. Common Raven are often overhead and easy to recognize by their deep voice and wedge-shaped tail. Lawrence's Goldfinch were found near Lajitas the winter of 1996-97.

Between Lajitas and Redford the land is characterized by ocotillo, prickly pear, and lechuguilla, typical plants of the Chihuahuan Desert. In spring Inca Dove, Common Ground-Dove, and Verdin are common, while Crissal Thrasher is uncommon; in winter watch for Sage Thrasher and Sage Sparrow.

At Redford, the Presidio agricultural region begins signaling a drastic change in the birdlife. White-winged Dove, a unique race quite a bit larger than other races, makes its appearance here. Northern Cardinal, Yellow-breasted Chat, and Painted and Varied Buntings are common. Check the ditches and drainage pileups for the Mallard/Mexican Duck hybrids. During migration this area can be teeming with waterfowl and shorebirds and sometimes White-faced Ibis. On the western edge of Redford is a packing shed surrounded by tall cottonwoods where Mississippi Kite has nested.

About nine miles northwest of Redford, at the junction of Alamito Creek and the Rio Grande, is a marshy area that can be overflowing with migrants. Baird's Sandpiper is usually fairly common in spring and fall. Look for them among the Western and Least Sandpipers. The tree tobacco near the river attracts several hummingbird species in late summer, including Anna's and Rufous.

Fort Leaton State Historical Park is on RR 170 between Alamito Creek and Presidio, and is well worth a visit. A fortified trading post dating back to the mid-19th century has been restored for historical study, and you can look for Gambel's Quail here. The park address is P.O. Box 1220, Presidio, TX 79845, (915) 229-3613.

PRESIDIO COUNTY

At Presidio turn north to Marfa on US 67 or continue on RR 170 to Ruidosa.

On US 67, the old mining town of Shafter is a worthwhile stop. Drive to the east edge of town to the tall cottonwoods along Cibolo Creek. Ask permission at the house to bird beyond the creek. Nesting birds include Cassin's and Western Kingbirds and occasionally Common Black-Hawk. Virginia's, Townsend's, Hermit, and Black-throated Gray Warblers have been recorded here in migration.

If going to Ruidosa, drive with care on RR 170 northwest of Presidio. Loose livestock are common, and the road undulates like a roller coaster for much of its 47 miles. The birding is best along this stretch if the departure from Presidio is made about 30 minutes before daylight. The most common birds along the road are White-winged Dove, Crissal Thrasher, Verdin, Cactus Wren, and Turkey Vulture. The only Presidio County flock of Black Vulture is found in this stretch. A pair of Harris' Hawks reside about three miles southeast of Ruidosa. The closer to Ruidosa, the more common Gambel's Quail become. There should be no problem finding Gambel's Quail before reaching Candelaria. Sage Sparrow have been seen in this area in winter.

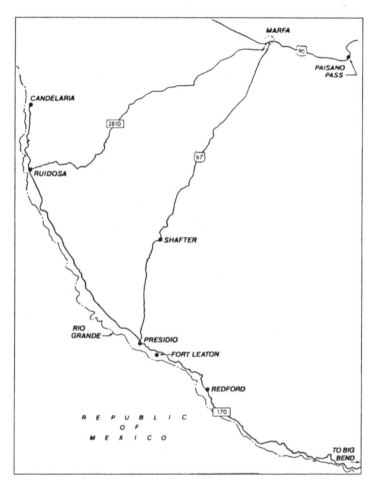

PRESIDIO COUNTY

The best birding is past Ruidosa to Candelaria. From May to October, flash floods are not unusual past Ruidosa. Do not drive into the area if the weather appears threatening. Scan the skies carefully anywhere along this stretch and up into the Chinati Mountains to the north. Zone-tailed Hawk, Common Black-

Hawk, and Prairie and Peregrine Falcons have all nested in this area. Golden Eagle are a regular sight, especially in migration.

An oxbow, a section of the former river channel, is a prominent feature near Candelaria. From mid-April to mid-May, when there is water, it can be alive with migrants in the runoff as well as in the bordering salt cedar. This is a good place for waterfowl, including Mallard/Mexican Duck hybrids and shorebirds. In the trees look for local nesters, such as Zone-tailed Hawk, Ladder-backed Woodpecker, Varied Bunting, Lesser Goldfinch, Common Yellowthroat, Yellow-breasted Chat, Summer Tanager, Bell's Vireo, Verdin, Hooded and Scott's Orioles, and sometimes Bullock's Oriole. Walking one of the sandy draws toward the Rio Grande should reveal some of these birds in abundance. In winter numerous sparrow species are present. During April and May, listen carefully for a high-pitched trill emanating from the salt cedars. Quietly stalk the trill, and perhaps there will be a Lucy's Warbler feeding in the trees. These birds nest in Texas in a small area around Candelaria, and I have been fortunate enough to have recorded them there. In migration the most common warblers in this section are Yellow-rumped (Audubon's), Wilson's, MacGillivray's, Townsend's, Virginia's, Black-throated Gray, Common Yellowthroat, and Yellow-breasted Chat. Lazuli Bunting has been recorded in migration.

RR 170 ends at Candelaria, but not the birding. Continue northwest on the gravel road that leads to some promising habitats, including ponds and taller trees. There is a creek where one can bird the dense brush and rocky slopes along the banks for birds. If the creek is flowing, cross only after making sure it is safe.

From Candelaria return to Ruidosa, and turn left (northeast) on the unpaved road toward the mountains. Follow this road into Pinto Canyon and up through the pass between the Sierra Vieja Rimrock and the Chinati Mountains. Phainopepla can be rather common in this stretch, especially around cottonwoods and junipers. In cottonwood and oak areas watch for Western Scrub-Jay. In winter Steller's Jay and Williamson's Sapsucker have been found. In the mountains birders are cautioned that all land away from the roadway is private property. DO NOT WALK OFF THE ROAD whether the land is fenced or unfenced.

After going over the pass, the road is paved (RR 2810) and leads to Marfa. The habitat here is high-elevation grassland, and again the birdlife changes. Watch for Golden Eagle, Prairie Falcon, and Pronghorn year-round. In all but the hottest months Lark Bunting should be present, and in winter the roadsides are host to lots of sparrows, including Brewer's, Clay-colored, Vesper, and Chipping, along with McCown's and Chestnut-collared Longspurs, which frequent the open short grass prairie. Baird's Sparrow should be looked for in grassy areas near brushy draws. Montezuma Quail occur in a few sheltered spots in the canyon area near Marfa, and sometimes flocks of Pinyon Jay can be found in winter. This is a good area to see migrant Yellow-headed Blackbird. Occasionally, Swainson's Hawk nest on power lines south and east of Marfa.

The birds listed on the checklist for the Big Bend National Park should be representative of Presidio County.

DAVIS MOUNTAINS

The Davis Mountains offer a contrast to the Chisos in Big Bend and the more northern Guadalupe Mountains. The difference is explained by the more abundant rainfall, more thickly forested areas in the higher elevations, the presence of a highly developed riparian system, and the greater extent of acres of montane grasslands.

This area offers much for the visitor besides birds: Fort Davis National Historic Site, Davis Mountains State Park, McDonald Observatory atop Mount Locke, and a scenic 74-mile drive that circles Mount Livermore (8,382 feet), the highest peak in the Davis Mountains.

The scenic drive is an excellent birding tour with a diversity of montane grasslands, pine forest, and rock outcrops. From Fort Davis, drive north on SH 118. The Fort Davis National Historic Site is at the edge of town, where the frontier fort, established in 1854 and abandoned in 1891, has been restored by the National Park Service.

Davis Mountains State Park

About four miles farther north is Davis Mountains State Park, with camping, picnicking, restrooms with hot showers, and Indian Lodge, a modern motel-type facility with restaurant and pool. The rates are reasonable. Reservations are recommended, (915) 426-3254.

The park, 2,677 acres, is in the foothills between the grasslands and the mountains. Birds in the area are representative of both habitats. There is a four-mile hiking trail connecting the park with the Fort Davis National Historic Site.

Common nesting birds in the park include Common Poorwill, Acorn Woodpecker, Western Scrub-Jay, Cassin's Kingbird, Scaled Quail, Bushtit, Curve-billed Thrasher, Cactus and Rock Wrens, Pyrrhuloxia, White-breasted Nuthatch, and Black-headed Grosbeak.

Be on the lookout in the camping area for Montezuma Quail; they often come down for water. This is the only park in Texas where this quail can be expected regularly. Although it is possible to see Montezuma Quail all along the scenic drive, it was on my fourth trip to the Davis Mountains that I saw my first one. Common Poorwill can be heard calling at night and can often be seen on the road by driving to the Scenic Overlook after total darkness. Listen in spring for the contrasting call of the Whip-poor-will.

In very cold weather high-altitude species, such as Steller's Jay, Mountain Chickadee, Townsend's Solitaire, and Dark-eyed (Gray-headed) Junco, sometimes descend into the lowlands of the park. In the Davis Mountains, Eastern, Western, and Mountain

MONTEZUMA QUAIL

Bluebirds can be found in winter, one of the few places in Texas where all three bluebirds can be expected. Look for Red-naped Sapsucker in winter also.

A bird checklist (1991) with 189 species is available at park headquarters. The address is Box 786, Fort Davis, TX 79734, (915) 426-3337.

Scenic Drive

The next stop, McDonald Observatory, is 13 miles to the west on SH 118. McDonald Observatory is owned by The University of Texas. The drive up Mount Locke, elevation 6,828 feet, to the telescopes, includes the highest point in the Texas highway system. Western Scrub-Jay is common, and Montezuma Quail can sometimes be seen on the drive up. At this elevation, the Mexican Pinyon Pine and oaks are the dominant trees.

The Lawrence E. Wood Picnic Area, another seven miles on SH 118, is an extensive roadside park maintained by the Texas Department of Highways and Public Transportation. I have always had good luck birding this roadside park. In summer Montezuma Quail, Phainopepla (some years), Hepatic Tanager, American Robin, White-breasted Nuthatch, and Grace's Warbler can be found; in migration western warblers such as Black-throated Gray, MacGillivray's, Townsend's, Hermit, and Virginia's, are all possible, as well as some eastern warblers. In winter watch for Mountain Chickadee, Lewis' Woodpecker, Williamson's Sapsucker, and Golden Eagle overhead.

If you cross a fence on this drive, you are on private property. PLEASE DO NOT CROSS FENCES without the owner's permission. Do not give birders a bad reputation by trespassing on private property.

Prairie Falcon are permanent residents and should be watched for anywhere along the drive. Zone-tailed Hawk and Common Black-Hawk both nest in the Davis Mountains and should also be watched for as you drive the loop; they move their nests from year to year, so be on the lookout. In general, Common Black-Hawk is in the vicinity of creek bottoms, and Zone-tails are likely almost anywhere, but neither is very common. In addition, Mountain Plover has been found nesting in the grasslands on the southern portion of the Davis Mountains loop.

After turning left on SH 166, you will soon get to Sawtooth Mountain (to the left). Watch for White-throated Swift overhead. On one February visit, I saw Montezuma Quail and Bald and Golden Eagles within 30 minutes in this area.

Continue on SH 166 back to Fort Davis. Make additional stops at Bloys Camp Meeting Ground (ask permission) and the Point of Rock Roadside Park. Dark-eyed (Gray-headed) Junco, Townsend's Solitaire, and sparrows can be found in winter. During migration the grounds can be teeming with birds. In winter there are usually Ferruginous Hawk overhead and McCown's and Chestnut-collared Longspurs in the grasslands along with Pronghorn.

If you are very lucky, you may also encounter a flock of Pin-yon Jay on the loop in winter. They are usually in a large flock (from dozens to hundreds), but they seem to be constantly on the move. Sometimes they are accompanied by Clark's Nutcracker. Be aware that these two species are irregular at best.

In winter in grassy areas and along creeks the following sparrows are common: Vesper, Cassin's, Dark-eyed (Slate-colored, Gray-headed, and Oregon) Junco, Chipping, Clay-colored, Brewer's, Black-chinned, Black-throated, Lincoln's, and Song. Less common are Grasshopper, Sage, Field, and White-throated. Watch for Baird's Sparrow in fall migration. Near water, check for Black Phoebe and Vermilion Flycatcher.

BALMORHEA STATE PARK

Balmorhea State Park, 45 acres, is near the town of Toyahvale, some 32 miles north of Fort Davis on SH 17, or 50 miles west of Fort Stockton off of I-10. The main feature of park is San Solomon Springs. The flow of 26,000,000 gallons of water per day from the bottom of the large swimming pool in the park supplies water to Balmorhea Lake, which in turn provides irrigation water to the adjoining area. In addition to swimming, the park has camping, picnicking, and cabins with bath and kitchen. Nesting Barn Swallow are very abundant and Cave Swallow nest under the eaves of some buildings. When they are on the nest, it is easy to get a clear, well-lighted look at them.

A bird checklist (1992) with 292 species covering the park, Balmorhea Lake, Balmorhea and vicinity, is available at headquarters. The park address is Box 15, Toyahvale, TX 79786, (915) 375-2370.

Balmorhea Lake, 573 acres, is three miles south of the town of Balmorhea, which is about four miles north of Toyahvale. Large permanent bodies of water are scarce in the Trans-Pecos; therefore, the large lake is a mecca for migrating and wintering shorebirds and waterfowl.

WESTERN GREBE

Western and Clark's Grebes are present in midwinter, when they are easily compared.

In addition, Horned Grebe, Common and Red-breasted Mergansers, Mallard/Mexican Duck hybrids, Cinnamon Teal, Common Loon, and Sage and Brewer's Sparrows have been recorded on recent Christmas Counts. Rarities recorded include Red-necked Grebe, Ross' Goose, and Yellow-billed, Red-throated and Pacific Loons. Most of the geese and ducks of Texas can be found in winter on the lake at one time or another.

The surrounding fields support a thriving population of Ring-necked Pheasant and Verdin, and in winter there are large numbers of sparrows, McCown's and Chestnut-collared Longspurs, Lark Bunting, Marsh and Sedge Wrens, and LeConte's Sparrow.

Raptors found on Christmas Counts include Golden Eagle, Red-tailed, Ferruginous, and Rough-legged Hawks, Prairie Falcon, American Kestrel, and Merlin.

Any birding trip to this part of Texas should include a visit to Balmorhea Lake.

GUADALUPE MOUNTAINS NATIONAL PARK

Guadalupe Mountains National Park, 86,415 acres on the Texas-New Mexico line, is one of the unique natural areas of Texas. The park contains the four highest peaks in the state. The mountains are an exposed portion of the Capitan Reef, an ancient barrier reef laid down at the edge of an inland sea some 200-plus million years ago. Guadalupe Peak, 8,749 feet, is the highest point in Texas. El Capitan, the southern end of the reef, is a sheer rise of some 2,000 feet from the desert below. It is visible for 50 miles, and is said to be the most photographed natural feature in Texas. Approximately 46,850 acres in the park are designated wilderness areas.

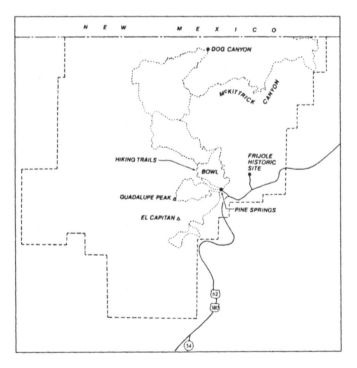

GUADALUPE MOUNTAINS NATIONAL PARK

The park is 55 miles southwest of Carlsbad, New Mexico, 110 miles east of El Paso on US 62-180, or 65 miles north of Van Horn on SH 54. There is no food, lodging, or gasoline in the park; the nearest facilities are 35 miles away.

Here the Rocky Mountains to the north meet the Chihuahuan Desert to the south. The canyons between the low and high country, especially McKittrick Canyon, have a mixture of plants and animals from the mountains as well as the desert.

Some common nesting birds of the higher elevations include Steller's Jay, Mountain Chickadee, Pygmy Nuthatch, Western Bluebird, Broad-tailed Hummingbird, Band-tailed Pigeon, Hermit Thrush, Violet-green Swallow, and White-throated Swift. Less common are Spotted and Flammulated Owls, Whip-poor-will, Blue-throated Hummingbird, Brown Creeper, Cooper's Hawk and, rarely, Northern Saw-whet Owl.

In the wooded canyons look for Cordilleran Flycatcher, Western Wood-Pewee, Warbling and Gray Vireos, Grace's Warbler, Western Tanager, Acorn Woodpecker, Spotted Owl, Olive-sided Flycatcher, and occasionally Magnificent Hummingbird. Virginia's Warbler can be found on dry canyon slopes.

Birds that nest in or near the desert are Black-throated Sparrow, Canyon Towhee, Scaled Quail, Rock Wren, Rufous-crowned Sparrow, Greater Roadrunner, Pyrrhuloxia, Black-chinned Sparrow, Scott's Oriole, and Crissal Thrasher. This is one of the few places in Texas where the Juniper Titmouse can be found regularly. I have seen them in the draw behind the ranger residence near Frijole Ranch and in Dog Canyon.

To see Guadalupe Mountains National Park, one must be prepared to hike. There are 80 miles of hiking trails. Two all-day hikes, one to the Bowl and one into McKittrick Canyon, are an excellent introduction to the park and to many birds as well.

No other place in Texas is like the Bowl. With an elevation of about 8,000 feet, the Bowl's 2,000 acres are surrounded by the highest peaks of the park. From Pine Spring Campground, it is about a 2.5-mile, steep and strenuous hike up to the Bowl. The increase in elevation is about 2,000 feet, but it is well worth the effort. Start early to avoid the heat of the day. When the rim is crossed from the canyon below, an abrupt vegetational change is immediately encountered. The very dry, rocky terrain with a scattering of Pinyon Pine, low shrubs, and cacti on the uphill hike suddenly becomes a dense forest of Ponderosa and Southwestern white pines, 100-foot tall Douglas firs, a few quaking aspen, and grassy meadows. Wildflowers are plentiful in summer. There is a pond or tank (sometimes dry) where many forms of wildlife come to drink at the head of South McKittrick Canyon. Wapiti (elk), mule deer, and other animals can be seen at the pond at dawn and dusk.

McKittrick Canyon has the only perennial stream in the park and is famous for its mixture of desert, plains, Rocky Mountain and south (Mexican) mountain plant species growing in close proximity. The fall colors of the Big-toothed Maples are spectacular. The McKittrick Canyon hike is the easiest hike for its length as well as the best hike in the park for the greatest variety of birds. Peregrine Falcon has nested on the high cliffs. Golden Eagle and Zone-tailed Hawk soar overhead. American Dipper have been recorded.

Manzanita Springs, a short distance behind the Frijole Historic Site, is the only place in Texas where I have seen a Northern Goshawk (can be found in the highlands as well).

A bird checklist is available at the Headquarters Visitor's Center, along with maps and other literature explaining the geology, history, and plants of the park.

The mailing address is Superintendent, Guadalupe Mountains National Park, HC 60, Box 400, Salt Flat, TX 79847-9400, (915) 828-3251. The park is in the mountain time zone.

EL PASO

El Paso, population 554,000, at the western extremity of Texas, is in the valley of the Rio Grande at the base of the Franklin Mountains, and is surrounded by the Chihuahuan Desert. The combined population of El Paso and Juarez, Mexico, just across the river, is more than 1.3 million. With an average rainfall of about eight inches, finding birds means finding a place where there is water. Nevertheless, there are a variety of habitats within a short drive from the city: mountains of more than 7,000 feet elevation, the river, some man-made ponds and lakes, and the desert.

Common nesting birds of El Paso County include Mallard/Mexican Duck hybrids, Gambel's Quail, Common Moorhen, Swainson's Hawk, Burrowing Owl, Lesser Nighthawk, White-throated Swift, Ash-throated Flycatcher, Say's Phoebe, Chihuahuan Raven, Verdin, Cactus, Canyon and Rock Wrens, Crissal Thrasher, Scott's Oriole, and Black-throated Sparrow. American Kestrel, Phainopepla, and Hooded Oriole are less common in summer.

A bird checklist for El Paso County and Adjacent Areas (1987) is available from El Paso/Trans-Pecos Audubon Society, P.O. Box 9655, El Paso, TX 79986, for 50 cents plus a stamped, addressed envelope.

Memorial Park

Memorial Park, in downtown El Paso, is a favorite of local birders for resident and migrant land birds. From I-10, drive north on Piedras Street six blocks. Turn right on Grant Street, which leads to the park.

Great-tailed Grackle, House Finch, and Inca and White-winged Doves can be found in any season. In spring, Wilson's, Yellow-rumped, and Orange-crowned Warblers, Bullock's Oriole, Black-headed Grosbeak, Western Tanager, and Western Wood-Pewee are common migrants. Watch also for Lazuli Bunting and MacGillivray's, Townsend's, Virginia's, and Yellow Warblers.

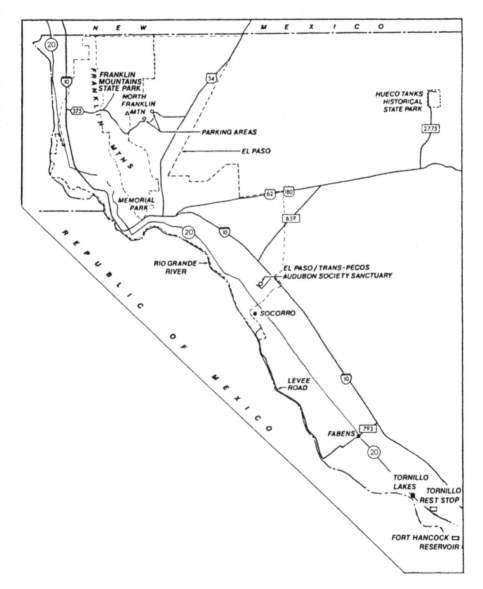

EL PASO

Fall is the time to look for montane invaders, including Williamson's Sapsucker, White-breasted and Pygmy Nuthatches, Mountain Chickadee, and Flammulated Owl. Some are sporadic. Look for Golden-crowned Kinglet and Red Crossbill in the pines around the Garden Center. This is also a good place for Cordilleran, Dusky, and Willow Flycatchers. Watch for the less-common Gray and Hammond's Flycatchers as well. Most of the spring warbler species are probably more common in fall.

In winter look for Dark-eyed (Oregon and Gray-headed) Junco, Lesser Goldfinch, Green-tailed Towhee, Red-breasted Nuthatch (rare but regular), and Red-naped Sapsucker. Arrive early in the morning (especially on weekends), or there will be more people than birds.

Franklin Mountains

The Franklin Mountains, just north of the city, have several peaks above 5,000 feet. The highest peak is North Franklin Mountain, at 7,172 feet.

Good birding can be had in the canyons of the Franklin Mountains off of Trans-Mountain Road (Loop 375), which crosses the mountains east to west north of the city. Golden Eagle may be seen soaring overhead anywhere in the Franklins. Common Poorwill is easier to find along Trans-Mountain Road than anywhere else around El Paso. Stop at any pullover after dark and listen for their calls. With a recorder it is possible to bring one in fairly close.

From I-10 in downtown El Paso, drive north on US 54 (Alamogordo exit), also known as the Patroit Freeway. After about 5.5 miles, US 54 branches off to the east. Continue straight on Patroit Freeway another 3 miles to the Trans-Mountain/Loop 375 exit. Drive west on Trans-Mountain Road for 0.9 mile to the turn out on the right. Walk straight toward the mountains, cross the flats and arroyos, and head northwest into the canyon. This is Indian Springs Canyon. Permanent residents to be found are Canyon Wren, Crissal Thrasher, White-throated Swift, Red-tailed Hawk, and Black-throated and Rufous-crowned Sparrows. Other nesting birds are Blue Grosbeak, Ash-throated Flycatcher, and Scott's Oriole.

In winter, in addition to the permanent residents, watch for Pyrrhuloxia (a few may nest), Lesser Goldfinch (may nest), Black-chinned (a few do nest far up the canyon), White-crowned, Chipping, and Brewer's Sparrows. Sage Thrasher are spring and fall migrants.

The next good birding canyon (there are other canyons in between) is Whispering Springs Canyon, which is 2.1 miles west of the stop above. The canyon is on the right, and there is a small pull-off to park a car. A trail leads up the dry wash. Farther up where the wash widens, desert willow becomes common. Higher, the canyon narrows into a small but lush oasis surrounding the longest flowing spring in the Franklins. Cottonwood, ash, and black walnut provide shade and nesting sites, as do the profuse tangles of grapevine. The birds are essentially the same as in Indian Springs Canyon, but Rufous-crowned Sparrow, Bewick's Wren, and hummingbirds are more common. Indigo Bunting nest here sporadically. During migration this canyon is very good for Virginia's and MacGillivray's Warblers.

Franklin Mountains State Park

Franklin Mountains State Park, 23,867 acres, is located at the north edge of El Paso and is bisected by Trans-Mountain Road (Loop 375). The entrance to the park is from West Cottonwood Road approximately 4.1 miles west of Whispering Spring Canyon. Facilities offered are day-use only hiking trails, picnicking, and restrooms.

West Cottonwood Road leads to West Cottonwood Springs Canyon, perhaps the best canyon for birds in the Franklins. Follow the road for 1.0 mile, turn right on a rocky dirt road near some old picnic shelters, and continue another 0.5 mile to a gate. Walk up the trail into the canyon. When the trail makes a sharp bend (almost a U-turn) to the left, continue straight on a much smaller trail that leads to the springs.

Nesting birds include Golden Eagle, Common Poorwill, White-throated Swift, Say's Phoebe, Violet-green Swallow, Verdin, and Crissal Thrasher.

Broad-tailed and Rufous Hummingbirds are abundant, while Calliope are uncommon in August and September. Townsend's and Black-throated Gray Warblers should be looked for here in fall. Hermit Warbler and Painted Redstart have been recorded. Black-chinned Sparrow is almost common in fall and winter and usually one can be found in summer. Watch the shrubby growth in the canyon for Hammond's Flycatcher, and for Green-tailed Towhee in migration. A Red-naped Sapsucker can often be found in the large trees near the spring in fall and Western Scrub-Jay can be common in fall and winter.

While a large number of species are not expected, such accidentals as Northern Goshawk, Band-tailed Pigeon, Flammulated and Northern Saw-whet Owls, and Greater Pewee, should be adequate incentive for bird seekers. Black and Vaux's Swifts have been reported but have not been documented.

A bird checklist (1989) with 152 species plus 6 hypotheticals is available at park headquarters. The address is P.O. Box 200, Canutillo, TX 79835-9998, (915) 566-6441.

El Paso/Trans-Pecos Audubon Society Sanctuary

The El Paso/Trans-Pecos Audubon Society has a bird sanctuary called Feather Lake in the "lower valley" of El Paso County. The lake is a City of El Paso stormwater detention basin and it provides a unique wildlife habitat in the city. To reach it, drive southeast on I-10 from downtown El Paso and take the Avenue of the Americas (Loop 375) exit. Stay to the right on Avenue of the Americas about 1.3 miles to the signal light marking the intersection with North Loop Drive (FM 76). Turn right, and drive a short distance to the lake on the left. Pull over here. The lake is surrounded by a chain-link fence, and a caretaker lives in a trailer inside. If the gate is locked, honk the horn, and the caretaker will open the gate. The lake is excellent for migrant and wintering waterfowl, including Cinnamon Teal, several species of migrant shorebirds, and various herons and egrets. White-faced Ibis is commonly seen in migration. American Bittern has been recorded rarely. Common Merganser is often present in winter and Tundra Swan will occasionally winter.

Rio Grande

The levee road along the Rio Grande from Fabens to Socorro offers the bird seeker an opportunity to bird irrigated farmland and the river. Drive southeast 30 miles on I-10 from its intersection with US 54 (Copia Street) to the Fabens exit. Turn right (south) on North Fabens Street to the dead end near the river, and go right (west) onto the levee road. Permanent residents are Gambel's Quail, Mallard/Mexican Duck hybrids, Great-tailed Grackle, and White-winged Dove. Northern Harrier, Prairie Falcon, and Ferruginous, Cooper's, and Sharp-shinned Hawks are seen in winter. Summer residents are Burrowing Owl, Blue Grosbeak, and Common Yellowthroat near the ditches.

Tornillo Lake, southeast of Fabens on SH 20, is good for shorebirds and waterfowl. From Fabens drive southeast on SH 20 11.4 miles. Breeders include Bell's Vireo, Summer Tanager, and Painted Bunting.

The Tornillo Rest Stop is on SH 20, 1.7 miles southeast of Tornillo Lake. There are large cottonwoods and picnic tables at the rest stop. Breeding birds include Yellow-breasted Chat and Bullock's Oriole plus the species mentioned at Tornillo Lake above. In winter look for Phainopepla, Red-naped Sapsucker, and Western Bluebird. This is also a favorable migrant location. Some unusual sightings here are Hermit and Prairie Warblers, Hepatic Tanager and Groove-billed Ani.

Continue east on SH 20 from the rest stop for 8.1 miles to the Fort Hancock Reservoir. This spot is 21.2 miles from Fabens. Drive on the dirt road up the large dirt dike on the right (south) and park. The gate is usually locked but DO NOT DRIVE IN EVEN IF IT IS OPEN. The water is not visible from the road.

This is private property but birding on foot is allowed. In winter look for Clark's and Western Grebes, Snow and Ross' Geese, Herring and Bonaparte's Gulls, ducks, etc. Osprey, Forster's and Black Terns, Franklin's Gulls, and numerous shorebirds can be found in migration. In fall huge flocks of swallows can often be encountered with Tree, Violet-green, Northern Rough-winged, Bank, Cliff, Cave, and Barn all represented. Cave Swallow nest in nearby culverts.

EASTERN EL PASO COUNTY

The Hueco Basin, in the desert east of El Paso, is a good place to look for Sage Sparrow from November through February, some years more fruitfully than others. From the intersection of US 62-180 and RR 659 drive east 7.5 miles to a paved road on the right. Turn off and park. The sparrows prefer patches of creosote bush, which are associated with a fair amount of grass and some salt-bush, as opposed to the bareground, well-spaced creosote bush areas that are common along the highway. They are somewhat shy, and seldom "pish" up into the open like the abundant Black-throated Sparrow. When flushed, watch where they land and rush to the spot, slowing down in the last several yards. If approached too slowly, the bird will run out of the area. If there are two or or more members in a birding party, the sparrow can be surrounded and pinned down. This is the best way to get a good view.

Sage Sparrow can also be found in the first mile of grasslands along RR 2775, the road from US 62-180 to Hueco Tanks State Historical Park. Cassin's Sparrow breed in this area as well. The area on both sides is very good for wintering sparrows, but this is private ranch land, and visiting birders should exercise appropriate behavior at all times.

HUECO TANKS STATE HISTORICAL PARK

Hueco Tanks State Historical Park, 860 acres, is about 32 miles northeast of El Paso. To reach the park, drive east on US 62-180, either from Montana Avenue downtown until it becomes US 62, or from I-10, about 10 miles southeast to RR 659 (Zaragosa Road), then northeast about 8.5 miles to US 62-180. From that point, go east 9 miles to RR 2775, which leads north about 6 miles to the park.

The park offers camping, picnicking (wood or charcoal fires are prohibited), restrooms with hot showers, hiking, and climbing. Abruptly rising from the surrounding desert are some unusual rock formations, the largest of which are in four "islands" 300 feet or more above the desert. For centuries Hueco Tanks has been a well-known landmark in this arid region. Rainwater trapped in the natural basins or *huecos* (Spanish for hollow) among the rocks was used by Indians, whose numerous pictographs are a featured highlight of the park, and later by settlers going west. The extensive Indian art is found in caves and on rock formations. Naturally, the trapped water is also a magnet for all forms of wildlife. In addition, several springs are located in the rocks.

Nesting birds at Hueco Tanks include White-throated Swift, Black-chinned Hummingbird, Ash-throated Flycatcher, Crissal Thrasher, Scott's Oriole, and Common Poorwill. Burrowing Owl and Barn Owl are sporadic nesters. Other summer residents are Swainson's Hawk and Lesser Nighthawk.

Migrants include Western Wood-Pewee, Rufous Hummingbird, Cassin's Kingbird, Cordilleran Flycatcher, Violet-green Swallow, Sage Thrasher, Virginia's, Black-throated Gray, Townsend's, and MacGillivray's Warblers, Black-headed Grosbeak, Broad-tailed Hummingbird, and Lazuli Bunting. In winter 1996-97 a flock of up to 10 Lawrence's Goldfinches wintered in the park.

In winter Black Phoebe, Mountain Chickadee, Mountain and Western Bluebirds, Townsend's Solitaire, Lesser Goldfinch, Pine Siskin, Lark Bunting, and Brewer's Sparrow have been recorded. One winter day I found my first Prairie Falcon at Hueco Tanks, perched high on one of the hills on the entrance road.

A bird checklist (1990) with 211 species is available at park headquarters. The address is 6900 Hueco Tanks Rd. #1, El Paso, TX 79936-8793, (915) 857-1135.

MONAHANS SANDHILLS STATE PARK

Monahans Sandhills State Park, 3,840 acres, is 6 miles northeast of Monahans on I-20, then north on Park Road 41. The park preserves a small portion of the sand hill country. There are large, barren sand dunes, some nearly 100 feet high, many of which are stabilized by vegetation, including the Havard Oak. Some of the oaks are hundreds of years old, although they are only 3-4 feet tall. The acorns are the size of silver dollars. The park offers picnicking, camping, restrooms with hot showers, a snack bar, a one-quarter mile nature trail, an equestrian trail, and a natural history interpretive center.

There are two good birding areas within the park. The mesquite thickets near the headquarters building and the nature trail (access through the building) are good places to see birds that are year-round residents of such habitat: Harris' Hawk, Ladder-backed Woodpecker, Verdin, Cactus Wren, Curve-billed Thrasher, Lesser Goldfinch, and Black-throated Sparrow. Sage Thrasher may be found in winter.

While driving through the park in winter, watch for hawks. Ferruginous, Northern Harrier, and American Kestrel are common. Prairie Falcon winter in the vicinity and are often seen in the park.

CURVE-BILLED THRASHER

It is 1.4 miles from headquarters to the souvenir stand, where a Say's Phoebe may usually be found. Turn left at the souvenir stand and drive to the end of the paved road; park at the picnic area. There is also an oil well pumping unit here. A road runs west from the picnic area. There is a bar across the road, but its purpose is to keep out vehicles, not hikers. Note the telephone poles along the road. Walk to the second pole, turn left (south) and walk across the dunes to a row of willow trees. The willows are not visible from the road but are only 50 yards distant. Boots are advisable. At the south end of the row of willows is a small seep, and the combination of trees and water in the sandy desert is a magnet for birds. This area is especially productive during migration. It is also a good place to see summer residents: Western Kingbird, Ash-throated Flycatcher, Bullock's Oriole, and Blue Grosbeak. Common Poorwill may be heard at dusk.

A bird checklist (1989) with 97 species is available at headquarters. The address is P.O. Box 1738, Monahans, TX 79756, (915) 943-2092.

3
Rolling Plains

The Rolling Plains region, about 14% of Texas, is defined here as that part of Texas that is underlain by Permian and Pennsylvanian deposits. The area is bounded on the west by the Llano Estacado, with the Caprock Escarpment marking a sharp boundary between the two. The West Cross Timbers and prairies of Central Texas and the Lampasas Cut Plains of the Edwards Plateau delineate the

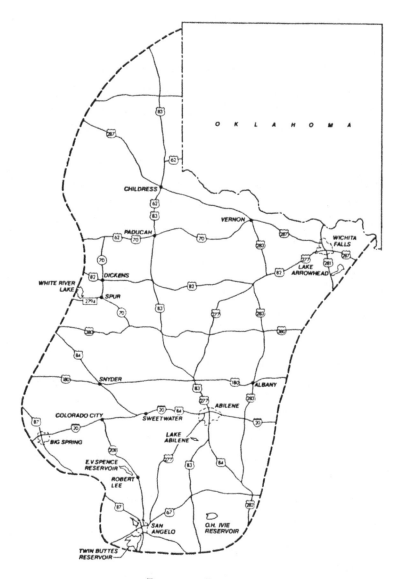

ROLLING PLAINS

eastern boundary, while the Edwards Plateau forms the southern boundary.

The area is mostly hilly, increasing in elevation from about 800 feet to 3,000 feet southeast to northwest. Most streams are intermittent and drought is common, with periodic catastrophic flooding. Two-thirds of the area is devoted to ranchland.

The dominant vegetation is mesquite-grasslands, where redberry juniper is widespread. In the riparian areas the vegetation is much like areas to the east, with cottonwood, pecan, cedar elm, hackberry, etc.

The area is a transition zone for eastern and western nesting bird species. Ruby-throated Hummingbird, Common Grackle, and Red-bellied and Downy Woodpeckers are shared with the Central Texas region. Common nesting birds found here and in the Llano Estacado and Trans-Pecos are Mississippi Kite, Scaled Quail, Common Poorwill, Golden-fronted Woodpecker, Ash-throated Flycatcher, Cactus and Rock Wrens, Lesser Goldfinch, Canyon Towhee, and Rufous-crowned Sparrow.

WICHITA FALLS

Wichita Falls, population 101,000, is located approximately 14 miles south of the Red River near the convergence of the Rolling-Plains and Central Texas. It is the largest city between Fort Worth and Amarillo.

Mesquite is the dominant woody plant in the uplands of the Wichita Falls area, with hackberry, cottonwood, and cedar elm in the stream bottoms.

Common nesting birds throughout include Great Blue Heron, Carolina Chickadee, Tufted Titmouse, Greater Roadrunner, and Scissor-tailed Flycatcher. Look for Grasshopper and Cassin's Sparrows, Verdin, and Bell's Vireo in the dry uplands in spring and early summer.

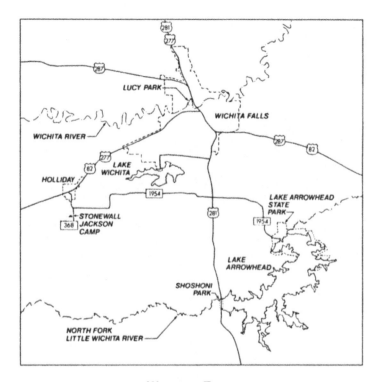

WICHITA FALLS

Lucy Park

Lucy Park, 156 acres, is operated by the City of Wichita Falls Parks and Recreation Department. It is located on the northern edge of Wichita Falls on the Wichita River. Picnicking, swimming, playgrounds, walking trails, and restrooms are available.

From downtown, drive north on Red River Expressway (US 277-281-287) to the Tourist Information exit. Drive south of the Tourist Bureau, park, and enter by the swinging bridge. If driving west on US 82-277, turn right (north) on Sunset Street to the park. River Bend Nature Center is under construction near the Sunset Street entrance to the park.

GREATER ROADRUNNER

Nesting birds in the park include Red-bellied, Red-headed, and Hairy Woodpeckers, Blue Jay, Mississippi Kite, Great Crested Flycatcher, Bullock's Oriole, Indigo Bunting, and Warbling Vireo.

In winter watch for Cedar Waxwing, Orange-crowned and Yellow-rumped Warblers, and Dark-eyed Junco.

Lucy Park is a good location for migrating land birds, including Swainson's Thrush, Philadelphia Vireo, and Black-and-white, Nashville, Yellow, and Wilson's Warblers.

Lake Arrowhead State Park

Lake Arrowhead State Park, 524 acres, is on the northwest shoreline of Lake Arrowhead. The lake is approximately 14 miles southeast of Wichita Falls on the Little Wichita River, and has 13,500 surface acres and 106 miles of shoreline. It is operated by the City of Wichita Falls as a municipal water supply.

To reach the park, drive south from Wichita Falls on US 281 eight miles to FM 1954, then go east eight miles to the park. Offerings include a boat ramp, boat docks, water skiing, fishing, swimming, picnicking, camping, restrooms with hot showers, equestrian trail, and two miles of hiking trails.

Habitats in the park and adjacent areas consist of rolling grasslands invaded by mesquite and other woody species, such as cottonwood, hackberry and wild plum; a heavily wooded riparian area along Sloop Creek in the northern portion of the park; and marshy areas along the lake shore.

Nesting birds include Red-tailed Hawk, Loggerhead Shrike, Western Kingbird, Eastern Bluebird, Bewick's Wren and Golden-fronted Woodpecker. In winter look for Ring-billed Gull, Northern Flicker, Double-crested Cormorant, Dark-eyed Junco, Pied-billed Grebe, and 23 waterfowl and 13 sparrow species. A drive by the spillway is sometimes productive.

A bird checklist (1997) with 204 species is available at headquarters. The address is Route 2, Box 260, Wichita Falls, TX 76301, (817) 528-2211.

Shoshoni Park

Shoshoni Park, 93 acres, is on the southwestern edge of Lake Arrowhead. It is operated by the City of Wichita Falls Parks and Recreation Department. There is no sign at the entrance. A boat ramp, picnicking, and fishing are available but there are no restrooms. The park is 12 miles south of Wichita Falls on US 281, or 1 mile north of Scotland.

Birds found here in summer include Downy Woodpecker, American Robin and Lark Sparrow.

Wintering species to be expected are Northern Harrier, Ruby-crowned Kinglet, and Harris' Sparrows.

Stonewall Jackson Camp

Stonewall Jackson Camp, 25 acres, a Girl Scout Camp and popular local bird location, is about 14 miles west of Wichita Falls. To reach the camp, drive south on US 281 for 8 miles. Turn west on FM 1954, drive 13.4 miles to FM 368, turn south and go .5 mile to the camp entrance on the east side of the road. Another way to get there is to go south from Holliday on FM 368 for 2.1 miles. There is usually a barricade to keep cars out, but hiking birders are welcome.

Nesting birds include Ladder-backed Woodpecker, Swainson's Hawk, Western Kingbird, and Painted Bunting.

In winter this is a good location for Brown Creeper, Brown Thrasher, American Goldfinch, Golden-crowned Kinglet, Spotted Towhee, and Field, Fox and Song Sparrows.

ABILENE

Abilene, population 110,000, is located in the north-central section of the state on I-20 between Fort Worth and El Paso. It is near the eastern extreme of the Rolling Plains, with the West Cross Timbers section of Central Texas just to the east. There are elements of the Edwards Plateau represented in the area, particularly the Callahan Divide, the division between the drainages of the Colorado and Brazos rivers. In the stream bottoms the vegetation and birdlife are representative of Central Texas, while western species are found in the uplands where the mesquite and short-grass prairies occur.

RARE BIRD ALERT, (915) 691-8981, operated by The Big Country Audubon Society.

Birding areas covered here include the town of Buffalo Gap, Abilene State Park and Lake Abilene south of the city, lakes north and east, and two city parks.

Buffalo Gap is about 10 miles south of Abilene on FM 89. On the roads in and around Buffalo Gap look for Curve-billed Thrasher and Bewick's Wren. Pyrrhuloxia have been reported in and around the town, and Bushtits are sighted occasionally.

As is true elsewhere in the state, White-winged Dove have moved into Abilene with nesting recorded in 1995.

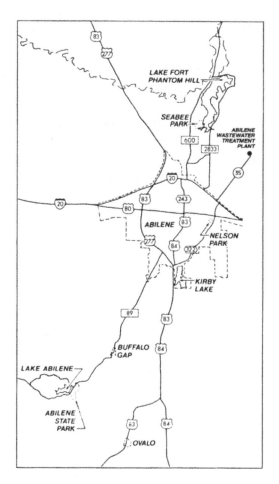

ABILENE

Abilene State Park

Abilene State Park, 621 acres, is about 4 miles south of Buffalo Gap (or 14 miles south of Abilene) on FM 89 in the low hills near the Callahan Divide. The park, a portion of which is preserved in a natural state, offers camping, screened shelters, a swimming pool with bathhouse, a one-mile hiking trail, and picnicking. The land birds of the park are most evident along the wooded sections of Elm Creek.

Nesting species include Mississippi Kite (present April to September), Yellow-billed Cuckoo, Common Nighthawk, Western Kingbird, Blue-gray Gnatcatcher, Loggerhead Shrike and House Finch. Less common are Turkey Vulture, Greater Roadrunner, Ash-throated Flycatcher, Western Scrub-Jay, Chihuahuan Raven, Brown Thrasher, Lesser Goldfinch and Black Vulture. Eight warbler species are listed on the park check-list as migrants, including MacGillivray's Warbler. In addition, 16 sparrow species have been recorded in winter.

MISSISSIPPI KITE

A bird checklist (1994) is available at headquarters listing 145 species occurring in the park or in the immediate vicinity. The address is 150 Park Road 32, Tuscola, TX 79562, (915) 572-3204.

Lake Abilene

Lake Abilene, 653 surface acres, is operated by the City of Abilene for municipal water supply. Bird seekers are welcome during daylight hours seven days a week. The entrance is on FM 89 across the highway from Abilene State Park. In winter Mallard, Gadwall, Northern Pintail, American Wigeon, Northern Shoveler, Canvasback, Ruddy Duck and American Coot are found. Redhead, Ring-necked Duck, Hooded Merganser, and Bufflehead are less likely. Woodlands consisting of junipers, live oaks and red oaks surround the lake. Eastern, Western and Mountain Bluebirds, and sometimes Canyon Towhee, can be found around the lake in winter.

Abilene Zoological Gardens

Abilene Zoological Gardens at Nelson Park, 13 acres, is on the east side of town on SH 36, just north of the municipal airport and West Texas Fairgrounds. It has a display of amphibians, reptiles, mammals and 49 species of birds. Bullock's Oriole nest and ducks winter on the ponds in the park. White-faced Ibis and Yellow-headed Blackbird have been recorded in migration.

Lake Fort Phantom Hill

Lake Fort Phantom Hill, 39,050 surface acres, is operated by the City of Abilene for recreation and municipal water supply. The lake is about six miles north of downtown Abilene between FM 600 (west side) and FM 2833 (east side). Seabee Park, 184 acres, is a City of Abilene park. It is a prime birding spot between FM 600 and the lake. The park has picnicking, camping, and fishing. The wintering ducks on the lake are the same species listed for Lake Abilene. Permanent residents are Great Blue Heron, Belted Kingfisher, Ladder-backed Woodpecker, and Blue Jay. American White Pelican, Sandhill Crane, American Pipit and many sparrow species are present in winter.

Will Hair Park

Will Hair Park is just north of downtown Abilene about one-half mile east of Loop 243 on SH 351 (Ambler Avenue). This 25-acre city park has picnicking, restrooms, a playground, and a nature trail. Winter residents include Spotted Towhee, White-crowned, White-throated, Field and Vesper Sparrows, Dark-eyed Junco, and sometimes Fox Sparrow.

Kirby Lake

Kirby Lake, 800 surface acres, is operated by the City of Abilene for municipal water. It is at the city's southern edge about 5 miles from downtown. From US 83-84 drive east on Loop 322 approximately 1.5 miles, then south on Maple Street to the entrance. Paved roads are on the east side; the dirt roads on the west side may be deeply rutted and uncertain after rain. There is a restroom near the Maple Street entrance. The lake is open to birders during daylight hours seven days a week.

Nesting species include Red-tailed and Swainson's Hawks, Eastern Phoebe, Cactus Wren, Painted Bunting, and Bell's Vireo.

The west shore is excellent for migrating shorebirds. Rarities include Black-bellied, Semipalmated, and Snowy Plovers, Whimbrel, Buff-breasted Sandpiper, and Hudsonian Godwit. Other accidental records are Roseate Spoonbill, Long-tailed Jaeger and Red Knot.

Ducks and sparrows are plentiful in winter. Horned and Clark's Grebes, Neotropic Cormorant, White-tailed Kite, Bald Eagle, Caspian Tern, and Marsh Wren are some examples of rare winter visitors.

City of Abilene Wastewater Treatment Plant

The City of Abilene Wastewater Treatment Plant is located on SH 351 northeast of Abilene about 6 miles north of the intersection of I-20 and SH 351. The plant is in the extreme southeast corner of Jones County near the community of Hamby. This is the most reliable location in the area for migrating shorebirds.

Nesting species include Black-necked Stilt, and Black-crowned and Yellow-crowned Night-Herons. Mountain Plover was recorded in April, 1996—a first sighting for the area. Peregrine Falcon occur in migration diving on shorebirds. In addition, herons, egrets, and numerous waterfowl can be found in season. The species list for Lake Abilene is applicable here.

A bird checklist for Taylor and southern Jones County is available for 50 cents plus addressed, stamped envelope from Big Country Audubon Society, Attn: Bird Checklist, P.O. Box 569, Abilene, TX 79604.

SAN ANGELO

San Angelo, population 87,000, is located at the southern extreme of the Rolling Plains, where the North, Middle, and South Concho rivers join to form the Concho River. The Edwards Plateau is just to the south. San Angelo is the major lamb, wool, and mohair distribution center for the state. Most of the area is devoted to ranching, except for the Lipan Flats area just east of the city where cotton and grain sorghum are grown.

Short-grass prairies with mesquite and other shrubs are the dominant vegetation near San Angelo, with mid-grasses and live oak and juniper on the Edwards Plateau to the south.

A field checklist to birds of the Concho Valley region, Texas (counties of Concho, Irion, Sterling, Tom Green and portions of Reagan, Glasscock and Schleicher), (1997) with 329 species plus 3 hypotheticals is available for 25 cents and a legal-size, stamped, addressed envelope from the San Angelo Nature Center, 7409 Knickerbocker Road, San Angelo, TX 76904.

Lakes

There is a series of man-made lakes in the San Angelo area: O.C. Fischer Lake, Lake Nasworthy, Twin Buttes Reservoir, E. V.

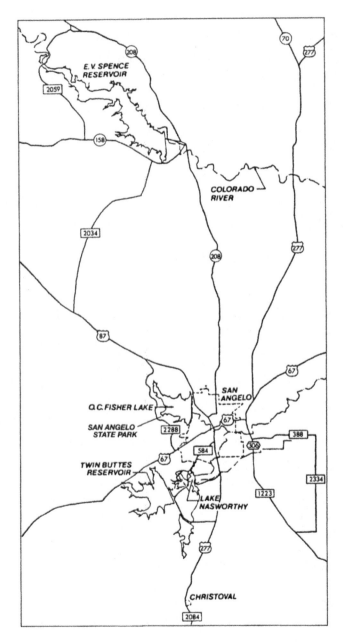

SAN ANGELO

Spence Reservoir, and O. H. Ivie Reservoir. All of the lakes have numerous waterfowl in winter and all are described below. There are 29 species on the local checklist including Greater White-fronted, Snow, and Canada Geese, Cinnamon Teal, Common Goldeneye, Hooded, Common, and Red-breasted Mergansers. The lakes have wooded and grassland areas of varying size as well as muddy shorelines creating the possibility for a variety of birds.

Lake Nasworthy

Lake Nasworthy, a constant level lake with 1,210 surface acres, is in southwestern San Angelo just below Twin Buttes Reservoir.

The lake is reached by driving south from town on FM 584 (Knickerbocker Road) about 6 miles, or west about 3 miles on Country Club Road from just south of the intersection of US 277 and US 87 (Loop 306). Most of the shoreline is leased to private residences, but there are many parks and other places where the lake can be birded. Do not trespass on private property. A spotting scope helps.

Most of the wintering water birds have been recorded on the lake including Cinnamon Teal, Wood Duck, Hooded Merganser, and Common Loon.

An excellent location for migrating Yellow-headed Blackbird and shorebirds is on an arm of Lake Nasworthy known locally as Ducote's Mud Flat. From FM 584 just south of the Lake Nasworthy bridge, drive left on South Concho Drive 0.9 mile to the mud flats. Do not cross the fence since this is private property. The best time to visit Ducote's Mud Flat is in the morning when the light is more favorable than in the afternoon. Birds found in migration include American Avocet, Long-billed Curlew, White-faced Ibis, Marbled Godwit, Hudsonian Godwit, and Willet plus most of the small sandpipers and plovers on the local checklist. A few Black-necked Stilt have nested in addition to being regular migrants.

Middle Concho Park

This park is on the Middle Concho River section of Lake Nasworthy just below the Twin Buttes spillway, and is just across the river from the San Angelo Nature Center Wilderness Trail. It is easily reached by going southwest from San Angelo on FM 584 (Knickerbocker Road) and turning right on Red Bluff Road at a convenience store. If you cross Lake Nasworthy bridge you have gone too far. Follow Red Bluff Road, keeping right all the way, to the entrance to the park. The park consists mainly of large, old pecan trees and mowed grassy areas. It is used quite extensively by fishermen who camp there at night. Just past the entrance kiosk (there is a small fee on summer weekends) you may turn left or right, or drive straight ahead and wind up in the lake. The left road dead ends shortly at the water edge but is excellent all year for Eastern Bluebird, and even (rarely) Vermilion Flycatcher. The right road, partly paved and partly graveled, goes to the spillway of Twin Buttes Dam. The north side of this road is a mesquite tangle with extensive undergrowth. In this undergrowth look for Canyon Towhee, and in winter White-crowned Sparrow. Other birds seen in winter include Red-naped and Yellow-bellied Sapsuckers, Eared Grebe, and numerous ducks. Green Heron are usually present during migration.

When you get to the spillway, there is a dirt road going off to the right. There is a gate that is sometimes locked, particularly at night and on weekends. If locked, walk in on this road for a few hundred yards. The hillside on the left is known by local birders as Gnatcatcher Hill. The rocky brush-covered hillside is good for Rock Wren in winter, and occasionally nesting Canyon Wren. For three years an Elf Owl was found in early July. Yellow-billed Cuckoo and Painted Bunting are common nesting species, and in 1994 a singing Varied Bunting was found. Pyrrhuloxia are found in the mesquite brushland across the road from Gnatcatcher Hill. If the gate is unlocked you may drive this road, turning right at the dam, and come out at the Middle Concho Pool on Twin Buttes

Reservoir. In winter, after leaving the dam watch for Green-tailed Towhee in the thick underbrush of the mesquite habitat.

San Angelo Nature Center

The San Angelo Nature Center contains excellent exhibits of area flora in its office/museum building at Lake Nasworthy. The center can be reached by going southwest on FM 584 (Knicker-bocker Road), crossing the Lake Nasworthy bridge and immediately turning right. The combination museum and office building is behind the Lake Nasworthy Marina. The center is open from 1 to 6 pm, Tuesday through Saturday, and a small fee is charged for entrance. The address is San Angelo Nature Center, 7409 Knickerbocker Road, San Angelo, TX 76903, (915) 942-0121.

The center also operates two nature trails. The wilderness trail is reached by continuing southwest on FM 584 past the entrance to Mathis Field Municipal Airport, then turning right on Spillway Road (the first paved road). Follow this road, always keeping left, for 2.0 miles to the marked parking area on the right. The trail is about one mile long and easy walking. There are several numbered markers and a leaflet describing each is available at the Nature Center Office. The trail has several different natural features. Part of the area has large pecan trees along the water line, with mesquite brush and heavy undergrowth in other parts. The front part of the area is a rocky hillside with scattered mesquite and juniper brush. Birds likely to be encountered are Cactus, Bewick's, and Carolina Wrens, Curve-billed Thrasher, Verdin, and White-winged Dove. Great Horned Owl are often seen resting in the big trees and the area also has Western Screech-Owl. Watch on the rocky hillside for Rufous-crowned Sparrow. Belted Kingfisher are commonly seen along the adjacent waterways. Summer residents are Scissor-tailed and Ash-throated Flycatchers, Eastern Phoebe, Blue Grosbeak, Bell's Vireo, and Yellow-breasted Chat. Wintering species include Swamp and Fox Sparrows, sometimes Golden-crowned Kinglet, Brown Thrasher, Hermit Thrush, Spotted Towhee and Sharp-shinned Hawk. Migrants usually include several warbler species including Nashville, Wilson's and Yellow Warblers, Least Flycatcher, Lazuli Bunting, and Clay-colored and Brewer's Sparrows. In winter, waterfowl are often seen on the lake from the trail. Also, look for Rock Wren on the rocky rip-rap below the end of the road. This wilderness trail is open 24 hours a day and permission is not required.

The San Angelo Nature Center Spring Creek Wetland Area is a new trail system that contains the same type of habitat as the Wilderness Trail, but also includes some marshy wetland area. The birds found are essentially the same as those on the Wilderness Trail except for the marsh-dwelling birds, such as rails. The wetland area is reached by continuing southwest on Knickerbocker Road from the Nature Center building to a locked entrance on the right, nearly opposite the Municipal Airport. This area is kept locked and permission to enter must be obtained from the office.

Twin Buttes Reservoir

Twin Buttes Reservoir, 9,080 surface acres, is just above Lake Nasworthy. The lake level varies often, creating mud flats.

To bird the South Pool area, drive past Lake Nasworthy and the Municipal Airport on FM 584 (Knickerbocker Road) until the road makes a left turn. Immediately after this, turn right at a sign for the community of Knickerbocker and cross the dam. After crossing the equalization channel at the bottom of the dam, turn left over a cattle guard onto a dirt road. This road winds around the south pool area. Check the salt cedar area for singing passerines, the mud flats for shorebirds, and the lake for waterfowl.

The Middle Concho Pool is reached by driving west on US 67 about 3.3 miles past the intersection with FM 2288. Turn left onto a hard surface road by a convenience store, and follow a camping sign into the park. This is a good winter birding location.

City of San Angelo

There are numerous favorable birding locations in the city. River Drive along the North Concho River from Santa Fe Park (Golf Course) north to the 19th Street bridge is lined with large trees and brushy areas, giving the opportunity to bird the river along with its margins. There are several turnouts along the drive for parking: for instance, Rio Concho Drive (an extension of River Drive) from downtown to Bell Street, and Fairmount Cemetery on Avenue N. Mississippi Kite nest in tall trees in the city. The southwest section of the city in the vicinity of Oxford Street has been a good general area.

Cave Swallow can be found nesting under most small bridges and culverts on US 67 west and US 277 south from San Angelo. A very easy location is the Red Arroyo bridge adjacent to Rivercrest Hospital on Arden Road about 0.8 mile east of FM 2288.

San Angelo State Park

San Angelo State Park, 18,000 acres, is located on the south, west, and north shores on O. C. Fisher Lake.

The entrances (one north and one south) are from FM 2288 west of San Angelo, between US 87 on the north and US 67 on the south.

The park, established in 1995, consists mainly of mesquite brushland with stands of pecan and black willow along the water edges. Access for birding is limited, but walk-in birding is allowed at many places with prior approval from park officials. Headquarters is open 8 am to 5 pm, Monday through Friday. Note that access is limited on weekends. Facilities include camping with hookups, tent camping, restrooms with hot showers, picnicking, a boat ramp, and a hiking trail.

In the mesquite brushland permanent residents include Greater Roadrunner, Cactus Wren, Verdin, Scaled Quail, White-winged Dove, both Western and Eastern Screech-Owls, and Cassin's and

Black-throated Sparrows. Some regular summer residents are Mississippi Kite, Swainson's Hawk, Common Poorwill, Cave Swallow, Bell's Vireo, Painted Bunting, and Orchard and Bullock's Orioles. Wintering species include American White Pelican, most waterfowl of the area, an occasional Merlin, Peregrine or Prairie Falcon, Sora, Bonaparte's Gull, Burrowing Owl (especially along the top of the dam), Sprague's Pipit (in short grass area inside the lake spillway), and numerous sparrows. Long-eared Owl have been recorded in early morning and/or late afternoon in winter. The area is also an excellent migration location.

A bird checklist (1997) with 251 species is available at headquarters. The park address is 3900-2 Mercedes Street, San Angelo, TX 76901-2630, (915) 949-4757. For camping reservations call (512) 389-8900.

Lipan Flats

Southeast of San Angelo between FM 308 on the north, FM 1223 on the south, Loop 306 on the west, and FM 2334 on the east, is an agricultural area called the Lipan Flats. The principal crops are grain sorghum and cotton. In late fall and winter look in the fields for Horned Lark, Mountain Plover, and longspurs. Most longspurs will be McCown's, but Chestnut-collared are also found, and less frequently Lapland. Prairie Falcons often perch on power poles. Mountain Plover are not as frequently found as the above, but if a farmer is plowing, scope the fields carefully, as freshly plowed fields often attract the birds. Song, Vesper, and Savannah Sparrow, and Northern Harrier are usually present.

Common Raven, which nest on utility poles west of the city, and Vermilion Flycatcher, which are common in summer near ranch windmills, are more easily found by driving along roads outside the city. In the sparsely vegetated rangeland listen for Common Poorwill at night during spring and summer. Lark Bunting is abundant throughout the area in winter.

E. V. Spence Reservoir

E. V. Spence Reservoir, 14,950 surface acres, created by a dam on the Colorado River, is north of San Angelo near the town of Robert Lee. The lake is owned and operated by the Colorado River Municipal Water District. To reach the reservoir, drive 30 miles north on SH 208 to Robert Lee, then west on SH 158 to the south shore of the reservoir, or drive north past Robert Lee on SH 208 to the county roads leading to the north shore. Taking FM 1907 west from downtown Robert Lee will lead to the north end of the dam.

Wintering ducks are plentiful. Gadwall, Northern Pintail, Green-winged Teal, American Wigeon, Northern Shoveler, Canvasback, Lesser Scaup, Bufflehead, and Ruddy Duck are the most common. Be on the lookout for Cinnamon Teal, Common Merganser, and Common Goldeneye. In winter look for Sandhill Crane, which roost in the shallow water at the upstream end of the reservoir in great numbers and are best seen in very early morning before they leave to feed (about sunup), and late afternoon when they return to roost. Eared and Horned Grebes are also present in winter.

The divide between the Concho and Colorado River watersheds has nesting Canyon Wren and Black-capped Vireo. To reach the divide drive south and west on SH 158 from Robert Lee to RR 2034, then south on RR 2034 about eight miles.

O. H. Ivie Reservoir

O. H. Ivie Reservoir is owned and operated by the Colorado River Municipal Water District. There are 19,200 surface acres at conservation pool level.

From Ballinger drive south on US 83 about 13 miles to FM 1929, then east on FM 1929 12 miles to the lake. From Paint Rock drive north on US 83 3.6 miles to FM 1929, then east on FM 1929 as described above. From Coleman take SH 206 to US

67, then west on US 67 to FM 503, and finally take FM 503 south to the lake.

This is a new lake where the avifauna is only beginning to be studied. It is located on the Colorado River just below its confluence with the Concho River, where Concho, Runnels, and Coleman counties meet.

After crossing the Concho River on FM 1929 from the west, there are several roads turning north toward the lake that lead to Concho and Kennedy parks. These parks offer a boat ramp, restrooms, and camping. Both areas have a privately owned marina with restaurant and motel, R.V. sites, etc. In Concho and Kennedy parks look for trailers where visitors are feeding birds. FM 1929 leads to FM 503, then turn north on FM 503 and drive a short distance to FM 2134, which leads to Padgitt Park. The park has a boat ramp, restrooms, and camping. The parks and the roads leading to the parks are all favorable for birds.

In December, 1996, 104 species were found at the lake in one day, including Common Loon, Horned Grebe, Red-breasted Merganser, Bald Eagle, Red-shouldered Hawk, Common Tern, Barred Owl, Chihuahuan and Common Ravens, Bushtit, Winter and Marsh Wrens, Mountain Bluebird, and Green-tailed Towhee.

Phone numbers are as follows: Kennedy Park concessionaire (915) 357-4776; Concho Park concessionaire (915) 357-4466; Lake Superintendent (915) 357-4486.

Christoval, Dan Brown's Ranch

Dan Brown, a rancher who is also an expert on archaeology, geology and gems, and a very good birder, feeds birds at his ranch and welcomes other birders to share. **He only asks that visitors notify him in advance of arrival.**

Directions to the ranch are: go south from San Angelo on US 277 about 17 miles, take Loop 110 through Christoval, then drive east from Christoval on RR 2084 1.8 miles to the gate on the right. The ranch house is less than a mile from the highway.

Mr. Brown has many hummingbird feeders, as well as feeders for other birds. Black-chinned Hummingbird is an abundant summer resident, and Ruby-throated and Rufous Hummingbirds migrate in late summer and early fall. He was recognized in 1994 and 1995 at the Hummer/Bird Celebration in Rockport for having fed more hummingbirds than anyone else in Texas. Scaled Quail and Wild Turkey are common, as well as many perching birds.

Mr. Brown has a guest house, Hummer House, that he rents to interested people by the day or longer. The house is completely furnished. The address is P.O. Box 555, Christoval, TX 76935, (915) 255-2254 (local call from San Angelo), fax (915) 255-2463.

WHITE RIVER LAKE

White River Lake, 1,800 surface acres, is operated by the White River Municipal Water District to supply water to neighboring cities. It is created by a dam on the White River, a tributary of the Brazos River.

To reach the lake from Lubbock, drive east on FM 40 for 37 miles to the end of the road, then go south on FM 651 for 7 miles. Turn east on FM 2794 and go about 8 miles to the lake, or go 13 miles west of Spur on FM 2794. A gravel road leads around both sides of the lake to many overlooks, boat launching sites, three campgrounds with running water and restrooms, and picnic areas. There is an entrance fee.

Located in the mesquite grasslands of the Rolling Plains, the lake is the largest permanent body of water for at least 75 miles in any direction. Bird habitats in addition to the lake include wooded dry water courses, or "draws", the adjacent marshes, and grasslands.

Nesting birds include Painted Bunting, Purple Martin, Western and Eastern Kingbirds, Curve-billed Thrasher, Orchard and Bullock's Orioles, and Scissor-tailed Flycatcher. Cassin's and Lark Sparrows are abundant in the grasslands surrounding the lake.

In winter, sparrows commonly found in the draws and the grasslands are Savannah, Rufous-crowned, Field, White-crowned, Fox, Song, and Dark-eyed Junco. Less common species include Vesper, American Tree, White-throated, Harris', and Lincoln's. Other possibilities are Chipping, Brewer's, Swamp, and Baird's Sparrows.

Long-eared Owl winter in the dense draws, usually only a few feet above the ground. This is one of the few places in Texas where I have seen Baird's Sparrow. A Northern Shrike was found here in late December, 1995.

Many wintering hawks can be found in the vicinity of the lake. Sharp-shinned, Cooper's, Red-tailed, Rough-legged, and Ferruginous Hawks, Northern Harrier, Golden Eagle, Prairie Falcon, and American Kestrel are all regular in winter.

The marshy areas support a dense growth of trees, shrubs, and thick herbaceous plants where Marsh Wrens are common in winter.

Water birds recorded in winter include Common Loon, Horned, Eared, and Pied-billed Grebes, Double-crested Cormorant, and about 12 waterfowl species. Red-breasted Mergansers are seen occasionally and Red-necked Grebe have been recorded.

HOODED MERGANSER

BIG SPRING

Big Spring, population 23,000, is on I-20 near the convergence of the Rolling Plains, Llano Estacado, and Edwards Plateau. The Trans-Pecos is only about 60 miles west. Birds from all these areas are possible near Big Spring.

Thousands of Sandhill Crane spend the winter in the area. The best way to see them is at One Mile Lake (more information following) and at playa lakes west of Big Spring. In the grasslands of the area look for Burrowing Owl and Horned Lark. The mesquite pastures provide habitat for Red-tailed Hawk, Scaled Quail, Greater Roadrunner, Golden-fronted and Ladder-backed Woodpeckers, Verdin, and Pyrrhuloxia. Mississippi Kite and Swainson's Hawk are common summer residents. Other nesting birds include Chihuahuan Raven, Ash-throated Flycatchers, Yellow-billed Cuckoo, and Chipping and Lark Sparrows.

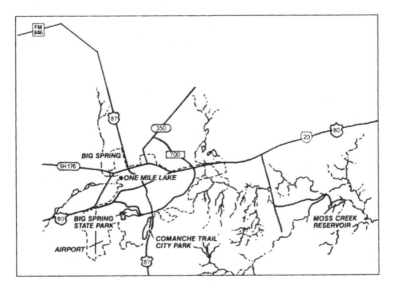

BIG SPRING

Some wintering hawks of the area are Sharp-shinned, Cooper's, Rough-legged, and Ferruginous Hawks, Northern Harrier, and Prairie Falcon.

When fall and winter rainfall is sufficient there are two roads that can be productive for Sandhill Crane, hawks and waterfowl. The roads are near the southern extremity of playas of the plains. The first is FM 846 through the community of Knott. Drive north from Big Spring 12.2 miles on US 87 to FM 846, then drive west. One February day while attending the "Cranefest" I saw four hawk species and nine duck species, along with dozens of Sandhill Cranes, on FM 846. The second is SH 176 northwest from Big Spring toward Andrews. Be sure to check the water crossing about 10 miles from Big Spring.

Several good birding spots are south of McMahon/Wrinkle Air Park. The areas can be reached by going west on I-20 (Business) 2 miles past US 87 to Airbase Road, turn left (south) and continue straight ahead 1.1 miles to Randolph Road. After passing the Westside Day Care building, turn right and drive past the prison facilities. Turn left on Parimeter Road to the grassland and mesquite pasture area where you can pull off for observation. Park and walk around the area about half a block west of the police training center. This is a good area for warblers, kinglets, Curve-billed Thrasher, Cactus and Bewick's Wrens, sparrows and other species in season. Great Horned Owl has been recorded here. Nineteen sparrow species have been recorded locally.

A bird checklist for Howard County (1988) with 274 species is available from the Big Spring Chamber of Commerce, P.O. Box 1391, Big Spring, TX 79721, or at Big Spring State Park. There is no charge for the check-list, but send a stamped, addressed letter-size envelope.

Big Spring State Park

Big Spring State Park, 382 acres, is located in the southwest section of Big Spring. To reach the park drive south on US 87 to FM 700, then west one mile to the park entrance. Facilities in-

CACTUS WREN

clude hiking trails, picnicking, restrooms, playgrounds, and a few camping spaces.

In the park there is a three-mile road around "Scenic Mountain" that can be driven or walked. This 200-foot-high limestone-capped mesa is the main attraction of the park for many visitors. There is a marked nature trail just after the drive starts up the mountain at the Prairie Dog Village. The trail with juniper, shin oak, mesquite, and hackberry is a good introduction to the native trees and plants of the area as well as the birds.

Nesting birds include Western Scrub-Jay, Cassin's and Rufous-crowned Sparrows. In winter look for Green-tailed, Canyon, and Spotted Towhees, Mountain Bluebird, and Rock Wren. The park address is #1 Scenic Drive, Big Spring, TX 79720, (915) 263-4931.

Comanche Trail Park

Comanche Trail Park, 432 acres, is owned and operated by the City of Big Spring. Facilities include a golf course, picnicking, restrooms, playgrounds, and a new "Kid Zone" playground. This has been a very popular local birding location.

To reach the park from Big Spring, drive south on US 87 past FM 700. The first entrance is a little over a city block on the west side, the second is about one mile on the right (west) and leads into the heart of the park.

Located on a shallow draw, the park provides abundant shelter, food, and water for birds.

Birds that nest regularly in the park are Lesser Goldfinch, Western Kingbird, and Scissor-tailed Flycatcher. There are also nesting records of Painted Bunting, Phainopepla, and Bell's Vireo. In winter look for Western Bluebird, Red-breasted Nuthatch, Townsend's Solitaire, Sage Thrasher, and Bushtit. A Greater Pewee visited for about three weeks in the fall of 1984.

Park in the main section of the park and walk north to "The Big Spring," after which the city was named, and then across the dam. This spring, the only one in a 30-mile radius, has provided a watering place for wildlife, Indians, explorers, and settlers. The natural area between the park and The Big Spring is an excellent birding location where most resident and migrant passerines can be found. Wintering species on the lake include American Wigeon, Bufflehead, Canvasback, Ruddy and Ring-necked Ducks, American Coot, Great Blue Heron, and Belted Kingfisher. Ring-billed Gull and Double-crested Cormorant have been recorded in recent years.

One Mile Lake

One Mile Lake is located in the northwest part of the city next to the railroad tracks. There are several sites from which to observe the lake. The first can be reached by driving west approximately one mile on W. Third Street (I-20 Business), turning right on Jones Street, and driving three blocks. The second site is reached by driving north on US 87 to the first light after crossing the viaduct (Sgt. Paredez), turning west (left), and going approximately six blocks, crossing the railroad tracks, turning left (one way) on Channing Street, and traveling south, following the tracks to the viewing location. A closer view of shorebirds and Sandhill Cranes can be reached by turning right (instead of left) after crossing the railroad tracks, driving to NW 7th, turning left and going almost to the end. Park on the street or park in the weedy lot area. While this is a great bird spot, caution is advised if entering this neighborhood alone.

One Mile Lake is the winter resting and roosting location for large numbers of Sandhill Crane. The cranes arrive in mid-October and spend the winter. Early morning and late afternoon are the best times to see them as they depart for and return from their feeding areas. Numbers depend on weather and water conditions but more than 6,000 have been observed in recent years. In addition, wintering species include American Avocet, White-faced Ibis, Black and Least Terns, Long-billed Dowitcher, Black-necked Stilt, Greater and Lesser Yellowlegs, Least, Western, Semipalmated, Solitary, and White-rumped Sandpipers, plus numerous ducks.

The City of Big Spring, with help from local birders, is working to improve this area to attract birds and birders.

Moss Creek Lake

Moss Creek Lake, southeast of Big Spring, has swimming, fishing, picnicking, boating, and an opportunity for sparrows, waterfowl, and numerous other species, especially in winter. To reach the lake drive east on I-20 about 7 miles to Moss Creek Lake Road, then turn south and drive 5 miles to the park entrance.

There are excellent birding spots on the last two or three miles of this drive, so keep a sharp look-out, especially at the bridge. Both sides of the lake provide good overlooks; the shoreline can be hiked also. In the winter Sandhill Crane fly over the lake in early morning on their way from a roosting area to feeding grounds. The checklist for the county has nineteen waterfowl species, most of which can be seen on Moss Creek Lake. The park is closed in December. There is an entrance fee.

4

Edwards Plateau

The Edwards Plateau region, approximately 17% of the state, is an elevated area of lower Cretaceous limestone. On the east and south the boundary is the prominent Balcones Escarpment. It runs south from west of Waco through Austin and San Antonio, then west to Del Rio. The northern limit, a very indistinct and discontinuous boundary, is where the limestone meets the Permi-

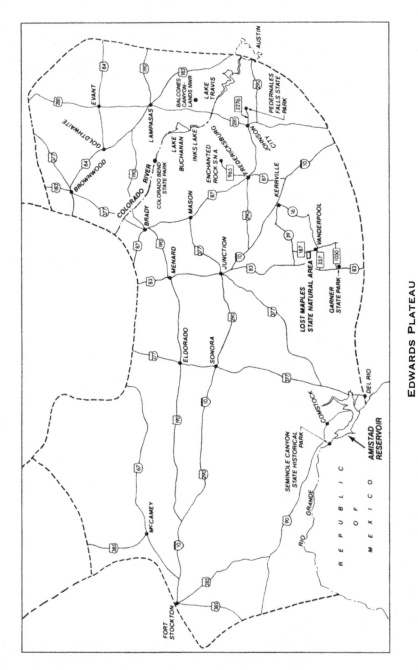

EDWARDS PLATEAU

an and Pennsylvanian deposits of the Rolling Plains. This line runs roughly south of San Angelo, northwestward more or less south of Midland and Odessa, then south to the Rio Grande through Fort Stockton.

The eastern and southern portion of the region bordering the Balcones Fault is the "Hill Country," also known as the Balcones Canyonlands, with deep canyons, numerous active springs, and thin, rocky soil. Between the Colorado, San Saba, and Pedernales Rivers is the Central Mineral Basin, also called the Llano Uplift. This is an ancient uplift of Paleozoic sedimentary and Precambrian igneous and metamorphic rocks, an exception to the general limestone deposits of the rest of the plateau.

Examples of these formations, which are among the oldest in the state, can be seen at Inks Lake State Park and Enchanted Rock State Natural Area. Elevation increases westward from 550 feet at Austin to more than 3,000 feet on the Stockton Plateau. Rainfall decreases from an average of 33 inches to 12 inches, east to west.

The region is underlain by massive limestone strata (in some areas several hundred feet thick), the soil is thin and rocky, and the terrain is hilly with many deep canyons, except the margins along stream valleys. Most of the region is devoted to cattle, sheep, and goat ranching. Hunters seeking the common white-tailed deer and wild turkey are an important income source for many ranchers.

Juniper and oak are the dominant woody plants. Formerly, the uplands were tall and mid-grasslands; now they are heavily invaded by woody plants. Bald cypress is common along the many perennial streams. There are numerous springs, which in turn create and feed many streams and rivers. The vegetation of the Stockton Plateau is similar to that of the low limestone ranges of the Chihuahuan Desert.

The unique nesting birds of the Edwards Plateau are Golden-cheeked Warbler and Black-capped Vireo. The vireo is found in two other regions of the state but is perhaps more common and widespread on the plateau. The Golden-cheeked Warbler is not known to nest anywhere else in the world. Birdwise, both eastern and western species are found. In the stream bottoms, eastern species extend their range westward. Examples of western species that are common nesters are Northern Rough-winged Swallow, Common Poorwill, Black-chinned Hummingbird, Western Scrub-Jay, Bushtit, Bell's Vireo, Golden-fronted Woodpecker, Lesser Goldfinch, and Rufous-crowned Sparrow.

In addition to the locations detailed in this chapter, bird checklists are available at the following locations: Enchanted Rock State Natural Area, north of Fredericksburg; Guadalupe River State Park/Honey Creek State Natural Area, between Boerne and New Braunfels; Hill Country State Natural Area, southwest of Bandera; and Kickapoo Cavern State Natural Area, north of Brackettville.

AUSTIN

Austin, the capital of Texas, population 501,000, is located on the Balcones Escarpment where the Colorado River passes from the Edwards Plateau to Central Texas. The birds of both areas are well represented. There are several large man-made lakes in all directions from the city. The Central Mineral Basin, between Burnet and Llano, is 50 miles northwest, and the "Lost Pines of Texas" at Bastrop is 30 miles east. These features make Austin an interesting area for birds.

RARE BIRD ALERT, (512) 926-8751, Travis Audubon Society.

There are more than 11,000 acres of parks administered by the Austin Parks and Recreation Department. Six parks, representing the different habitats in and around Austin are to be preserved as natural areas. Natural area acquisition is continuing. Most of the parks are along creeks with wooded areas that provide favorable bird habitats. Eastwoods Park has long been a favorite for migrating warblers and other land birds. The park is located on Waller

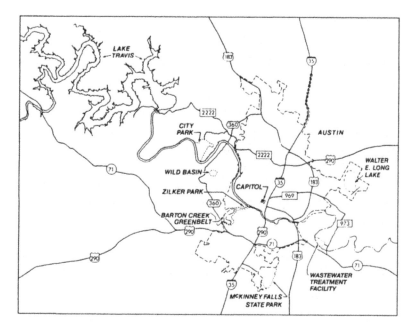

AUSTIN

Creek at the intersection of 26th Street and Harris Park Boulevard, only a couple of blocks from The University of Texas campus.

In the Austin area many species are at the periphery of their range. Red-bellied Woodpecker, Ruby-throated Hummingbird, and Blue Jay nest in the city and are common east; while Golden-fronted Woodpecker, Black-chinned Hummingbird, Western Scrub-Jay, Black-capped Vireo, and Golden-cheeked Warbler are at the eastern edge of their range. Other species found west of the city but rarely seen in the east are Bullock's Oriole, Lesser Goldfinch, Rufous-crowned Sparrow, Common Poorwill, Ash-throated Flycatcher, Vermilion Flycatcher, Verdin, Bushtit, and House Finch. The Blue Jay seems to be moving west with urban development.

Zilker Park

Zilker Park, 350 acres, is located on the south shore of Town Lake and is bisected by Barton Creek. To get there, go west from downtown on Barton Springs Road or south on Loop 1 (MoPac Boulevard). Barton Springs flows 37,000,000 gallons of water per day at 68° F year-round. The pool is a gathering spot for swimmers in great numbers, especially on summer weekends, but it is large enough to accommodate them. The park has ball fields, an excellent garden center with a Japanese garden, hike-and-bike trails, picnicking, and a miniature railroad, but no camping. Up Barton Creek two-plus miles to Loop 360 is the Barton Creek Greenbelt, an excellent place to hike and look for birds of the area. Here, Canyon, Bewick's, and Carolina Wrens, and Belted Kingfisher, are permanent residents. On Town Lake, Wood Duck can be found in summer; in winter Gadwall, Lesser Scaup, Amer-

CANYON WREN

ican Coot, and Pied-billed Grebe are very common. Other duck species are less common, except during migration.

Wild Basin Wilderness Preserve

Wild Basin Wilderness Preserve is a 227-acre Travis County preserve owned by Travis County and managed by the Committee for Wild Basin for the purpose of keeping a segment of the Texas Hill Country in its natural state for educational purposes. Located in the hills west of Lake Austin, the preserve is in the upper drainage of Bee Creek. The creek is usually dry, but in the rainy season it can be full and is very scenic.

To reach the preserve, drive southwest from Austin on Loop 1 (MoPac Boulevard) to RR 2244 (Bee Caves Road), then go west about four miles to Loop 360. Turn north and drive on Loop 360 for three-quarters of a mile to the entrance.

Golden-cheeked Warbler, Black-capped Vireo, and Yellow-breasted Chat nest at the preserve. Guided and self-guided tours are available. Approximately 5,000 school children, led by volunteers, tour the preserve annually. There is an interpretative center where maps are available and nature items are for sale.

Picnicking and pets are not allowed at the preserve.

The address is 805 N. Capital of Texas Highway, Austin, TX 78746, (512) 327-7622.

Golden-cheeked Warbler and Black-capped Vireo

On the Edwards Plateau immediately west of the city, locally called the "Hill Country," the Golden-cheeked Warbler can be found where mature Ashe juniper (cedar) and oaks occur. It is the only bird that nests solely in Texas. Golden-cheeks summer in a narrow area from as far north as Dinosaur Valley State Park southwest to near Del Rio. This narrow band follows and is just west of the Balcones Escarpment. Mature Ashe juniper is being ravaged daily by housing developments and cedar-clearing, conditions that cause the bird to be on the Endangered Species List of the U.S. Department of the Interior.

97

BLACK-CAPPED VIREO

In the immediate Austin area, City Park has been another fa-vored location for finding Golden-cheeked Warbler. City Park is at the end of City Park Road, which is west off RR 2222 a short distance north of the intersection of Loop 360 and RR 2222.Gold-en-cheeks can be found in City Park along Turkey Creek, the only creek that crosses City Park Road. There is a trail up the creek that should be walked until the Golden-cheeks are heard. The creek is near the entrance to the swimming and camping portion of City Park, about five miles from RR 2222.

Travis Audubon Society owns and manages a 600-plus acre sanctuary where Golden-cheeked Warbler spend the summer. Per-mission to enter and directions should be obtained from the sanc-tuary manager, (512) 219-8425.

Hornsby Bend Wastewater Treatment Facility

The Hornsby Bend Wastewater Treatment Facility has been the best location in the area for migrating shorebirds and wintering waterfowl. Entry regulations change from time to time.

To reach the facility drive east from I-35 on FM 969 (MLK Blvd.) about 8 miles to FM 973, then south on FM 973, 3.3 miles to the entrance road on the right, or from SH 71 east of the city go 1 mile north on FM 973. On the drying basins shorebirds can be very abundant in July through October, then again in March, April, and May. Some birds are present all year. During these times as many as 23 species of shorebirds have been recorded on a single day. At least 41 shorebird species have been recorded here over the past 25 years. Waterfowl are present in large numbers in winter, mostly Northern Shoveler, Green-winged Teal, and Lesser Scaup. Black-bellied Whistling-Duck have nested in recent years.

A bird checklist for the facility is available at the entrance to the City of Austin Water and Wastewater Building, or from the Travis Audubon Society.

At Lake Walter E. Long, 1.5 miles north of the intersection of FM 973 and FM 969, waterfowl winter and Least Bittern and Pied-billed Grebe have nested. Osprey are usually present in spring and fall. The lake is surrounded by woods and grasslands. There is an entrance fee to enter the lake property, where there are picnic tables and a boat ramp. In fall and winter check below the dam from FM 973 where Virginia Rail, Sora, Hooded Merganser, Swamp Sparrow and Common Yellowthroat are found in or near the abundant cattails.

There are several state parks within a one-hour drive of Austin, each offering a completely different habitat for birds. These are McKinney Falls State Park (Edwards Plateau and Blackland Prairies), Pedernales Falls State Park (Edwards Plateau), Palmetto State Park (swamps and woody river bottom in the Post Oak Savannah of Central Texas), Bastrop and Buescher State Parks (Lost Pines of Central Texas), and Inks Lake State Park (Central Mineral Basin of the Edwards Plateau). Each is described more fully elsewhere in this book.

A bird checklist for the Austin Region (1994) with 393 species is available from the Travis Audubon Society, 5401 Martin Luther

King, Jr., Blvd., Austin, TX 78759, for 50 cents plus a stamped, addressed envelope. The Austin Region is defined as a circle with a radius of 60 miles centered in Austin.

INKS LAKE STATE PARK

Inks Lake State Park, 1,201 acres, is located 9 miles west of Burnet on SH 29. The park has picnic sites, camping with restrooms and hot showers, screen shelters, fishing, boating, golfing, hiking trails, and water skiing. The park is on Inks Lake just south of Lake Buchanan and is in the Central Mineral Basin, also called the Llano Uplift. Precambrian gneiss, schist, and granite are found on the surface here, some of the oldest exposed rock in the state.

Nesting birds of the area include Canyon Towhee, Cactus Wren, Verdin, Black-throated Sparrow, Bell's Vireo, Orchard Oriole, and Golden-cheeked Warbler. Osprey migrate regularly in spring and fall; they sometimes linger along the Colorado River.

The U.S. Fish Hatchery is an excellent location for wintering waterfowl. The hatchery is approximately 1 mile south of Inks Lake State Park on PR 4 and is open to visitors Monday through Friday during working hours and on Saturday morning.

A bird checklist for Inks Lake State Park, which includes the Fish Hatchery and Longhorn State Park (1994) with 139 species is available at park headquarters. The address is RR 22, Box 31, Burnet, TX 78611.

Lake Buchanan

In winter, Lake Buchanan and Inks Lake host Red-breasted Merganser, Common Loon, Horned Grebe, Herring, Ring-billed, and Bonaparte's Gulls, Forster's Tern, and a small wintering colony of Bald Eagle.

The Vanishing Texas River Cruise, accommodating 180 passengers, conducts year-round tours on Lake Buchanan. From mid-November to mid-March the cruise is the best opportunity to see

BLACK-THROATED SPARROW

eagles. To reach the cruise dock, drive west from Burnet on SH 29 three miles to RR 2341, turn right (north) and drive 13.5 miles to the well-marked entrance. For information write P. O. Box 901, Burnet, TX 78611, or call (512) 756-6986.

RR 690 and RR 2341 east of Lake Buchanan and SH 261 and RR 2241 west of the lake are good roads to check out the land birds around the lake. The partially developed subdivisions can be walked for the nesting species mentioned above and wintering sparrows. Lake Buchanan is 32 miles long and 8 miles wide.

PEDERNALES FALLS STATE PARK

Pedernales Falls State Park, 5,211 acres, is typical Edwards Plateau habitat with oaks and junipers (cedars) on the dry uplands and bald cypress and sycamores along the river, creeks, and intermittent streams. Approximately 90% of the acreage is being allowed to return to a natural condition. The park is 14 miles east of

Johnson City on RR 2766. From Austin, drive west 28 miles on US 290, then go 6 miles north on RR 3232.

Camping, restrooms with hot showers, primitive camping areas, picnicking, canoeing, fishing, swimming, and backpacking are available at the park. There are nine miles of Pedernales River frontage in the park. At the falls the river descends over a vast area of Paleozoic rock.

Nesting birds include Yellow-billed Cuckoo, Green and Belted Kingfishers, Chuck-will's-widow, Ladder-backed Woodpecker, Carolina Chickadee, Bushtit, Bewick's, Carolina, and Canyon Wrens, White-eyed Vireo, Orchard Oriole, House Finch, and Chipping and Field Sparrows. Wild Turkey are abundant, and are sometimes seen in the campground in early morning or late afternoon. White-tailed deer are very common.

From the middle of March to the middle of June, look for Golden-cheeked Warbler nesting in the park. Good places to look are at the top of the bluff along the river on the Pedernales Hill Country Nature Trail, on the trail between the parking lot and the overlook at the falls, and along the trail to the Primitive Camping Area.

A bird checklist for the park (1991) with 203 species is available at headquarters. The address is Route 1, Box 31-A, Johnson City, TX 78636, (512) 868-7304.

BALCONES CANYONLANDS NATIONAL WILDLIFE REFUGE

Balcones Canyonlands National Wildlife Refuge is located in Travis, Burnet and Williamson counties about 30 miles northwest of Austin. The refuge is in the acquisition and planning stage. It is hoped that it will eventually be 46,000 acres in extent. In early 1997, 14,000-plus acres in 20 separate tracts were acquired. The refuge, when completed, will preserve a prime example of the Edwards Plateau flora and fauna near a major city.

There is no public access, but it is hoped that by early 1998 selected tracts will be opened to public visitation, particularly tracts

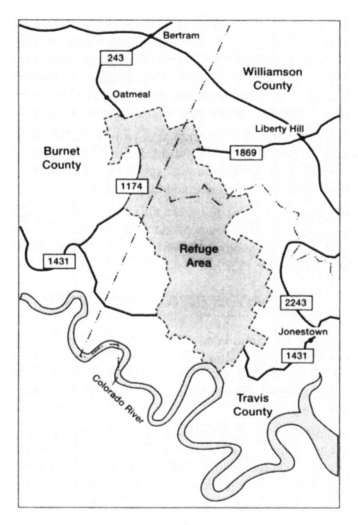

BALCONES CANYONLANDS NATIONAL WILDLIFE REFUGE

with nesting Golden-cheeked Warbler and Black-capped Vireo. When opened, it is urged that visitors stay on marked trails not only to avoid harassment of the birds but also because portions of the refuge are home to rattlesnakes, chiggers, poison ivy, etc., particularly the vireo habitat.

Breeding birds of interest in addition to the Golden-cheeked Warbler and Black-capped Vireo are Ladder-backed Woodpecker, Ash-throated and Vermilion Flycatchers, Western Scrub-Jay, Yellow-breasted Chat, White-eyed Vireo, Black-and-white Warbler, Painted Bunting, Field, Lark, Rufous-crowned, and Black-throated Sparrows, Canyon Towhee, House Finch, and Lesser Goldfinch.

The preliminary bird checklist has more than 200 species including 16 hawks, 7 vireos, 19 warblers, and 21 sparrows. In addition to the bird list, there are also preliminary lists of plants, butterflies, mammals, amphibians and reptiles.

Interested persons should contact the refuge office for information on when tracts will be opened to the public or for times of guided tours. The address is 10711 Burnet Road, Suite 201, Austin, TX 78758, (512) 339-9432.

COLORADO BEND STATE PARK

Colorado Bend State Park, 5,328 acres, is located on the Colorado River at the junction of San Saba, Lampasas, and Burnet counties. To reach the park from Lampasas, drive west on RR 580 24 miles to Bend, then go south on gravel road for 6 miles, following the signs.

The park lies in a transitional area between two major vegetational areas, the Cross Timbers and Prairies to the northeast and the Edwards Plateau to the southwest. Facilities include picnicking, primitive camping, hiking trails, fishing, and boat ramp.

Most visitors probably come to the park to fish in the river. The park is also of interest to cave explorers as there are numerous limestone caves. Contact the park office for information on cave tours.

Of most interest to birders is that both Golden-cheeked Warbler and Black-capped Vireo are nesting species in the park. Golden-cheeked Warbler are most easily found either along the Colorado River or Spicewood Creek. The Black-capped Vireo, on the other

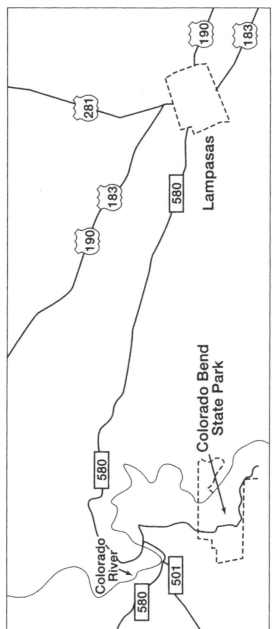

COLORADO BEND STATE PARK

hand, is in an area of the park closed to the public. Check at the office for current regulations.

The best birding location is along the river where the diverse woodland supports a variety of species.

Nesting species in addition to the above are Wild Turkey, Common Poorwill, Belted Kingfisher, Golden-fronted Woodpecker, Eastern Phoebe, Ash-throated and Great Crested Flycatchers, Cactus and Canyon Wrens, Bushtit, Yellow-throated and Red-eyed Vireos, Summer Tanager, Painted Bunting, Indigo Bunting, and Black-throated Sparrow.

Bald Eagle are frequent winter residents perched in large trees along the banks or in canyons of the river from November through early March. Other birds found in winter are Downy Woodpecker, Yellow-bellied Sapsucker, Hermit Thrush, Cedar Waxwing, Spotted Towhee, and a dozen or so sparrow species.

Common Raven visit the park occasionally from the west.

A bird checklist (1993) with 157 species is available at headquarters. The park address is Box 118, Bend, TX 76824, (915) 628-3240.

KERRVILLE

Kerrville, population 19,000, is in the heart of typical Hill Country habitat 66 miles west of San Antonio on I-10. It is that part of the Edwards Plateau sometimes called the Balcones Canyonlands, with deeply dissected canyons, clear springs, thin soil, "cedar brakes" with oak, and large ranches with an abundance of white-tailed deer and wild turkey. The altitude of more than 1,600 feet creates what many local residents say is the best year-round climate in the state. The many springs of the area create creeks which flow into the Guadalupe River. Along the river there are many resorts and dude ranches that attract numerous vacationers in summer and hunters in fall. The river is a magnet for migrants and water birds.

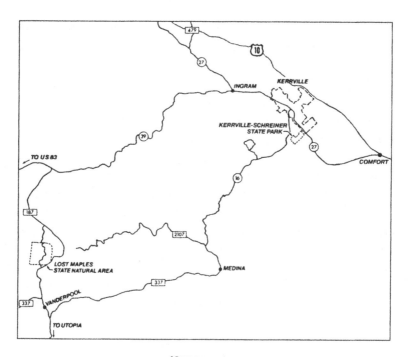

KERRVILLE

The area around Kerrville is an excellent place to look for two Texas specialities: Green Kingfisher and Golden-cheeked Warbler. The warblers can be heard singing from late March to early June, while the kingfishers are permanent residents along the river and clear streams.

Eastern Phoebe, Northern Parula, and Yellow-throated Warbler nest throughout the Kerrville area and are most easily found at stream crossings in the tall bald cypress. They have been found on the county road along Cypress Creek just west of the town of Comfort, and along Prison Camp Road just west of the town of Camp Verde. Comfort is 10 miles southeast of Kerrville on SH 27, and Camp Verde is 14 miles south on SH 173. Another good place is RR 2107, which follows the meanderings of the Medina River (with several crossings) for 8.5 miles to a dead end. RR

2107 is west of SH 16, 3.4 miles north of Medina or 20 miles south of Kerrville.

Kerrville-Schreiner State Park

To reach the Kerrville-Schreiner State Park, 517 acres, drive south of Kerrville on SH 16 for .5 mile to SH 173, then go east 2.5 miles to the entrance. Camping, restrooms with hot showers, screen shelters, picnicking, boat ramp, fishing, swimming in the adjacent Guadalupe River, and 2 miles of hiking trails await the visitor.

The park has one section along the river and another in the uplands. Wild turkey and white-tailed deer wander along the park roads and in the campground and are easily seen in the early morning and late afternoon. In fall migration warblers, vireos, and orioles, etc., are found in the trees and brush east of the loop bridge near the river. Across the river from this park is a county park where cormorants and kingfishers perch in the dead cypress trees in the lake.

A bird checklist (1991) with 146 species is available at headquarters. The address is 2385 Bandera Highway, Kerrville, TX 78028.

Scenic Drive

There are many scenic drives in the Kerrville area where birding can be excellent in all seasons. For an all-day, 150-mile loop trip west from Kerrville, take SH 27 to Ingram, and go west on SH 39 along the South Fork Guadalupe River to RR 187. Turn south to Lost Maples State Natural Area and Vanderpool. Proceed west on RR 337 over the divide to Leakey, turn south on US 83 to Garner State Park, and then return north on US 83 to RR 1050. Go east to Utopia, and then north on RR 187 back to Vanderpool. From Vanderpool, go east on RR 337 to Medina, then north on SH 16 back to Kerrville. Between Medina and Kerrville Golden-cheeked Warblers can be found near the Guadalupe-Medina River divide. This trip should produce at least 70 bird species any time of the year.

Permanent residents to be watched for along the loop include Canyon Towhee, Ladder-backed Woodpecker, Common Raven, Wild Turkey, Vermilion Flycatcher, Eastern Bluebird, Western Scrub-Jay, Cactus, Canyon, and Rock Wrens, Black Phoebe, Pyrrhuloxia, Verdin, and Field, Chipping and Black-throated Sparrows. In spring and summer there are Acadian Flycatcher, Hooded and Scott's Orioles and rarely Zone-tailed Hawk. Wintering birds include Ferruginous Hawk, and Vesper and Lincoln's Sparrows. Sparrows less commonly found in winter are Harris', White-throated, Fox, Grasshopper, LeConte's, Swamp, and Song. Some winters Red-headed Woodpecker are found. Recently Blue Jay have become frequent winter residents, sometimes in large numbers.

There are several worthwhile stops along the loop, and brief descriptions of these sites follow.

The Kerr Wildlife Management Area, about 23 miles west of Kerrville on RR 1340, is a favorable location for Black-capped Vireo and other Edwards Plateau species. From Kerrville, drive west on SH 27 to Ingram, take SH 39 west of Hunt, then drive west on RR 1340 about 12 miles to the entrance.

LOST MAPLES STATE NATURAL AREA

Lost Maples State Natural Area, 2,174 acres, 4 miles north of Vanderpool on RR 187, is one of the natural areas in the Texas Parks and Wildlife Department system. The area was established to preserve an isolated population of big-toothed maple, the most extensive stand of this species east of the Guadalupe Mountains approximately 400 miles away.

The fall colors, always beautiful and sometimes spectacular, are usually best during the first two weeks of November. There is a strenuous six-mile loop hiking trail along Cann Creek and the Sabinal River, the two streams in the park, and the high ground between. The trail provides a good example of the flora and fauna of this section of the Edwards Plateau. In addition, the park offers camping, restrooms with hot showers, picnicking, and a primitive campground. The developed section is a very small percentage of the park.

Nesting birds include Golden-cheeked Warbler, Black-capped Vireo, and Green Kingfisher. There are not many places in the state where these three Texas specialities nest in such a small area. April and May should be the best time to find all three. Other common nesters include Ash-throated Flycatcher, Bushtit, Common Raven, Greater Roadrunner, Ladder-backed Woodpecker, Orchard Oriole, Black Phoebe (in the near vicinity if not in the park), Western Scrub-Jay, Blue-gray Gnatcatcher, Pyrrhuloxia, Scott's Oriole, Lesser Goldfinch, and Canyon Towhee. Watch for Zone-tailed Hawk from February through July among the many Turkey Vulture soaring overhead.

This part of Texas, especially west of the park, is the wintering ground for numerous Golden Eagle (November to March), and they are occasionally seen flying over the park.

A bird checklist (1996) with 197 species is available at park headquarters. The address is HC01, Box 156, Vanderpool, TX 78885, (830) 966-3413.

GREEN KINGFISHER

UVALDE

Uvalde is located where US 90 and US 83 intersect about 80 miles west of San Antonio, a few miles south of the Balcones Escarpment. Here Edwards Plateau and South Texas birds meet with good representation of both types within a half-hour drive, plus a few eastern and western species. At the Texas Ornithological Society meeting in Uvalde, May 7-9, 1992, 192 species, plus 10 hypothetical species, were recorded within 50 miles of the city.

An excellent spot to headquarter while birding the Uvalde area is Neal's Lodges, P.O. Box 165, Concan, TX 78838, (830) 232-6118, located about 23 miles north of Uvalde and 7 miles south of Garner State Park. Start by purchasing *Birder's Guide to Concan, Texas (and Surrounding Area)* by June Osborne, a detailed guide to birds, birding and other information of the area, at the lodge store. Mrs. Osborne has conducted birding tours and classes in and about Concan annually since 1987. The grounds of the lodges are a mecca for local birds with its unique setting along the Rio Frio. Green Kingfisher, Black-capped Vireo, and Golden-cheeked Warbler are summer residents.

Garner State Park

Garner State Park, 1,419 acres, is located on US 83, 10 miles south of Leakey and 31 miles north of Uvalde. The park offers camping, screen shelters, restrooms with hot showers, cabins, 6 miles of hiking trails, picnicking, and swimming. This is a delightful spot on the clear, spring-fed Frio River, which has immense bald cypress lining its banks in the heart of a scenic section of the Edwards Plateau.

Birds that are present year-round, either in the park or in adjacent areas, include Bushtit, Western Scrub-Jay, Pyrrhuloxia, Common Raven, Canyon Towhee, and Verdin.

In summer be on the lookout for Hooded and Scott's Orioles, Yellow-throated Warbler, White-winged Dove, Bronzed Cowbird, Vermilion Flycatcher, and Groove-billed Ani. Zone-tailed Hawk

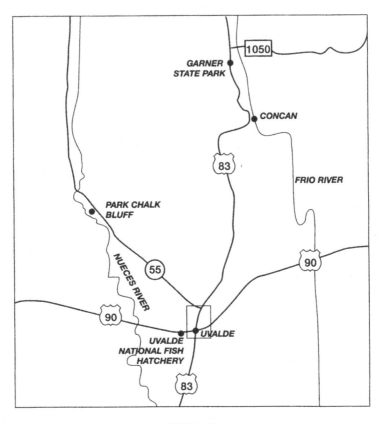

UVALDE

and Lesser Nighthawk are occasional in summer. If Black Phoebe and Green Kingfisher are not found in the park, check the river crossings north and south of the park where they are sometimes more easily found. Look for Harris' Hawk on US 83 between the park and Uvalde.

The park is very popular on summer weekends. For birding, any other time is better.

A bird checklist (1996) with 179 species is available at headquarters. The address is HCR #70, Box 599, Concan, TX 78838, (830) 232-6132.

Park Chalk Bluff

Park Chalk Bluff, a privately owned park, is about 15 miles northwest of Uvalde on SH 55. Watch for the entrance on the west side of the highway before SH 55 crosses the Nueces River. Cabins with hot and cold water, camping, restrooms, and a boat ramp are available.

A series of bird habitats is present here including woodlands, brush, ponds, and the river. The one-mile entrance road with typical south Texas brush is worthy of careful scrutiny for Bell's Vireo, Cactus Wren, Curve-billed and Long-billed Thrashers, and Black-throated Sparrow. Between the uplands and the river are a series of terraces, each a different habitat. Among the tall trees look for perching birds and along the river check for Green and Belted Kingfishers and Black Phoebe. Spring is a delightful time here with Red-shouldered Hawk, Common Ground-Dove, Cave Swallow, Lesser Goldfinch, Brown-crested Flycatcher, Black-chinned Hummingbird, Brown Thrasher, Bank and Northern Rough-winged Swallows, Yellow-throated Warbler, Yellow-breasted Chat, and Olive Sparrow. Rarities recorded here include Ringed Kingfisher, Rufous-capped Warbler, and Great Kiskadee.

If planning to stay overnight call ahead, (830) 278-5515, for reservations. There is an entrance fee.

Uvalde National Fish Hatchery

The Uvalde National Fish Hatchery is located west of Uvalde south of US 90. From the intersection of US 90 and US 83 in downtown, drive about 1.6 miles on US 90 to FM 481, turn left (south) and drive 2 miles on FM 481 to the entrance.

Walking the levees between the ponds is the best way to bird this location. Do not drive where signs say "Authorized Vehicles Only."

This is the best place locally for shorebirds, such as Least, Pectoral, Semipalmated, Western, and Spotted Sandpipers. This location can be good for a variety of birds as 58 species were recorded here on May 7–9, 1992, during the Texas Ornithological

Society meeting in Uvalde. On May 9, 1992, the first and only Collared Plover for the United States was found here. I was there on the 7th and may have seen that bird without realizing it was different. It stayed for four days and was well documented.

Cave Swallows

Cave Swallows are rapidly expanding their nesting range. Look for them from April to July. Formerly thought to be confined in Texas to a few caves on the Edwards Plateau and the Trans-Pecos, they are now found using highway culverts from San Angelo and Junction on the north, to the El Paso area on the west, the Gulf of Mexico on the east, and the Rio Grande on the south. The caves on the plateau are still being utilized. In West Texas they are found under bridges east and west of Fort Stockton on I-10, at Lake Balmorhea State Park, and along the Gulf Coast from Sea Rim State Park south to the Kingsville area. On US 90 a good location is the culvert at the rest stop just west of Uvalde.

JUNCTION

Junction, population 2,700, is located on I-10 about 121 miles west of San Antonio at the confluence of the North Llano and South Llano Rivers, hence the name of the town. South Llano River State Park and Walter Buck Wildlife Management Area, City Park in downtown Junction, and the Texas Tech University campus south of town are worthwhile birding spots.

South Llano River State Park and Walter Buck Wildlife Management Area

The South Llano River State Park and Walter Buck Wildlife Management Area, a 2,630-acre tract, lies on the west central Edwards Plateau. As the name implies the South Llano River flows through the tract. From Junction, drive south on US 377 about 4.5 miles to the entrance.

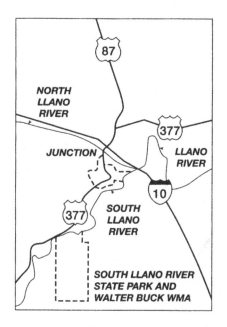

JUNCTION

Resident species include Green Kingfisher, Golden-fronted and Downy Woodpeckers, Common Raven, Verdin, Bushtit, Cactus and Rock Wrens, and Rufous-crowned Sparrow.

In summer look for Yellow-billed Cuckoo, Black Phoebe, Eastern Wood-Pewee, Acadian, Vermilion, Ash-throated, and Great Crested Flycatchers, Blue-gray Gnatcatcher, White-eyed, Bell's, Black-capped, Yellow-throated, and Red-eyed Vireos, Yellow-breasted Chat, Indigo and Painted Buntings, Cassin's Sparrow, Scott's Oriole, and Lesser Goldfinch. Gray Vireo has been recorded in summer. At night listen for Common Poorwill (uplands) and Chuck-will's-widow (riparian areas).

The woodlands along the river are favorable for passerine migrants.

The day use area in the park is closed from October 1st to April 1st to provide maximum protection for the large Wild Turkey winter roost.

The park offers camping, restrooms with hot showers, picnicking, and hiking. A bird checklist (1994) with 157 species is available at headquarters. The address is HC 15, Box 224, Junction, TX 76849, (915) 446-3994.

Texas Tech University Campus

The Texas Tech University campus is along the South Llano River between South Llano River State Park and Junction. To reach the campus from Junction drive east on US 83, cross the river bridge, and turn right on RR 2169 about one-half mile past the old bridge. The campus is at the end of RR 2169.

Check in at the first building on the right and pay a nominal fee for birding. There is one mile of river bottom, which is a good alternative to the State Park for riverine habitat, especially when the day use area is closed in the park.

Junction City Park

City Park in Junction has good river-bottom habitat on the east side of the river. From downtown turn left on RR 2169 after crossing the old bridge, then take the first dirt road to the left and down to the river bottom. Lesser Goldfinch and Green Kingfisher are residents. Summer residents include Blue Grosbeak and Summer Tanager. Some species found in migration are Western Tanager, Black-and-white and Chestnut-sided Warblers.

SEMINOLE CANYON STATE HISTORICAL PARK

Seminole Canyon State Historical Park, 2,173 acres, is located about 40 miles west of Del Rio, or 8 miles west of Comstock on US 90. The park was established to protect Indian pictographs that date back 10,000 or more years. The pictographs in the canyon near the headquarters can be seen only on guided tours. Time should be allowed to study the excellent exhibit in the headquarters building, which depicts the early history of the area.

Camping and picnic areas are provided. The flora and fauna are a mixture of the Edwards Plateau to the north, Chihuahuan Desert to the west, and South Texas to the east. Average annual rainfall is less than 18 inches.

The best birding opportunities are on a 3.5 mile hiking trail from the camping area south along an old road to Amistad Reservoir, which forms the southern boundary of the park.

Common summer birds include Turkey and Black Vultures, Harris' Hawk, Wild Turkey, Common Poorwill, Common Nighthawk, Green Kingfisher, Black and Say's Phoebes, Ash-throated Flycatcher, Common and Chihuahuan Ravens, Verdin, Cactus and Rock Wrens, Sage Thrasher, Hooded Oriole, Pyrrhuloxia, and Cassin's and Black-throated Sparrows. Other summer records are Zone-tailed Hawk, Peregrine Falcon, White-winged Dove, Lesser Nighthawk, White-throated Swift, Varied Bunting, and Canyon Towhee. Waterfowl and shorebirds should be looked for along the shore of the lake during spring and fall migration and in winter.

The address is P.O. Box 820, Comstock, TX 78837, (915) 292-4464.

5

Central
Texas

The Central Texas region, about 19% of the state, is the part of Texas between the Pineywoods to the east and the Rolling Plains to the west. The eastern boundary is the beginning of the pine forests of East Texas, roughly from Texarkana through Tyler, Palestine, and west of Huntsville to near Victoria. The southern boundary is very broad and indistinct but generally follows the San Antonio River northwest to San Antonio. The prominent Balcones

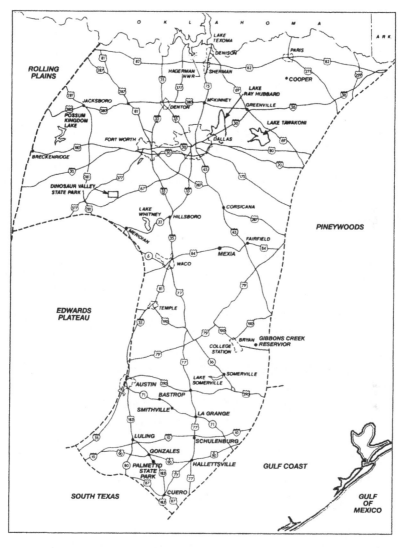

CENTRAL TEXAS

Escarpment is the western boundary from San Antonio north through Austin, Temple, and Waco. The line then proceeds west from the Glen Rose area to north of Brownwood, then north to just east of Wichita Falls.

The region consists of alternate prairies, woodlands, and savannahs underlain with Tertiary and upper Cretaceous deposits. The land becomes more hilly from east to west. The elevation increases from 150 feet in the southeast to about 1,500 feet in the northwest.

The major vegetation areas from east to west are the Fayette Prairies, Post-oak Savannah, Blackland Prairies, East Cross Timbers, Grand Prairie, West Cross Timbers, and North Central Prairie. Originally, tall grasses dominanted the savannahs and prairies. Ranching, farming, and urbanization have occurred to the extent that very little, if any, virgin prairie is preserved. The timberlands, mostly post oak and blackjack with a wide variety of other trees and shrubs in the stream bottoms, provide habitat for many of the breeding birds.

Birdwise, the region is a transition zone between the Gulf Coast and Pineywoods (south and east), and the Rolling Plains and Edwards Plateau (west). The numerous man-made lakes attract and provide habitat for many migrating shorebirds and wintering waterfowl.

Eastern species that reach or approach their western limit in the region include Red-shouldered Hawk, Acadian Flycatcher, Blue Jay, Indigo Bunting, Brown Thrasher, Common Grackle, Red-bellied Woodpecker, and Ruby-throated Hummingbird. Western species to be found are Greater Roadrunner, Western Kingbird, and Bell's Vireo.

Locations with bird checklists not included herein are Lake Mineral Wells State Park and Lake Brownwood State Park.

HAGERMAN NATIONAL WILDLIFE REFUGE

Hagerman National Wildlife Refuge, with 11,319 acres (3,000 of marsh and water, and 8,000 in uplands and farmland), is on the south shore of Lake Texoma about 12 road miles west-southwest of Denison; 17 road miles northwest of Sherman; or 6.5 miles from Pottsboro. From US 75 in Sherman, drive west on US 82 three

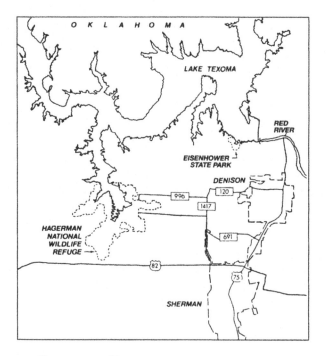

HAGERMAN NATIONAL WILDLIFE REFUGE

miles to FM 1417. Go north past the FM 691 intersection for 1.5 miles, then west on Refuge Road for 6 miles to the refuge headquarters. FM 1417 can also be reached from Denison by driving west on either FM 120, or FM 691 past Grayson County College.

Lake Texoma, formed by the Denison Dam on the Red River, has 580 miles of shoreline and 89,000 surface acres at power pool level. The Army Corps of Engineers has a vast array of recreational areas with camping, boat ramps, drinking water, picnicking, and restrooms. In Texas there are 19 such facilities; an additional 25 are in Oklahoma.

The refuge is on the Big Mineral Arm of Lake Texoma. The eastern half of the refuge is part of the Blackland Prairie, while the western portion is in the East Cross Timbers. Some of the dominant trees of the Eastern Cross Timbers are elms, eastern red cedar, pecan, hickory, willow, oaks, hackberry, cottonwood, osage orange (sometimes called bois d'arc), box elder, and green ash.

The primary objective of the refuge is to preserve the natural state of the plant and animal species in the area and to provide wintering and resting areas for migratory waterfowl of the Central Flyway. Five goose species, twenty-one duck species, and Tundra Swan have been seen on the refuge in winter, with large numbers of Canada Goose and Mallard. Snow and Greater White-fronted Geese are more common in migration. Ross' Goose is a common winter resident. Brant have been recorded but are very rare. Another rare winter visitor is Western Grebe. Wood Duck and Mallard nest at the refuge.

The marshes and mud flats provide habitat for shorebirds during migration, with 36 species recorded on the refuge checklist. Fall migration starts the first week of July. Regular migrants include Baird's, Pectoral, and Stilt Sandpipers, Greater and Lesser Yellowlegs, Semipalmated, Western and Least Sandpipers, Long-billed Dowitcher, and Common Snipe. Less frequent are Solitary, Spotted, Upland and Buff-breasted Sandpipers, Willet, Long-billed Curlew, Hudsonian and Marbled Godwits, Ruddy Turn-

WOOD DUCK

stone, Sanderling, Dunlin, Short-billed Dowitcher, and Wilson's Phalarope. Recent rarities include Virginia Rail, Snowy and Mountain Plovers, Whimbrel, and Red Knot.

Sandy Point Access Area, at the north end of the road on the west side of the refuge, is an excellent observation point for finding Bald Eagle fishing over the lake from late October through March. This is also a good place to look for Common Goldeneye, Common Merganser, Horned Grebe, and Bonaparte's Gull. Other waterfowl winter and migrate in lesser numbers, especially if the lake level is high enough.

Twenty-eight warbler species are on the refuge checklist, plus four accidentals. Most are seen only during migration; species that have been recorded nesting are Black-and-white, Prothonotary, and Kentucky Warblers, Louisiana Waterthrush, Common Yellowthroat, and Yellow-breasted Chat.

Nesting species include Pied-billed Grebe, Mississippi Kite, Broad-winged and Swainson's Hawks, and Grasshopper and Lark Sparrows.

Pileated Woodpecker are occasionally found in the woods at the Big Mineral Access Area and in the northwest corner of the refuge near Sandy Creek and Brushy Creek. Look for White-breasted Nuthatch in the same locations, near the Sandy Creek bridge on the west side of the refuge, and from the Meadow Pond west to the refuge boundary at the old steel bridge.

Seventeen sparrow species are on the refuge checklist. Watch for them mostly in winter on the road to the refuge. Sparrows usually common in winter are Harris', Field (nest also), Savannah, Fox, Song, White-throated, and White-crowned. LeConte's Sparrow are regular but uncommon.

The prairies and roadsides of North Texas are wintering areas for Horned Lark and all four species of longspurs. McCown's and Chestnut-collared are the most numerous; Lapland and Smith's harder to find. Approaches to the refuge, its grassy fields, and indeed, all roads in this part of Texas should be checked.

There is no camping on the refuge, but there are three picnic areas with restrooms.

A bird checklist (1992) with 273 species plus 43 accidentals is available at refuge headquarters. Check at the Visitor's Center for recent bird sightings and for the displays and exhibits. Guided bird tours from the Office/Visitor's Center are conducted each Tuesday and most Thursdays starting at 8:30 am. The address of the refuge is Route 3, Box 123, Sherman, TX 75092, (903) 786-2826.

Eisenhower State Park

Eisenhower State Park, 475 acres, is about 10 miles northwest of Denison and has camping, picnicking, a boat ramp, and restrooms with hot showers. The habitat is much more limited than at Hagerman National Wildlife Refuge.

HEARD NATURAL SCIENCE MUSEUM
AND WILDLIFE SANCTUARY

The Heard Natural Science Museum and Wildlife Sanctuary is south of McKinney, which is on US 75 thirty miles north of Dallas.

To reach the museum from McKinney drive south on SH 5 about 3 miles to FM 1378, then east 1 mile. From Dallas take US 75 north to Exit 38 and follow the brown and white directional signs to the entrance.

RARE BIRD ALERT FOR NORTH TEXAS, (817) 237-3209.

The 287-acre wildlife sanctuary features riparian woodlands, wetlands, and upland tallgrass prairies. Bottomland woodlands contain climax communities of burr oak, black walnut, cedar and American elms, and many other species. Wood Duck, Hooded Merganser, Prothonotary Warbler, and Red-eyed Vireo nest in this habitat. Dickcissel, Blue Grosbeak, Indigo and Painted Buntings can be heard singing from the tallgrass prairie and prairie edge habitat during the spring and summer months. The museum monitors a bluebird trail of nearly 30 nesting boxes on the sanctuary. A

McKinney Area

50-acre wetland attracts more than 2,000 breeding herons and egrets of 7 species throughout the spring and summer. Concentrations of waterfowl can be observed on the wetlands during the fall and winter months when this area hosts as many as 1,000 ducks and geese of 15 different species. Most of the sanctuary is maintained in a relatively undisturbed natural condition and is available for ecological research. There are over five miles of trails. Guided trail tours are offered on Saturdays and Sundays. Reservations for group tours are required in advance.

The museum operates the oldest continuously run, currently active bird banding station in the state of Texas. Most banding is conducted during spring and fall migration. The museum also operates a raptor rehabilitation center and raptor education outreach program, which utilizes live birds.

In the museum building there are natural history exhibits featuring fossils of north central Texas, sea shells, rocks and minerals, plant and animal ecology, art exhibits, a nature store, and classrooms. An extensive educational program is available for all ages, including a special summer Biology Camp.

The sanctuary is open Monday through Saturday from 9 am to 5 pm and Sunday from 1 pm to 5 pm. Admission is $3 for adults and $2 for children. The nature trail is available until 4 pm daily. The museum is closed on major holidays.

For information contact the museum by phone at (972) 562-5566, by fax at (972) 548-9119, or visit the Heard's home page at http://www.heardmuseum.org. The address is One Nature Place, McKinney, TX 75069-8840.

DALLAS

Dallas, population 1,390,000, in the center of north Central Texas, is one of the leading financial, manufacturing and transportation cities in the nation. Dallas County, 859 square miles, has the highest population density in the state, yet the city is said to have more parkland per person than any other major city in the United States. The county is within the Trinity River drainage basin and is part of the Blackland Prairie vegetational area except for the extreme northwestern corner of the county, which is a part of the East Cross Timbers. Providing habitat for many bird species, the City of Dallas and Dallas County now have 22,500 acres of parkland. There is an additional 28,000 acres in the City Open Space Program, which has 30 new sites. This does not include Dallas County Open Space land nor 27,000 city-owned water acres.

RARE BIRD ALERT FOR NORTH TEXAS, (817) 237-3209.

The Birds of North Central Texas by Warren M. Pulich, Texas A&M University Press (1988), brings together information on the status and distribution of the birds of the thirty-two counties of north central Texas.

White Rock Lake

White Rock Lake, six miles east of downtown Dallas, offers many different habitats such as water, woodlands, and marshy

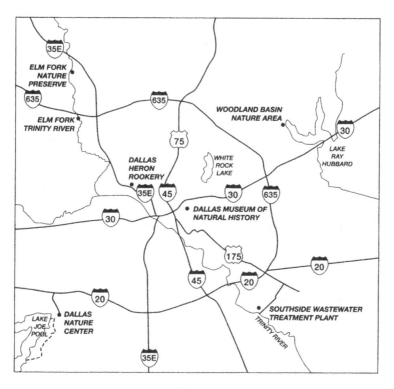

DALLAS

areas. If there is time for only one birding stop in Dallas, this area would be a good choice. More than 220 species have been recorded on and around the lake.

To reach the lake from downtown, drive east on I-30 to East Grand (Exit 49A), then go northeast on East Grand to the lake. The street name changes along the way to Garland Road (SH 78). This accesses the south end of the lake and East Lawther Drive. The east side of the lake can also be reached by continuing on Northwest Highway to Buckner Boulevard at the next traffic light, then driving south on Buckner to Garland Road. To reach the lake from the northern half of Dallas, see the West Lawther Drive section below.

The lake is approximately two miles long and one mile wide, and is surrounded by parks maintained by the Dallas Parks and Recreation Department.

The following areas are a rundown of good birding spots around the lake.

White Rock Spillway: In spring and fall the White Rock Spillway serves as a foraging area for sandpipers and plovers. Black Tern show up in late summer. Hundreds of Ring-billed Gull and Double-crested Cormorant are winter residents, along with Gadwall, Mallard, and Ruddy Duck. Bonaparte's Gull are recorded regularly. The woods here are a remnant of the original flood plain forest of White Rock Creek, whose abandoned channel may still be seen.

The Dallas Arboretum and Botanical Garden: This 66-acre estate is adjacent to the lake off Garland Road. It is being developed and maintained by a society with partial support from the city. The woodlands around and to the rear of the mansion are especially good for spring migrants, warblers, Rose-breasted Grosbeak, Baltimore Oriole and Warbling Vireo. There is an entrance fee except on Friday afternoon.

East Lawther Drive: This side of the lake is good for winter residents such as Redhead, Canvasback, and occasionally Eared and Horned Grebes. American White Pelican have wintered for several years. The light is best in the morning. East Lawther is divided into segments separated by wooden gates, making it necessary to return to Garland Road between segments.

West Lawther Drive: To reach the north end of White Rock and the west side of the lake take the West Lawther Drive exit from

Northwest Highway (Loop 12) East. West Lawther leads around the lake. Along the shore close to the road are several pull-offs where waterfowl, gulls, and Wood Duck can be found. Little Gull has been a visitor several times in recent years. Afternoon provides the best light for birding this side of the lake.

Upper White Rock Creek: From Mockingbird Lane north Upper White Rock Creek is home to Green-winged Teal, Great Horned and Barred Owls, and Eastern Screech-Owl. White Rock Lake will be dredged from this end of the lake beginning in August-September, 1997, with projected completion in 1999. This will not affect access except when loading or unloading dredge.

Old Fish Hatchery. This heavily wooded area adjacent to the spillway is owned by the Dallas Water Utilities and, with the co-operation of Dallas County Audubon Society, is now a fenced bird sanctuary. The entrances will be from Winsted Drive (northwest off Garland Road below the spillway) and at the old Water Pump Station with tall chimney at the northwest side of the area.

Although the hatchery has been abandoned for many years, the ponds are still in evidence and some often have water. Mallard and Wood Duck are usually present in the first ponds after entering the gate to the left of the parking lot on Winsted. Downy and Red-bellied Woodpeckers are permanent residents. Migrants include warblers, Baltimore and Orchard Orioles, Swainson's Thrush, Gray Catbird and occasionally Rose-breasted Grosbeak. Yellow-crowned and Black-crowned Night-Herons have nested here.

In the open area at the end of the ponds toward the water building look for wintering Field, Fox, Song, Harris', White-throated and White-crowned Sparrows. Rusty Blackbird sometimes make an appearance near the ponds in winter.

Be alert for copperhead snakes in spring and summer. A black mink is an unusual but possible sighting.

Near the Water Company Building, now a computer center, beyond the parking lot and across the street to the left there is a

HARRIS' SPARROW

small flock of Monk Parakeet. They nest in the horizontal beams of the metal structure at the electrical power station. There is a path to the dam from either side of the sanctuary.

White Rock Creek Hike-and-Bike Trail: This trail winds through the floodplain forest of White Rock Creek from Hillcrest and Lyndon B. Johnson Freeway in North Dallas and around the lake. Woodland birds abound in the large cottonwood, box elder, willow, and elm trees that shade the path. Be alert for the hikers and bikers.

Dallas Heron Rookery

The rookery is located about 3.5 miles northwest of downtown Dallas. It has been preserved and protected since 1938 in the shadow of the ever-expanding University of Texas Southwestern Medical Center. The main entrance is at 5323 Harry Hines Boulevard, where information can be obtained at a kiosk. The campus is severely congested weekdays and weekend visits are suggested using the entrance below.

From downtown drive north on I-35E (Stemmons Expressway) to Exit 432A, Inwood Road. Take Inwood Road north to the second traffic light and turn right on Campus. The wooded area on the left is the rookery, which ends at the Tennis Building and Courts. On weekends on-street parking is permitted. If a Security Officer is in the area, birding visitors are requested to identify themselves and the purpose of their visit.

Paved walks lead almost all the way around the green area surrounding the rookery and a few passerines may be found. Egret and heron populations vary with weather conditions, but Great, Cattle, and Snowy Egrets are usually present. Little Blue Heron and Black-crowned Night-Heron may be expected also. Entry into the wooded rookery is prohibited.

The best look into the life of these birds is obtained on weekends only from the second floor of the parking garage across from the tennis courts, where the nesting activity can be viewed at eye level. Nest building is from mid-April to early May, followed by incubation and the feeding of young. The birds arrive by March 20th and leave by October 1st.

Dallas Nature Center

The Dallas Nature Center, 650 acres, is located southwest of the city at the edge of the unique White Rock Escarpment. From the intersection of I-35E and I-20 drive west on I-20 to Exit 458, then south about 3 miles to the entrance on the right.

Grounds are open dawn to dusk, Tuesday through Sunday, and admission is free. The Mary Alice Bland Butterfly Garden is being developed. The property is noted for its variety of wildflowers. A native plant nursery and gift shop are at the site. Habitats include rolling prairie, ponds, and oak-juniper woodlands. There are 7 miles of trails varying in altitude from 250 feet to 750

CATTLE EGRET

feet. Eastern Screech-Owl and Great Horned Owl are permanent residents. Painted and Indigo Buntings are present in summer.

Call the office for information on bird walks, special events, etc. The address is 7171 Mountain Creek Parkway, Dallas, TX 75249 (972) 296-1955.

Dallas Museum of Natural History

The Dallas Museum of Natural History in Fair Park is most easily reached by driving east from downtown on I-30 (R. L. Thornton Freeway) to the 2nd Avenue Exit (Fair Park), driving right onto Robert B. Cullum Boulevard, then going left at the Grand Avenue entrance through metal gates. Parking is available on the right. The museum entrance is across the street.

There are 30 bird dioramas including the extirpated, or extinct, Ivory-billed Woodpecker and the Attwater's Greater-Prairie Chicken.

At present the museum's outstanding collection of mounted Texas birds is in storage with 6,900 study skins and mounted bird specimens, ranking it as one of the largest scientific Texas bird collections. Many of these birds were collected as early as the 1880s. The collections are now cataloged on computer. There is also a collection of bird nests and eggs and an extensive ornithological library that includes subscriptions to every major ornithological periodical.

The Mudge Library, one of the top four illustrated bird libraries in the United States, is housed at the museum. There are 4,000 volumes, some dated as early as 1555, including the complete works of Gould, as well as books by Audubon, Wilson, Sharpe, Lear, Gatesby, Baird, and others.

These outstanding resources, of great interest to scientists and serious bird students, are available to the public for examination by appointment. Interested persons may contact the Collections Manager or Chief Curator of the Museum at (214) 421-3466.

Lake Ray Hubbard

Lake Ray Hubbard in eastern Dallas and western Rockwall counties is formed by a dam on the East Fork Trinity River and is operated by the City of Dallas for municipal water supply. At conservation pool level there are 22,745 surface acres. Facilities include camping, marinas, and fishing.

The lake attracts numerous gulls, terns, and waterfowl, especially in winter. Herring, Bonaparte's, and Ring-billed Gulls are common. Franklin's Gull are regular migrants. Forster's, Caspian, and Black Terns have been recorded.

A popular birding area is Woodland Basin Nature Area, 300 acres, on the west side of the lake. From downtown Dallas drive east on I-30 to I-635, then north about 5 miles to Centerville Road (Exit 11A). Go east on Centerville Road 3.8 miles to Miller Road and drive 0.5 mile east on Miller Road to Rowlett Creek. There is a sign, "Woodland Basin Nature Area," on the right. There is a boardwalk from the parking lot where many land birds can be found. If the lake is low, mudflats can be present on which herons, egrets, rails, shorebirds, and waterfowl can be seen. This is also a good location for migrating spring warblers.

East on Miller Road one-fourth mile from the Woodland Basin Parking Lot is the entrance to Rowlett Nature Trail, which is 1.3 miles long on the east side of the Rowlett Creek arm of the lake. Approximately 200 bird species have been recorded at Woodland Basin and this nature trail should average 55 to 60 species a day.

Southside Wastewater Treatment Plant

Southside, known to veteran birders as "Log Cabin," is located on the eastern edge of Dallas near the point I-20 from the east and I-635 (Lyndon B. Johnson Freeway) from the north merge. Where US 175 crosses this junction, take US 175 east (Kaufman Exit), continue east 2 miles, turn right on South Belt Line Road, then drive 1.5 miles past Foot Hill Road to the entrance on Log Cabin Road on the right. The gates are open from 6 am to 6 pm, Monday through Friday, except holidays. Weekdays register at the front entrance of Administration Building (Level 2) taking the elevator to the desk on the 3rd floor. To arrange a Saturday or Sunday visit, call the Supervisor at (972) 670-0400 on the day before the planned visit and set a definite arrival time so the plant phone will be answered and the gate opened. On weekends use the open parking lot at the rear of the building, enter through the lunch room, and register at the office on the left (Level 1).

This is probably the most reliable birding spot in the Dallas Metroplex. Excepting periods before and after migration, there is always some special bird or bird behavior to be seen here. In 1988 Southside began a mult-million dollar transformation from old-style sewage pond drying-beds to a new process facility that resembles a large park. Construction of levees and water storage ponds is ongoing and birders are cautioned to watch for heavy equipment and trucks. Visitors are permitted to drive anywhere on the grounds, including the levee at the rear of the area and the dike roads that go around the ponds, if gates are open. Be careful to leave room for work trucks to pass, and avoid construction areas.

During spring and fall migration, there is a constant changing parade of shorebirds and wading birds. Found every year are Black-bellied Plover and American Golden-Plover; Stilt, Solitary, Buff-breasted and Upland Sandpipers; and occasional Ruddy Turnstone, Sanderling, and Willet. Red and Red-necked Phalaropes have been recorded but are rare. Depending on rainfall, shorebirds are best found at the drying bed across from the Administration Building down to the gravel dike. Fall migration begins in July.

Up to sixteen duck species are regularly seen. Most spend the winter, while Mottled Duck are present in small numbers in summer. In late August and September there may be Wood Stork early in the morning (there were 80 or so in 1996) and Roseate Spoonbill is occasional. Other birds to watch for are American White Pelican (winter), Peregrine Falcon (migrant), and herons and egrets (spring and summer). This is a good Rusty Blackbird spot in winter. Nesting birds include Black-necked Stilt, Common Moorhen, and probably Black-bellied Whistling-Duck. The endangered inland race of the Least Tern has successfully nested here for several years.

CEDAR HILL STATE PARK

Cedar Hill State Park, 1,810 acres, is located along the east shore of Joe Pool Lake about 16 miles from downtown Dallas. The park can be reached by driving west on I-20 to Exit 457 (FM 1382), then south on FM 1382 following signs to the entrance. From US 67 south of I-20, drive to FM 1382, then north to the entrance.

Park attractions include camping, picnicking, restrooms with hot showers, fishing, swimming, and hiking trails. The best birding is to the left on West Spine Road where Painted Bunting is resident during late spring and summer. West Spine ends at areas closed to the public; go right and check out areas at circular ends of roads in both directions. Habitats along the trails are woodlands, ponds, grasslands and a vista or two. The park checklist has 14 sparrow species. Lark Sparrow nest, Clay-colored are spring and fall migrants, and the rest are winter residents, mostly in the grasslands. Check the woodlands for migrating passerines, including warblers, and the lake for waterfowl.

A bird checklist (1990) with 193 species and trail maps is available at headquarters. The park address is P.O. Box 941, Cedar Hill, TX 75104, (214) 291-3900. There is an entrance fee.

ELM FORK NATURE PRESERVE, CARROLLTON

The City of Carrollton has reserved a 38-acre natural area bordering the Elm Fork of the Trinity River. To reach the site drive north on I-35E approximately 4.6 miles north of I-635 (Lyndon B. Johnson Freeway), exit west on Sandy Lake Road, then go 1 mile west to the entrance.

The railhead for the 1.5-mile walking trail is in the northwest corner behind the McInnish Sports Complex.

The trail leads through Trinity River woodlands where there are several small ponds frequented by ducks, especially in winter, and favorable habitats for migrants and wintering sparrows. The trail is open every day from one hour before sunrise to one hour after sunset. Volunteers lead bird walks on Saturdays and occasional night hikes on an irregular basis. Call (972) 446-3667 for information about walks.

LAKE TAWAKONI

Lake Tawakoni, 20,614 surface acres at operating level, is on the Sabine River in Hunt, Rains, and Van Zandt counties, 9 miles northeast of Wills Point. It is operated by the Sabine River Authority for municipal water, industrial use, and irrigation.

The most popular birding areas are near the dam, which can be reached from Dallas by driving east on I-20 approximately 48 miles to FM 47, then north on FM 47 through Wills Point to the dam. An alternate route from Dallas is east on US 80 to Wills Point. From Greenville go southeast on US 69 about 30 miles to Wills Point, then south 7 miles to the Sabine River Authority Headquarters Building. The office is located in the small red brick building on county road 1480, north of the dam.

Smith's Longspur

The lake area is the most reliable and accessible public area in Texas for Smith's Longspur, but there is a lot more to see here than the longspurs, especially rare water birds. Check the shortgrass in the old airstrip, which runs parallel to the dam, for the longspur. This field can be located by looking for the "AIRSTRIP CLOSED" sign, which is posted near the road a hundred yards or so east of the Sabine River Authority office. It is recommended that the entire field be walked carefully until the birds flush. They often circle overhead a few times before they settle down some distance away. With great good luck, they may be seen walking in the grass. Some years, Sprague's Pipit winter in this field.

Smith's Longspurs have been seen consistently in a large cattle pasture nearby. To get to this location drive north from the dam area on SH 47, turn left on Rains County Road 1475 and follow this unpaved road until it dead ends at a small turn-around at the entrance to the Thousand Trails Campground. Park here and climb over or under the barbed wire fence to your left. This is private property but birders have been welcome. This field is fairly large, and the longspurs can be anywhere in the field. At times they seem to prefer the slightly taller grass closer to the edge of the lake. Sprague's Pipit often winter here.

On the far eastern side of this field is a small wooded cove surrounded by a patch of little bluestem grasses overgrown with small bushes. These grassy fields are owned by the Dallas County Audubon Society, and are a good place to consistently find wintering LeConte's Sparrow and Sedge Wren. To reach the field, simply walk across the large cattle pasture where the Smith's Longspur are and carefully climb through the fence.

The Dam

One of the better birding locations at the lake is the dam, which is closed to the public. Birders, however, are welcome from 8:00 am through 4:30 pm, Monday through Friday. Stop by the office to obtain permission. From fall through spring, drive the dam to search for Common Loon, Horned Grebe (hundreds), Red-breasted Merganser (dozens), and Common Goldeneye, as well as a host of other ducks and gulls. Rarities that have been found here include Red-throated and Pacific Loons, Western and Red-necked Grebes, Oldsquaw, Harlequin Duck, Black, White-winged and Surf Scoters, Parasitic and Long-tailed Jaegers, Black-headed Gull, Sabine's Gull, and Black-legged Kittiwake.

When driving the dam frequent stops for scanning with a scope are recommended. Turn around at the spillway.

There are many other very good birding spots. A few are mentioned briefly here.

County Road 1480

West of the headquarters building drive to the end of county road 1480. Park in the parking area but do not block the metal gates. It is permissible to cross the fence to the south and west of the road but not north. PLEASE RESPECT PRIVATE PROPERTY. This has been a favorable hawk migration site. Look for shorebirds along the lake. In fall some passerines migrate in large numbers near this spot to avoid flying over the lake.

Old Sabine River Channel

The woods below the dam along the old Sabine River channel have been favorable for spring and fall migrants such as warblers. Prothonotary and Kentucky Warblers are summer residents. To reach these woods, park in the parking lot just west of the river channel below the spillway area and walk across the bridge. There is a pedestrian entrance near the gate past the river channel.

Holiday Marina and Old Van Zandt County Park

The Holiday Marina and the Old Van Zandt County Park are found by driving south on SH 47 from the dam and continuing past the spillway area. After a short distance turn north at the Holiday Marina sign. There is a public access boat ramp located at the end of the first road on the right, and the Old Van Zandt County Park can be reached from this location by climbing the closed gate and following the path.

To reach the Holiday Marina continue straight for a few hundred feet and park beside (but do not block) the boat ramp. There is a small convenience store and restroom facilities. This is private property but birders have always been welcome. Patronizing the store may help keep birders welcome. Scan the lake for loons, gulls and terns. A Red-necked Grebe was recorded near the boat ramp from November, 1993, to February, 1994.

Although closed to vehicular traffic, the Old Van Zandt County Park is good for woodland birding and scanning the water, so carry a scope along. Park in the parking lot, climb the metal gate, and then follow the fishermen's trail to the woods beyond. In winter and during migration watch for Marsh Wren. Virginia Rail and Sora are rarities. Pine Warbler are sometimes seen in the oak trees in winter even though east of their normal range in the Pineywoods.

When driving around the lake, keep an eye open for the rare but resident Crested Caracara, especially early in the morning.

To explore other areas of the lake, maps are available at local convenience stores.

COOPER

Cooper is on SH 24 about 25 miles south of Paris or 24 miles northeast of Commerce. Birding locations are Cooper Lake State Park and Cooper Lake. The lake is a U.S. Army Corps of Engineers impoundment located in Hopkins and Delta counties on the South Sulphur River just south of the city of Cooper. The 19,300-acre lake was completed in 1991 for flood control, recreation, and to provide additional water conservation.

Cooper Lake State Park

Cooper Lake State Park is divided into two units, Doctor's Creek Unit and the South Sulphur Unit.

Doctor's Creek Unit, 466 acres, is on the north side of the lake. Attractions are camping, playground, fishing, picnicking, hiking, a boat ramp, and swimming. There are 6.2 miles of shoreline. To reach the unit drive east from Cooper for 1 mile on SH 154, then south 2 miles on FM 1529 to the park entrance. The address is Route 1, Box 231-A15, Cooper, TX 75432, (903) 395-3100.

South Sulphur Unit, 2,560 acres, is on the south shore of the lake. The park has 25.5 miles of shoreline, camping, screen shelters, modern cabins, fishing piers, picnicking, boat ramps, swimming, 8 miles of hiking trails, and horseback riding. To reach the unit from Cooper drive east 1 mile on SH 154, then south on FM 1529 5 miles to SH 19, then south 5 miles to FM 71, then west 4 miles to FM 3505, and finally north 1 mile to the entrance. The address is Route 3, Box 741, Sulphur Springs, TX 75482, (903) 945-5256.

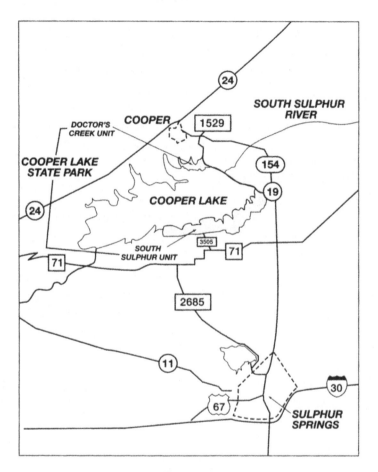

COOPER

Cooper Lake

The area below the dam, from the Doctor's Creek Unit of the Cooper Lake State Park to the spillway and the U.S. Army Corps of Engineers office, is currently designated as a Watchable Wildlife area. The habitat ranges from dense bottomland hardwood to uplands dominated by post-oak savannah. Park at the spillway parking lot or in the parking lot for the state park. AB-SOLUTELY NO BIRDING IS PERMITTED FROM THE DAM.

In winter the eastern red cedars provide habitat for owls and large flocks of American Robin, along with Orange-crowned and Yellow-rumped Warblers. LeConte's Sparrow and Sedge Wren are found in the grassy areas. Wild Turkey has been introduced. The first White-tailed Hawk for northeast Texas appeared here after a recent prescribed burn.

Ring-billed, Bonaparte's and a few Herring Gulls are regular in winter, while Franklin's Gull migrate through. Rarities recorded include Laughing, Black-headed, Little, Thayer's and California Gulls.

Another worthwhile area is the Tira Boat Ramp. Look for the signs and the road directly across from the Army Corps of Engineers office on the east side of the lake. This winding road leads through several old fields that were once cattle pastures. The successional habitats are excellent for wintering sparrows including Fox and Harris' Sparrows.

Yellow-breasted Chat have become summer residents along the road to Tira Boat Ramp. Fish Crow are occasionally found along the South Sulphur River.

FORT WORTH

Fort Worth, population 471,000, is located on the Grand Prairie at the eastern edge of the West Cross Timbers. The city is bisected by the Clear Fork Trinity River and the West Fork Trinity River, which join near downtown to continue east as the West Fork Trinity River. An agricultural, transportation, and manufacturing center, the city also has world-famous art museums, spacious city parks, several large man-made lakes, and the Fort Worth Nature Center and Refuge. This last is one of the finest examples of natural habitat preservation by any city in Texas.

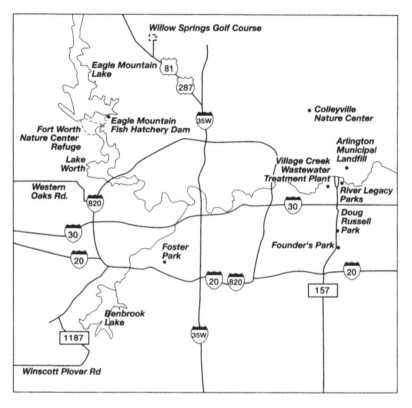

FORT WORTH

A bar graph checklist of the birds of Tarrant County is available from the Fort Worth Nature Center, 9601 Fossil Ridge Road, Fort Worth, TX 76135, (817) 237-1111, for $2.00 plus stamped, addressed envelope.

Birds of Tarrant County, second edition, by Warren M. Pulich, 1979, is an annotated account of the birds of the county.

RARE BIRD ALERT FOR NORTH TEXAS, (817) 237-3209, is sponsored by the Dallas County, Fort Worth, and Prairie & Timbers (McKinney) Audubon Societies.

Fort Worth Nature Center and Refuge

The Fort Worth Nature Center and Refuge, 3,412 acres, is northwest of the city on Lake Worth. To reach the refuge, drive 2 miles northwest of the Lake Worth bridge on SH 199 (Jacksboro Highway) to the entrance on the right. It is open 9 am to 5 pm, Tuesday through Saturday, and noon to 5 pm Sunday, except on City of Fort Worth holidays. From Memorial Day through Labor Day, Saturday hours are 7 am to 5 pm. The refuge is closed on Mondays. There are over 20 miles of trails (from 0.5 to 7 miles long) through a wide variety of habitats. These include woodlands with a half-dozen oak species, river bottoms, prairies, extensive marshes, and the lake. Buffalo have been reintroduced to an enclosed area and are thriving. White-tailed deer, beaver, coyote, and bobcat are also resident, but not in enclosed areas. Canoeing is allowed on the river, lake, and marshes and is the best way to see the birds of these areas. A 900-foot boardwalk over Lotus Marsh (wheel chair accessible) has been provided to allow visitors to view the marsh from above.

Start at the Hardwicke Interpretive Center, where there are natural history exhibits, trail maps, classes, workshops, an herbarium, guided trail walks, an excellent natural history library, etc. Books and bird checklists are for sale covering the nature center, Tarrant County, and much more. Check with the office for programs available. There is no entrance fee to the refuge.

The Center features a picture window overlooking a courtyard where water and food are provided for wildlife. Binoculars, books, and seating are available for the observer. Twenty to twenty-five bird species per day come in to feed in winter including Fox Sparrow, Yellow-bellied Sapsucker, Red-breasted Nuthatch, and Purple Finch. One October day, a male Black-throated Blue Warbler graced the courtyard. Other visitors are gray fox, raccoon, opossum, eastern fox squirrel, and white-tailed deer.

In summer, check the hummingbird feeders for Black-chinned and Ruby-throated Hummingbirds. Year-round, keep an eye out for Wild Turkey, which were reintroduced several years ago. The nature center grounds are one of the best places in the county to find these shy birds, especially in early morning in the spring.

Directly north of the Hardwicke Center is the Trinity River, which can be birded by trail or by car. A scenic road runs along the river from the Lotus Marsh Boardwalk to Greer Island. Here, along the river and just below the nature center building, listen in spring and summer for Yellow-throated Warbler, Prothonotary Warbler, and Northern Parula. These birds are best seen in the vicinity of the Cross Timbers levee. Keep an eye on the skies in spring and summer for Anhinga (rare), which nested here in 1987.

The drive upriver leads to the Lotus Marsh Boardwalk. Stop, look, and listen along the way in the winter months for Rusty Blackbird and Winter Wren. The boardwalk itself is a good vantage point year-round for Wood Duck, Red-shouldered Hawk, and Barred Owl. In summer look for nesting Yellow-crowned Night-Heron, Yellow-billed Cuckoo, and White-eyed Vireo. A spotting scope is highly recommended. Scan the skies for Mississippi Kite. In winter look for Cinnamon Teal (rare) and Hooded Merganser with the ducks on the river. The nearby river-bottom trail is a great place to look for the rare American Woodcock.

From the parking lot of the Lotus Marsh Boardwalk, hike north along the former Equestrian Trail. This trail follows the river channel north through some of the best river-bottom woodland in North Texas. Winter residents include Hairy Woodpecker, Eastern Phoebe, Brown Creeper, and Golden-crowned Kinglet. Some summer residents are Great Crested Flycatcher, Red-eyed Vireo, and Summer Tanager. When Carolina Chickadee and Tufted Titmouse are encountered, examine the titmice carefully, particularly in drier post-oak woodlands. Many will be the eastern race, a few the western race (Black-crested), but intergrades between the two races are sometimes present. In migration, look for warblers including Ovenbird, Canada and Mourning Warblers. The trail eventually intersects a power line cut, creating an edge habitat between forest, field, and river. Indigo and Painted Buntings (summer) and Swamp, Song, and Lincoln's Sparrows (winter) are found here in addition to many previously mentioned species. Red-headed Woodpecker are sometimes seen here.

Greer Island is located downriver from Lotus Marsh at the opposite end of the refuge. A causeway connects the island with the main road. When lotus plants inundate either side of the causeway, look for Least Bittern, Common Moorhen, and (rarely) Purple Gallinule in summer. When the lake level is low a wide variety of shorebirds can be present along with rarities such as Roseate Spoonbill, Tricolored Heron, and White Ibis.

Eagle Mountain Fish Hatchery and Dam

Located in northwest Fort Worth, the 78 acres of the Eagle Mountain Fish Hatchery and the adjacent dam to Eagle Mountain Lake are an excellent place to bird between late summer and spring. All ducks that migrate through or winter in the area can usually be found here.

Before planning a visit, call the Fort Worth Audubon Society, (817) 237-7791, to obtain the latest combination to the gate. Also, call the Tarrant County Water Control district office, (807) 237-8585, for permission to climb the dam.

Despite a "No Trespassing" sign at the hatchery entrance, birders are welcome to enter under an agreement between the Fort Worth Audubon Society and the Tarrant County Water Control district offices.

To reach the hatchery from I-820 (Jim Wright Expressway), exit at Azle Avenue (Exit 10B) and drive west. After 1 block turn north on FM 1220 and go about 2 miles, then left (west) onto Ten Mile Bridge Road. After 3.7 miles, turn north onto Eagle Mountain. Circle and go 0.6 mile to the entrance on the right.

In late summer, watch for the possibility of Tricolored Heron, Roseate Spoonbill, and White Ibis. Migrants include American White Pelican on the lake, Least Bittern (in lotus ponds), White-faced Ibis, Osprey, Mississippi Kite, Tree and Bank Swallows amongst the more numerous Barn, Northern Rough-winged, and

Cliff Swallows, plus rarities like Broad-winged Hawk, Peregrine and Prairie Falcons.

Between October and April, the hatchery is a dependable area for numerous waterfowl species including Cinnamon Teal, Canvasback and Greater Scaup. In migration, check any White-faced Ibis carefully. Glossy Ibis is fast becoming an annual visitor and has occurred in the winter months as well. The first accepted Glossy Ibis for Texas was found here in 1983.

The cattail marsh located near the east end of the hatchery has traditionally been good for Sora in migration and Virginia Rail and Marsh Wren in winter. A tape of rail calls is usually needed to elicit a response.

Many other rarities have shown up at the hatchery over the years including Surf Scoter, Laughing Gull, Lesser Black-backed Gull, and Sedge Wren.

The adjacent dam creating Eagle Mountain Lake is an excellent vantage point from which to scan for migrating hawks, cranes, and other species. There is a step ladder to get over the fence separating the fish hatchery from the dam.

From the dam, look for loons, Horned Grebe, mergansers, and Bonaparte's Gull on the lake in winter.

Benbrook Lake

Benbrook Lake, 3,770 surface acres at conservation pool level, a U.S. Army Corps of Engineers flood control and water conservation project, is approximately 12 miles southwest of downtown Fort Worth. From downtown, drive west on I-30 to US 377, then southwest on US 377 to the lake.

The lake has about 40 miles of shoreline and 6 parks, with camping, picnicking, fishing, boat ramps, marinas, and restrooms. The developed parks total 2,896 acres, with another 1,578 acres undeveloped. It is easy to spend a whole day birding around the lake. The creek bottoms are wooded, some short-grass prairie is preserved, and the lake itself offers many birding opportunities.

From I-820 and US 377, drive south 1.3 miles to a traffic light and a sign that indicates "Benbrook Dam." Turn left (east) on Winscott Road, formerly Lakeside Drive. After 0.4 mile Beach Road to the right leads generally south along the western shore of the lake. Continuing on Winscott Road another 0.3 mile, a second road to the right (Lakeside Drive) leads below the spillway, past the Pecan Valley Golf Course and around the east side of the lake. Continuing on Winscott Road (past Lakeside Drive) for another 0.5 mile will lead to Memorial Oak Road. Turn right at the sign for Memorial Oak Park and park in the parking lot at the end of the road. Birding opportunities abound in the wooded areas on either side of the river in this park. This is usually an excellent park for finding passerine migrants in spring and fall. The woods are good in winter also. Barred Owl and Red-shouldered Hawk are resident species.

From the intersection of Winscott and US 377, Holiday Park can be reached by driving south on US 377 4.4 miles and turning left at the sign "Holiday Park" just before the bridge over Clear Fork Trinity River. This is a camping area, therefore it is necessary to advise the attendant in the entrance booth that birding is the objective of the visit. Turn right immediately after passing the entrance booth and drive south to the boat launch ramp. The shallow bay here is one of the better birding spots at the lake. Light is best in the morning. Scan the dead trees in the water with a scope in late summer and early fall for Neotropic Cormorant, which has become a regular visitor. A well-established Great Blue Heron rookery exists directly across the bay from the boat launch. A drive north from the entrance booth will lead to a road block. The open woodlands along this drive between the road and the lake can result in good birding also.

Rocky Creek Park on the southeast side of the lake and Mustang Park at the southern end offer more extensive woodlands and less visitor use. Mustang Point in Mustang Park offers a good vantage point for scanning the lake with a scope. Red-breasted and Common Mergansers can sometimes be found in winter.

Mountain Bluebird were found here in 1994. Some portions of Mustang Park are closed in winter.

Scan the lake for Horned Grebe and Bonaparte's Gull, which can be found in good numbers in winter. Rare gulls recorded are Sabine's, Laughing, and Black-legged Kittiwake. Common Goldeneye are sometime present in winter. Look for Osprey in migration. All the parks are good for wintering sparrows plus other land birds. The cottonwoods and willows lining the lakeshore, especially at Holiday Park, can be good places to search for nesting Warbling Vireo and Orchard Oriole.

Driving around the lake one fall day, I found Pied-billed Grebe, Double-crested Cormorant, Great Blue Heron, Northern Shoveler, Gadwall, Bufflehead, Turkey Vulture, Northern Harrier, Red-tailed Hawk, American Kestrel, American Coot, Lesser Yellowlegs, Least Sandpiper, Common Snipe, Ring-billed Gull, Eastern Screech-Owl, Belted Kingfisher, Red-bellied Woodpecker, Yellow-bellied Sapsucker, Downy Woodpecker, Blue Jay, Carolina Chickadee, Bewick's Wren, Ruby-crowned Kinglet, Northern Mockingbird, Loggerhead Shrike, Orange-crowned Warbler, Northern Cardinal, Spotted Towhee, Field, Song, Lincoln's, White-crowned, and Harris' Sparrows, Dark-eyed Junco, American Goldfinch, and House Sparrow.

The address of the Benbrook Lake Manager is P.O. Box 26059, Fort Worth, TX 76116, (817) 292-2400.

Winscott-Plover Road

Nearly every raptor recorded in Tarrant County has at one time or another been spotted along this road, which parallels the county line south of Lake Benbrook. The road transects a large expanse of rolling prairie used primarily as ranch land. From US 377 and I-820 in Benbrook, drive south on US 377 6.4 miles to FM 1187. Turn left (east) on FM 1187 and go 4.1 miles, then turn right (south) on Winscott-Plover Road and proceed 1.7 miles to the railroad tracks. Immediately after crossing the tracks, turn right again onto the east-west (unmarked) portion of Winscott-Plover Road. It is this stretch going west that is the most productive for finding birds of prey. Red-tailed Hawk, Northern Harrier, and American Kestrel predominate in winter as does Swainson's Hawk in summer, but White-tailed Kite, Ferruginous and Rough-legged Hawks, Golden Eagle, Crested Caracara, Merlin, and Prairie Falcon have been recorded. For two months following widespread grass fires in the spring of 1996, American Golden-Plover, Upland Sandpiper, and Long-billed Curlew congregated to take advantage of the fresh new growth. While in the area in winter, look also for Short-eared Owl, Lark Bunting, Lapland, McCown's, and Chestnut-collared Longspurs, and Brewer's Blackbird.

Foster Park

Foster Park, located at the intersection of Trail Lake Drive and South Drive in southwest Fort Worth, is one of the best locations in the county for passerine migrants. From I-20 in southwest Fort Worth, take Exit 434B (Trail Lake Drive), drive north 0.7 mile to Granbury Road, cross Granbury and proceed 0.2 mile to South Drive. Turn left on South Drive and immediately park on the right. There are open woodlands, many brush areas, and a flowing stream. Walk the hike and bike trail. Thirty or so warbler species and seven vireo species have been recorded.

Northwest Tarrant County

Perhaps the best area for longspsurs in the region exists in far northwest Tarrant County in the vicinity of the Willow Springs Golf Course. To reach the golf course, go north on I-35W from I-820 to US 287. Drive northwest on US 287 about five miles to the Willow Springs exit, follow Willow Springs Road north to the golf course. A cold, blustery day in January or February is best. Obtain permission in the clubhouse to walk the golf course. Here is the best chance for McCown's Longspur in addition to Lapland, and perhaps a few Chestnut-collared Longspur. Horned Lark are usually common. Driving the back roads in this area such as Blue Mound Road or Willow Springs Road will sometimes yield large flocks of longspurs. Look for flocks of McCown's and Lapland

Longspurs in the plowed fields and Chestnut-collared Longspurs in the taller grassy fields. Lark and Grasshopper Sparrows (summer), hawks and LeConte's Sparrow (winter), and Lark Bunting (occasional in winter) can also be found in this area.

Western Oaks Road

This dead end road is reached from I-820 by taking Exit 5B (Silver Creek Road), between White Settlement Road and Lake Worth in west Fort Worth. From I-820 take Silver Creek Road for 2.3 miles to Western Oaks Road, then go west. In winter especially, small numbers of Rufous-crowned Sparrow can usually be found at the end of this road, the only known site in the county for this species. Chuck-will's-widow (early summer) and Eastern Screech-Owl (year-round) can be heard calling before first light. Harris' Sparrow are numerous along the road in winter. During late winter and early spring, the real attraction here is to look and listen for American Woodcock in courtship flight at dawn and dusk.

ARLINGTON AND EASTERN TARRANT COUNTY

Village Creek Wastewater Treatment Plant

The extensive drying beds of this sewage disposal plant were formerly one of the top inland shorebird locations in the state and produced many excellent records. The plant is located in the Trinity River bottoms east of Fort Worth in Arlington. Changing technology is claiming the life of these drying beds; however, until they are gone completely, birders are still welcome dawn to dusk, seven days per week.

To reach the facility, take Exit 26 (Fielder Road) from I-30, drive north on Fielder Road 1.3 miles to Green Oaks Blvd., then right (east) on Green Oaks Blvd. 0.3 mile to the entrance on the left.

While shorebirding may be a shadow of what it once was, quite a few species of sandpipers can still be found, particularly after rains have saturated the beds. If there is sufficient standing water, the beds attract a large number of long-legged waders in migration and several species of waterfowl in winter. Traditionally, the beds have been the best place in the county to find (in season) Black-bellied Whistling-Duck, Cinnamon Teal, Common Moorhen, Black-necked Stilt, Hudsonian Godwit, Buff-breasted Sandpiper, Short-billed Dowitcher, and Rusty Blackbird.

Two very rare species found here include Texas' only record of Sharp-tailed Sandpiper in May, 1991, and a Ruff in 1995. Other recent rarities are White Ibis, Glossy Ibis, Mottled Duck (summer), and Ross' Goose.

Unlike the beds, the cattail marsh located at the south end of the property has continually improved in recent years. It is the best place around to look for American Bittern (migration), King Rail (rare in summer), Virginia Rail (winter), Sora (migration), Marsh Wren (winter), and Swamp Sparrow (winter).

Founder's Park

Founder's Park is located just north of the larger Vandergriff Park in south Arlington at the southeast corner of Matlock Road and Arkansas Lane. The location is a short distance south of the intersection of Spur 303 and FM 157. This unassuming little park consists mainly of a tree-lined creek, but perhaps due to an oasis effect and an ample number of fruiting mulberry trees, it can be an excellent place to find migrating songbirds in April and May. Among the many migrants recorded each spring are some notable rarities including Vermilion Flycatcher, Cerulean Warbler, and Scarlet Tanager. Check the mulberry trees for Rose-breasted and Black-headed (rare) Grosbeaks.

Doug Russell Park

Doug Russell Park is situated on the west side of Cooper Street in the heart of The University of Texas at Arlington campus. Many of the same species described for Founder's Park can be found here.

Colleyville Nature Center

The Colleyville Nature Center (unmanned) is a recent addition to the park system and consists of several self-guided nature trails winding along either side of Little Bear Creek in Colleyville. Larger than both Founder's and Doug Russell Parks, it has much to offer the visiting birder. In its short history, well over 20 warbler species have been recorded including Golden-winged and Hooded Warblers. Red-breasted Nuthatch have been found in winter. To reach the park from northeast I-820, take Exit 22A (SH 26), drive northeast on SH 26 4.8 miles, turn left on Glade Road and go 0.6 mile to Mill Creek Drive, then turn left and follow Mill Creek Drive through a subdivision for 0.3 mile to the park entrance.

River Legacy Parks

River Legacy Parks (formerly Rose-Brown-May Parks), 626 acres, is located in Arlington behind the newly-opened River Legacy Living Science Center. To reach the parks and the center from I-30 take Exit 26 (Fielder Road), drive north on Fielder Road 1.3 miles to Green Oaks Blvd., turn right (east) and drive 1.1 mile to the entrance on the left (the entrance to the Parks precedes the entrance to the Living Science Center). Comprised of several parks in one, River Legacy is one of the finest city parks in the Dallas/Fort Worth metroplex and succeeds in catering to birders and naturalists as well as to bicyclists and roller-bladers. Included in the 28 miles of trails are nearly 20 miles of unpaved woodland trails open to foot travel only.

The many trails through the river bottom woodland provide excellent opportunities for birding, especially in spring. Over 25 warbler species have been recorded including Mourning, Swainson's and Hooded Warblers. Other finds include Black-billed Cuckoo, Yellow-throated and Philadelphia Vireos, Lazuli Bunting, and Black-headed Grosbeak. Broad-winged Hawk, Yellow-bellied Flycatcher, several species of thrushes, Gray Catbird, and Orchard and Baltimore Orioles are regular migrants. Red-shouldered Hawk, Barred Owl, Great Crested Flycatcher, Red-eyed, Warbling, and White-eyed Vireos, and Summer Tanager are among the summer residents. Wood Duck can often be seen on the Trinity River and on the creeks that feed it.

The Living Science Center is a state-of-the-art nature center with natural history exhibits, a multi-purpose room, and a gift shop. Entrance to an exhibit hall featuring a high definition, interactive, simulation of a seasonal canoe ride down the Trinity River costs $3 for adults and $2 for children 2–18. Entrance to the remainder of the center and to the parks is free. The Living Science Center is open 9 am to 5 pm, Tuesday through Saturday, while the parkland is open seven days per week, daylight hours only. The phone number of the center is (817) 860-6752.

Arlington Municipal Landfill

Located in north Arlington at the intersection of Mosier Valley Road and FM 157 about 2.0 miles south of SH 183 is one of the best landfills in the metroplex for gulls. Among the countless number of Ring-billed Gulls and the handful of Herring Gulls present in fall, winter, and spring, a rarity occasionally appears. For example, Mew, California, and Thayer's Gulls have been recorded. Franklin's Gulls migrate through by the thousands in spring and fall.

DINOSAUR VALLEY STATE PARK

Dinosaur Valley State Park, 1,274 acres, is near Glen Rose about 60 miles southwest of Fort Worth. From Glen Rose drive one mile west on US 67, then northwest 2.8 miles on FM 205 to the park entrance. Facilities include picnicking, camping, restrooms with hot showers, fishing, swimming, hiking, and birding. The park was established to preserve some of the best fossil footprints of dinosaurs known to exist. There are three types of tracks represented: the sauropods, the theropods, and the ornithopods.

Two special birds are present in summer: the Golden-cheeked Warbler and the Black-capped Vireo, although the vireo numbers

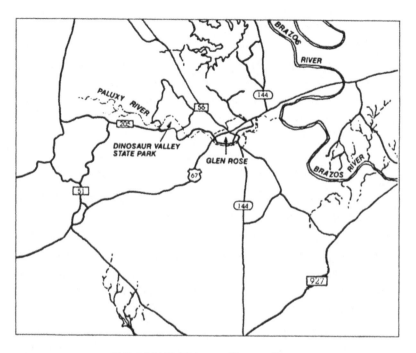

DINOSAUR VALLEY STATE PARK

may be decreasing. This is one of the northernmost active nesting sites for the warbler and also one of the northernmost in Texas for the vireo. Look for the warbler, April through June, along Denio Creek Trail and the Ridge Trail. The vireo also occurs along the Ridge Trail from April through July. Most of the birds of the park are eastern species but the following western birds are near the eastern edge of their range: Common Poorwill, Black-chinned Hummingbird, Ladder-backed Woodpecker, Canyon Wren, Bell's Vireo, and Rufous-crowned Sparrow. Rufous-crowned Sparrow is fairly common in brush along the Paluxy River. Lesser Goldfinch and House Finch are rare but can sometimes be found in summer.

In winter watch for Northern Flicker, Hermit Thrush, Pine Siskin, American Goldfinch, Spotted Towhee, Harris', Field, Fox, Song, Lincoln's, White-throated, and White-crowned Sparrows, and Dark-eyed Junco. LeConte's Sparrow have been found in the tall grassy field upstream from the picnic area. The equestrian trail leads to this large field.

A bird checklist (1991) with 151 species and a map of the hiking trails is available at headquarters. A nice feature of the checklist is that it details the best bird spots in the park. The address is P.O. Box 396, Glen Rose, TX 76043, (817) 897-4588.

WACO

Waco, population 107,000, is in the heart of Central Texas at the western edge of the Blackland Prairies near the Balcones Escarpment.

The story of Waco begins with the Brazos River. The Huaco Indians originally established their village on its banks at Indian Spring Park. Visitors to Indian Spring Park will discover a world of history, natural beauty, fun, and good birding.

Birding opportunities in and around Waco are enhanced by the extensive farmlands (hawks and sparrows in winter), several large man-made lakes (waterfowl and shorebirds), and wide and heavily wooded river bottomland (land birds). In the Bellmead area just north of Waco and west of US 84, Cattle Egret have had a large rookery for several years with more than 3,000 birds. Nesting with them are Great and Snowy Egrets and Little Blue Herons, but in much smaller numbers. Short-eared Owl winter around the golf course near the new Veterans Hospital.

A bird checklist, 1997, for McLennan County is available from Strecker Museum, Baylor University, Waco, TX 76798, for $1.00 plus stamped, addressed envelope.

Cameron Park

Fort Fisher is just south of the Brazos River on IH 35. It is operated by the Waco Parks and Recreation Department and has excellent facilities for fishing, boating, picnicking, and camping. The Homer Garrison Memorial Texas Ranger Museum and the

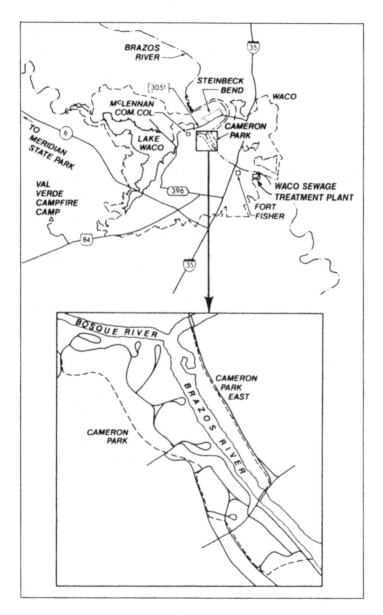

WACO

Texas Ranger Hall of Fame are here, and both are well worth a visit. For camper hook-up information, write to the Waco Parks and Recreation Department, P.O. Box 1370, Waco, TX 76703, or call (817) 754-1433.

To reach Cameron Park from Fort Fisher, drive northwest on University Parks Drive for 2.5 miles. A sign indicates "William Cameron Park," but if the sign is missed, the horse stables on the left will indicate that the park has been reached. Cameron Park, 680 acres, also operated by the Waco Parks and Recreation Department, is spread on both sides of the Brazos River. At the upper end of the park, the Bosque River joins the Brazos, which can be seen from Lover's Leap. Lover's Leap is one of three cliffs inside the park. From this high vantage point, one can view for miles the farmlands and plains to the east of the city.

The cul-de-sac at Proctor Spring is a good place to start birding among the majestic old sycamore, elm, oak, pecan, and cottonwood trees for resident land birds and migrants. During spring migration, the height of warbler passage usually occurs in the first two weeks of May. Starting near the picnic pavilion, follow the stream back toward Lindsey Hollow, and look for birds in the tops of the trees. Migrants found include *Empidonax* flycatchers, Eastern Wood-Pewee, Veery, Swainson's and Gray-cheeked Thrushes, Baltimore, Bullock's, and Orchard Orioles, Scarlet Tanager, Rose-breasted Grosbeak, "Solitary," Bell's, Philadelphia, and Warbling Vireos as well as warblers. Black-headed Grosbeak and Black-billed Cuckoo have been recorded but are very rare.

The Redwood Shelter, Cameron Park Clubhouse, and Junior League Anniversay Park Pavilion are areas in the park accessible by reservation only and with a small rental fee. However, there are numerous other beautiful picnic spots throughout the park that are free. Across the road from the Redwood Shelter is a large mulberry tree. When there are ripe berries on the tree, there is a good chance of seeing migrants plus a few lingering wintering species, such as Pine Siskin, Lincoln's Sparrow, American Goldfinch, and

Cedar Waxwing. Painted Buntings sometimes nest here as well as directly across the river in Cameron Park East.

Another land bird location is the South Bottom Playground. From the car bridge, check the creek for Green Heron (a summer resident) and migrating Northern Waterthrush. Overhead watch for Northern Rough-winged Swallow (summer resident), and migrating Mississippi Kite, Franklin's Gull, and Broad-winged and Swainson's Hawks. In recent years Wood Ducks have nested in one of the tall cottonwood trees on the bank of the stream near the bridge.

The pecan and oak trees all along the South Bottom Playground are excellent locations for finding warblers. During migration, Nashville, Black-throated Green, Blackburnian, Chestnut-sided, Bay-breasted, Wilson's, American Redstart, Black-and-white, and Yellow Warblers, Common Yellowthroat, and Yellow-breasted Chat are usually recorded. Less common are Tennessee and Canada Warblers, and Northern Parula. Blackpoll Warbler is very rare. Look for nesting Pied-billed Grebe and Belted Kingfisher along the water's edge. Shorebirds and waterfowl have been seen in migration along the river.

Nesting species in the park are Carolina Wren, Eastern Screech-Owl, Barred and Great Horned Owls, Black-chinned Hummingbird, Ladder-backed Woodpecker, Eastern and Western Kingbirds, and Summer Tanager.

In the winter the following birds can be found in the park: Northern Flicker, Yellow-bellied Sapsucker, Brown Creeper, Blue-gray Gnatcatcher, Hermit Thrush, Purple Finch, Dark-eyed Junco, White-throated Sparrow, Yellow-rumped and Orange-crowned Warblers, and Cedar Waxwing. Chipping Sparrow and Greater Roadrunner can be found in the higher areas of the park in summer. Rare winter visitors include Winter Wren, Red-headed Woodpecker, and Red-breasted and White-breasted Nuthatches.

The best time for bird seekers to visit Cameron Park on weekends is early morning, before the picnickers arrive with their loud music and frisbees flying in all directions. It is generally very crowded on Saturdays and Sundays, beginning around 1 pm and continuing until late evening. However, there is usually no problem on weekdays, except toward the end of May when school picnics prevail.

Steinbeck Bend Area

The Steinbeck Bend area has consistently produced good birding in all seasons. Though within the Waco city limits, the area is rural. Formerly devoted to cropland farming and grazing, this big bend of the Brazos River just north of Cameron Park is now an area of widely spaced private homes with a few cattle.

From Cameron Park, drive east on Herring Avenue (FM 1637), and cross the bridge over Lake Brazos. Turn left onto Lake Brazos Drive at the second traffic light. Eastern and Western Kingbirds, Scissor-tailed Flycatcher, Dickcissel, and Painted and Indigo Buntings are easily heard and seen in spring and summer

SCISSOR-TAILED FLYCATCHER

between the traffic light and the bridge over the Brazos River. The woods west of the road are in Cameron Park East. From the traffic light, drive north 1.8 miles, and turn right at the traffic light onto Lake Shore Drive. After 0.3 mile, turn left at the first road, where there is a small abandoned barn and windmill. Though unmarked at the end of the loop, this is Old Steinbeck Bend Road (not to be confused with Steinbeck Bend Road). From this point, make a right turn at each intersection until back at the starting point, thus completing a loop.

The loop can also be reached from the intersection of IH 35 and Industrial Boulevard (FM 3051) by driving west on Industrial Boulevard and crossing the river. The loop is reached in about 0.5 mile. Fence rows, open fields, and wood margins along the 2.5-mile loop provide good habitats for a diverse group of bird species.

During spring migration (April and early May), the following birds have been recorded on the loop: Upland Sandpiper (in large numbers in the open fields), Black Tern, Barn and Cliff Swallows, Eastern and Western Kingbirds, *Empidonax* flycatchers, Baltimore, Bullock's and Orchard Orioles, Dickcissel, Indigo and Painted Buntings, Cattle Egret, Nashville and Yellow Warblers, Common Yellowthroat, and White-crowned and Grasshopper Sparrows. Bobolink are occasionally sighted migrating with the abundant Dickcissel.

Sometimes water stands in these fields for days after heavy rains. On such occasions, shorebirds and wading birds not usually found in abundance in the area can congregate in great numbers. One particularly rainy spring, Wilson's Phalarope, Long-billed Dowitcher, Pectoral Sandpiper, Common Snipe, Little Blue Heron, Greater and Lesser Yellowlegs, Northern Pintail, Northern Shoveler, and Blue-winged Teal were all seen feeding in the shallow water for a period of two weeks or more. In recent years, during the first two weeks of May Yellow-headed Blackbird have stopped over to feed with mixed flocks of Brown-headed Cowbird, Red-winged Blackbird, and Great-tailed and Common Grackles.

During winter, look for American Goldfinch feeding in the dried weeds along the fence rows with wintering Harris', Lincoln's, White-throated, White-crowned, Savannah, and Vesper Sparrows.

McLennan Community College

The campus of McLennan Community College, 160 acres owned and operated by McLennan County, is located on the crest of a heavily wooded bluff that commands a magnificent view of the valleys of the Brazos and Bosque rivers. The athletic fields, woods, and frontage along the river offer another opportunity for birding in the city.

From the Steinbeck Bend area, drive southwest on Lake Shore Drive to the Bosque River bridge. Just after crossing the bridge, turn left at the first traffic light (College Drive), then go left again at the first street (Cameron Street). Park in the parking lot next to the athletic field house beneath the shade trees. Near the river there is an amphitheater.

In spring and summer this is a good area in which to see Great Crested Flycatcher, Red-eyed and White-eyed Vireos, Red-bellied Woodpecker, and an occasional Red-headed Woodpecker. In summer listen for Chuck-will's-widow calling at night in the heavily wooded areas around the campus. Whip-poor-will can sometimes be heard in April and May.

Near the river in summer look for Little Blue Heron, American Coot, and Pied-billed Grebe. Up river there are Cliff Swallow in-great abundance under the bridge. Opposite the marina, the woods on both sides of the road offer excellent habitat for Painted and Indigo Buntings from late April to early August.

Next, walk or drive up the hill and turn left at the first intersection. Search the wood margins all around the perimeter of the large parking lot at the top of the hill. This is another favorable location for migrating warblers (same species as mentioned in the Cameron Park section). Watch for Inca Dove year-round and Black-chinned and Ruby-throated Hummingbirds in summer.

Camp Val Verde

Camp Val Verde, a 400-acre camp located 12 miles west of Waco, is owned and operated by the Huaco Council of Camp Fire, Inc. To reach the camp from the intersection of IH 35 and Valley Mills Drive, go west on Valley Mills Drive for 2.2 miles to Waco Drive (US 84), then drive 9.5 miles to the Val Verde Road exit. Drive north on Val Verde Road 2.5 miles to the camp. There are signs along the road with directions.

The camp is situated on the Middle Bosque River in a predominately agricultural area. There are two shallow ponds and one small lake on the property as well as flowing streams during rainy seasons. Permission from the Camp Fire office is required to enter.

Numerous campsites and small cabins with faciles are available for rent. These are scattered throughout the camp. To obtain information or permission for access to the premises for birding, write: Huaco Council of Camp Fire, Inc., Community Services Building, Suite 205, 201 West Waco Drive, Waco, TX 76707; or call (817) 752-5515.

Permanent resident birds of the area include Inca Dove, Greater Roadrunner, Red-headed and Ladder-backed Woodpeckers, Eastern Bluebird, Eastern Phoebe, Loggerhead Shrike, Common Grackle, Great Horned and Barred Owls, Eastern Screech-Owl, Brown Thrasher, Great Blue and Little Blue Herons, Belted Kingfisher, and Black Vulture.

Wintering species include Sharp-shinned and Cooper's Hawks, Northern Flicker, Field, Chipping, White-throated, Fox, Lincoln's, and Harris' Sparrows, Golden-crowned Kinglet, American Goldfinch, Dark-eyed Junco, Brown Creeper, Yellow-bellied Sapsucker, Common Snipe, Winter and House Wrens, and Purple Finch. Occasionals are Groove-billed Ani, Vermilion Flycatcher, Green-tailed Towhee, and Say's Phoebe. The wintering species are especially abundant and easy to find around the gravel pit area.

Some summer residents are Great, Snowy, and Cattle Egrets, Chuck-will's-widow, Black-chinned Hummingbird, Eastern and

Western Kingbirds, Great Crested Flycatcher, Orchard Oriole, Dickcissel, White-eyed and Red-eyed Vireos, Summer Tanager, Red-headed Woodpecker, and Barn and Northern Rough-winged Swallows.

Migrating birds recorded at the camp include Black-and-white, Yellow, Tennessee, Blackburnian, Bay-breasted, and Canada Warblers, Yellow-breasted Chat, American Redstart, Bullock's Oriole, Rose-breasted Grosbeak, Grasshopper and LeConte's Sparrows, Wood and Swainson's Thrushes, Least Flycatcher, Eastern Wood-Pewee, "Solitary" and Warbling Vireos, Blue-gray Gnatcatcher, Gray Catbird, American Pipit, Spotted, Semipalmated, and Upland Sandpipers, Lesser Yellowlegs, Mississippi Kite, and Sandhill Crane. Black-throated Sparrows, not usually found in the Waco area, have been recorded here. Wild Turkey are increasing in the camp.

Lake Waco

Lake Waco is located at the northwest city limits of Waco. It has a shoreline of 60 miles (7,270 surface acres at conservation pool level) and is operated by the U.S. Army Corps of Engineers. The lake impounds water from the North, Middle, and South Bosque rivers for the purposes of flood control, water conservation, and municipal water supply. Extra dividends derived from the lake include favorable fish and wildlife habitats, and recreational facilities for water sports, hunting, fishing, boating, and birding.

The lake is surrounded by eight Corps of Engineer parks, most of which have camping, restrooms, picnicking, and boat ramps. The north shore can be reached from IH 35 on the north side of Waco. Drive west from the Lake Shore Drive exit on Industrial Boulevard (soon becomes Lake Shore Drive) approximately four miles to Airport Road. From Waco's south side, take the Valley Mills exit, then go west on Valley Mills Drive approximately 3.5 miles until the road turns north and becomes Lake Shore Drive. To get to the parks on the south and west shoreline, drive northwest about 4 miles on SH 6 from south of Waco. Signs on the right give directions to the lake.

Airport Park, with its extensive woodlands and protected shoreline, is a good place to start birding the lake. From Lake Shore Drive turn north on Airport Road. Drive north to FM 3051, west to the dead end, then right (north) to the lake headquarters soon found on the right. Maps and bird information can be obtained from the lake rangers at headquarters. The beach area of Airport Park is on the left about 0.1 mile past headquarters. Airport Road is approximately 1 mile west of the McLennan Community College campus on Lake Shore Drive.

Soon after crossing the Bosque River bridge when driving north on Airport Drive, there is a large pecan grove and soccer fields on both sides of the road where Eastern Bluebird, Great Horned Owl, Red-tailed Hawk, Loggerhead Shrike, and Red-headed and Ladder-backed Woodpeckers are permanent residents. This is a part of Bosque Park.

The beach area is an excellent place for migrating shorebirds, wintering waterfowl, and gulls. During winter, the gate is locked; however, visitors can park at the entrance and walk in. Most wintering gulls are Ring-billed and Bonaparte's, with Franklin's as a regular migrant, but several rarities have been recorded. A Little Gull was a visitor in January, 1989, and a regular visitor each winter from 1989 through 1994. Other gulls recorded making rare appearances are Sabine's, Thayer's, California, Black-headed, and Laughing. Other unexpected species are Wood Stork, Roseate Spoonbill, White-winged Scoter, and Tundra Swan.

Some migrants that have been recorded are American Avocet, Common, Least, Black, Caspian, and Forster's Terns, Upland, Spotted, Least, Baird's, Buff-breasted and Western Sandpipers, Sanderling, Dunlin, Ruddy Turnstone, Northern and Louisiana Waterthrushes, American White Pelican, Sandhill Crane, Willet, Swainson's Hawk, Greater and Lesser Yellowlegs, Semipalmated Plover, Canada Goose, Marbled and Hudsonian Godwits, and

White-faced Ibis. Black Skimmer and Brown Pelican have been seen occasionally.

Wintering species along the shore, on the water, and in wooded areas include American Pipit, Northern Pintail, Redhead, Green-winged and Blue-winged Teals, Gadwall, American Wigeon, Canvasback, Northern Shoveler, Double-crested and Neotropic Cormorants, Osprey, Dark-eyed Junco, Lincoln's and Vesper Sparrows, and Northern Flicker. Near the bathhouse in the beach area, Horned Lark, McCown's, Chestnut-collared, and Lapland Longspurs are found some winters.

An excellent new birding location at the lake is the Army Corps of Engineers Research Area near the intersection of Steinbeck Bend Road and Airport Drive, about one block east of the Corps office. A permit is required for entry, but the permit is free and can be obtained at the Corps office. There is a wildlife viewing structure on a bench above the pond, which is an old borrow pit from the construction of the dam. It is one of the best spots in the county for observing large numbers of wintering waterfowl, most local herons and egrets, as well as Osprey, Bald Eagle, and other species.

Summer birds at or near the lake include Little Blue Heron, Snowy, Great, and Cattle Egrets, Great Crested Flycatcher, Grasshopper Sparrow, Barn and Cliff Swallows, Baltimore and Bullock's Orioles, Red-eyed Vireo, Dickcissel, Eastern and Western Kingbirds, Chuck-will's-widow, and Broad-winged Hawk.

The wooded areas of Airport Park and Waco Marina are good locations for spring and fall warbler migration. The area designated as 185 Park is especially good for Eastern Bluebird, shorebirds, herons, and White-faced Ibis. In winter, hawks are usually present west of the lake.

Speegleville I, II, and III Parks, on the west shore, are reached by driving northwest from Waco on SH 6 and provide the most developed facilities for camping. Woodpeckers are found year-round near the Bosque Bend Club House in Speegeville I Park. Northern Flicker are easily seen in winter. This is also where American White Pelicans have been found on numerous occasions in both winter and spring. Hawks, Osprey, and land birds are frequently found in the Speegleville Parks. Mountain Bluebird and Bald Eagle have also been seen in winter.

The address of the Reservoir Manager is Route 10, Box 173-G, Waco, TX 76708, (817) 756-5359.

Waco Sewage Treatment Plant

From IH 35 drive east on University Parks Drive to LaSalle Drive, continue on University Parks Drive for 1.7 miles to FM 434, and turn left (north) on FM 434. After crossing SH 6 (Loop 340), drive 0.6 mile to an unmarked paved road, turn left and drive to the entrance. To reach the ponds, take the first left after the headquarters building.

This is the best place in the Waco area for concentrations of shorebirds in winter and during migration. Peak times are July to August in fall, and March to April in spring. Some shorebirds are present nearly all year. Most commonly recorded are Spotted, Baird's, Least, Semipalmated, Western, and Pectoral Sandpipers, Wilson's Phalarope, and Greater and Lesser Yellowlegs. White-rumped Sandpipers are common in late spring. Black-necked Stilts have nested in recent years. Depending on the water level waterfowl can also be found in fall, winter and spring. Watch for Red-shouldered Hawk in the trees in the area.

MERIDIAN STATE PARK

Meridian State Park, 502 acres, is approximately 42 miles northwest of Waco by way of SH 6, or about 4 miles southwest of Meridian on SH 22. The park is near where the West Cross Timbers and Grand Prairie of central Texas meet the Lampasas Cut Plains of the Edwards Plateau. There is an abundance of Ashe juniper in the uplands, while the vegetation of the floodplain along Bee Creek is similar to that expected in East Texas. The creek has been dammed to form Bosque Lake (70 surface acres), which attracts many shorebirds and waterfowl, particularly in migration.

Camping, restrooms with hot showers, picnicking, swimming, fishing, boat ramps (12-hp limit), and hiking trails are offered.

Many eastern and western species occur in the park. This is near the northern limit of the nesting range of the Golden-cheeked Warbler. From mid-March through June, the Golden-cheeked Warbler is usually found in the Ashe juniper in the northwest section of the park above the lake.

Permanent residents include Black Vulture, Greater Roadrunner, Barn Owl, Great Horned Owl, Eastern Screech-Owl, Ladder-backed Woodpecker, Carolina and Canyon Wrens, Brown Thrasher, Eastern Bluebird, Lesser Goldfinch, and Rufous-crowned Sparrow. In summer look for Chuck-will's-widow, Common Poorwill, Western Kingbird, Great Crested Flycatcher, Northern Rough-winged Swallow, Blue-gray Gnatcatcher, White-eyed, Bell's, and Red-eyed Vireos, Black-chinned and Ruby-throated Hummingbirds, Black-and-white Warbler, Yellow-breasted Chat, Orchard Oriole, and Summer Tanager.

In addition to the transient waterfowl and shorebirds attracted to the lake, many land birds migrate through the area. Nineteen warbler species have been recorded, most as migrants, and 14 sparrow species, most of which winter.

A bird checklist (1989) with 207 species is available at headquarters. The address is P.O. Box 188, Meridian, TX 76665, (817) 435-2536.

MEXIA

The Mexia area, about 40 miles east of Waco on US 84, has several birding locations well worth a visit. Lake Mexia, west of town on US 84, has wintering ducks, gulls and terns. In late summer Wood Storks have been found. Many species can be seen from the US 84 causeway over the lake.

Fort Parker State Park, 1,458 acres, is 6 miles south of Mexia on SH 14. Facilities include camping, screen shelters, hiking

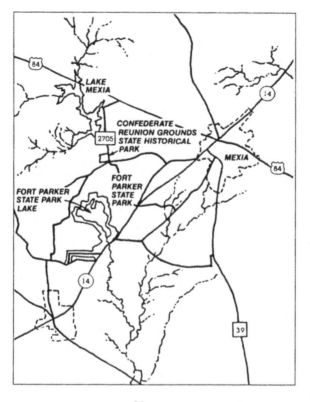

MEXIA

trails, restrooms with hot showers, picnicking, boat ramp, and fishing in Lake Fort Parker. There are over 700 acres of rolling woodlands where Eastern Bluebird is numerous. Check for White-breasted Nuthatch in winter.

The park address is RR 3, Box 95, Mexia, TX 76667, (817) 562-5751.

A third bird spot is the Confederate Reunion Grounds State Historical Park. Drive south of Mexia about 4.5 miles on SH 14, then 2.5 miles west on FM 2705. The site was a Confederate veteran meeting place for over 50 years, with as many as 5,000 said to be in attendance at one time. With 78 acres of gently rolling oak woodlands where Jack's Creek joins the Navasota River, there are good land bird opportunities. There are trails, restrooms and picnicking areas.

ALCOA LAKE

Alcoa Lake, 880 acres, is owned and operated by the Aluminum Company of America as part of their manufacturing plant near Rockdale in Milam County. The west side of the lake can be reached by driving west from Rockdale on US 79 about 5.5 miles to FM 1786, then south on FM 1786 to the plant. Stop at the security office and obtain permission to enter. To reach the east side of the facility from Rockdale, drive south on FM 487 about 3 miles, then southwest on FM 2116 to the lake. Weekends and holidays are the best times to visit due to the industrial traffic present during working hours.

This warm-water lake has had a small summer population of American White Pelican and Anhinga plus a few resident American Alligator with at least one large individual. Ring-billed and Bonaparte's Gulls and waterfowl are found in winter. Rarities recorded include Western Grebe, White-winged and Surf Scoters, and Sabine's Gull.

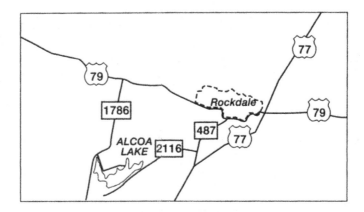

ALCOA LAKE

BRYAN-COLLEGE STATION

The Bryan–College Station metropolitan area, population about 110,000 (plus 42,000 students at Texas A&M University), is located in the eastern portion of the Post-Oak Savannah vegetational area of Central Texas. The Navasota River is 10 miles to the east and the Brazos River is 10 miles to the west. Hence, the area is easily accessible to bottomland hardwoods, floodplain croplands, upland woodlands, and pastures.

Common nesting birds include Cattle and Great Egrets, Little Blue Heron, Red-tailed and Red-shouldered Hawks, Barred, Great Horned and Eastern Screech-Owls, Red-bellied and Downy Woodpeckers, Eastern and Western Kingbirds, Scissor-tailed Flycatcher, Cliff Swallow, American Robin, and Painted Bunting. Common Moorhen breed on Country Club and Finfeather lakes in Bryan.

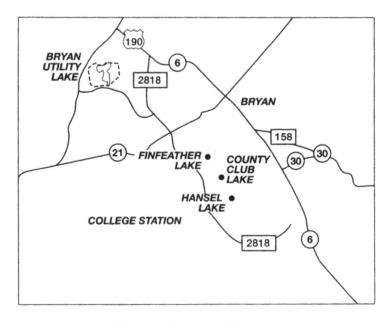

BRYAN–COLLEGE STATION

Northern Shoveler, Gadwall, Ring-necked Duck, Lesser Scaup, Ruddy Duck and Bufflehead commonly winter on area lakes. Double-crested Cormorant often winter on these lakes also.

Gibbons Creek Reservoir

Gibbons Creek Reservoir, created to provide cooling water for a power generation plant, is located east of College Station. To reach the reservoir, drive east on SH 30 about 15 miles to FM 244, then north on FM 244 to the entrance. Check in at the boat ramp. Restroom facilities are available. Bald Eagle is a regular, but rare winter resident. A pair nested here in the past. Osprey are found in migration and sometimes in winter.

Bryan Utility Lakes

Bryan Utility Lakes are located about 10 miles northwest of Bryan. From the intersection of SH 21 and FM 2818 (west loop around the cities), drive north on FM 2818 1.3 miles to FM 1687, then west on FM 1687 about 3 miles to the entrance.

Camping, picnicking, restrooms, and a boat ramp are available. There is an entrance fee.

This is the best local area for shorebirds, especially when the water level is down.

Bryan–College Station Parks

There are many municipal parks in the cities, two with modest reservoirs. Country Club Lake is located at S. College Avenue and Villa Maria. Access is best gained by driving one block north of the above intersection to Roundtree and the Astin Recreation Area. Finfeather Lake is about 1.5 miles northwest of Country Club Lake. From Country Club Lake drive north on College Avenue to Carson Street, turn west (left) and go to Fountain Street. Drive north on Fountain to Atkins Street, then east. Finfeather Lake will be to the left. Hensel Park, a Texas A&M University facility, is situated just north of University Drive and S. College. Woodland birds can be found nesting here. Hensel Park, along with Bee Creek Park in College Station, provides some of the best habitat for migrating passerines. Bee Creek Park is located at the end of Anderson Street, one block south of Southwest Parkway.

LAKE SOMERVILLE

Lake Somerville, 11,460 surface acres at conservation pool level, is located near SH 36 just east of Somerville between Brenham and Caldwell. This U.S. Army Corps of Engineers impoundment on Yegua Creek is a mecca for fishing and other recreational water activities. The lake is designed for flood control, municipal and industrial water supply, and recreation. The Corps of Engineers has seven parks on the lake, two of which are undeveloped. There are facilities for picnicking, camping with restrooms, and boat ramps.

Lake Somerville is in the Post Oak Savannah of Central Texas. Several bird habitats are represented in the parks: grasslands, understory thickets, extensive mud flats, woodlands along the many creeks, and the open water of the lake.

Regular nesting birds include Blue Jay, Lark Sparrow, Eastern Screech-Owl, Barred and Great Horned Owls, Red-bellied, Red-headed, and Downy Woodpeckers, Carolina Chickadee, Tufted Titmouse, Red-shouldered Hawk, Common Grackle, and Painted Bunting.

Wintering birds usually present are Gadwall, Northern Pintail, Green-winged Teal, American Wigeon, Northern Shoveler, Ring-necked Duck, Lesser Scaup, Bald Eagle, Double-crested Cormorant, and many sparrow species.

Shorebirds can be found anywhere along the shoreline, but near Overlook Park and those sections of the lake where boats are excluded are particularly good. Once in early May I saw a migrating Hudsonian Godwit at Rocky Creek Park.

Other birds recorded are Neotropic Cormorant, Roseate Spoonbill, Osprey, Wood Stork, and American White Pelican. Unexpected birds recorded include Curve-billed Thrasher, Reddish Egret, Brown Pelican, and Royal Tern.

Having a boat for access to the western portion of the lake where waterfowl, herons and egrets congregate will greatly increase the bird possibilities.

The address of the Corps of Engineers Resident Manager is P.O. Box 548, Somerville, TX 77879.

Lake Somerville State Park

Lake Somerville State Park is at the western end of the lake. This recreation area is divided into two non-contiguous units: Birch Creek, 3,140 acres, on the north shore, and Nails Creek, 2,830 acres, on the south. Camping, restrooms with hot showers, picnicking, nature trails, and boat ramps are available. Check with the park office for access and permission to bird the wildlife management area adjacent to and west of the parks, where passerine birding is different than in the parks. Yellow-throated Vireo, Northern Parula, Hooded and Swainson's Warblers have nested in the wildlife management area. Kentucky Warbler is a posssible nesting species. Migrating warblers include Black-and-white, Blue-winged, Magnolia, Blackburnian, and Chestnut-sided.

The address of the Birch Creek Unit is RR 1, Box 499, Somerville, TX 77879-9713, (409) 535-7763; Nails Creek Unit, RR 1, Box 61-C, Ledbetter, TX 78946-9512, (409) 289-2392.

BASTROP AND BUESCHER STATE PARKS

Bastrop State Park, 3,503 acres, is about 30 miles east of Austin on SH 71 in the "Lost Pines of Texas." The park is one mile east of Bastrop and can be reached from either SH 21 or SH 71 by way of Loop 150, which connects the two highways. Facilities include two campgrounds, picnicking, restrooms with hot showers, a swimming pool, golf course, cabins, group barracks with mess hall, a grocery, and hiking trails. The park preserves a disjunct stand of loblolly pines in the western section of the Post-Oak Savannah vegetational area some 180 miles west of the Pineywoods.

As might be expected, some nesting birds typical of the Pineywoods are found here, such as Pileated Woodpecker, Pine and

Black-and-white Warblers, and Northern Parula. Hairy Woodpecker is found occasionally. In winter Red-breasted Nuthatch and Golden-crowned Kinglet are usually present. Red Crossbill is a very rare winter vagrant. Barred Owl, Red-shouldered Hawk, and Common Grackle are more common in the Bastrop area than in Austin.

Park Road 1, which connects Bastrop and Buescher state parks, is 13 miles long with an easement 200 feet wide along its length: the road is a park in itself. On Alum Creek, the only flowing creek which crosses Park Road 1, Hooded and Kentucky Warblers nest regularly. Rarities include Green Violet-Ear (summer), Hammond's Flycatcher (winter), and Swainson's Warbler (nesting).

Buescher State Park, 1,017 acres, is 2 miles northwest of Smithville near SH 71. The park has a 25-acre lake, screen shelters, campground, restrooms with hot showers, a picnic area, and a recreation building. The wooded creek bottom leading to the lake offers the best variety of resident and migrating birds. While Black-chinned Hummingbird nests abundantly in Austin, the nesting hummingbird in Bastrop and Buescher state parks is the Ruby-throated. Hardwoods are more common in Buescher than at Bastrop, principally blackjack, live, and post oaks.

The University of Texas Environmental Science Park, a cancer research facility, is located in Buescher State Park.

LAKE BASTROP

Lake Bastrop, 906 acres, is operated by the Lower Colorado River Authority as part of a power generating plant. Numerous waterfowl winter on the lake and the woodlands around the lake provide habitat for nesting Red-shouldered Hawk, wintering Bald Eagle, and numerous other species in all seasons. The Lower Colorado River Authority operates North Shore and South Shore Parks at the lake.

North Shore Park is reached from Bastrop by driving north on SH 95 about 3 miles to FM 1441, then driving east on FM 1441 2.4 miles to the entrance. The park offers camping, fishing, a boat ramp, swimming, picknicking, and a store. The most famous bird noted here was a Blue-footed Booby from December, 1994, to April, 1995.

South Shore Park, 784 acres, is located on the south shore of Lake Bastrop. To reach the park from Bastrop drive northeast on SH 21 about 4 miles from the intersection of SH 95 and SH 21 to the road leading to the park. Located in oak-pine woodlands but with extensive water frontage, wintering waterfowl and shore-birds in migration add species not found in Bastrop and Buescher state parks. Offerings include camping with water and electricity, hiking trails, a lakeside observation platform, a boat ramp, fishing, and a bathhouse.

There is a combined bird checklist (1996) with 276 species for Bastrop and Buescher state parks, including Lake Bastrop, available at all headquarters. The park addresses are: Bastrop, Box 518, Bastrop, TX 78602, (512) 321-2101; Buescher, P. O. Box 75, Smithville, TX 78957-0075, (512) 237-2241; for reservations at Lake Bastrop, North Shore, call (512) 321-3307, for South Shore, (512) 321-5408.

PALMETTO STATE PARK

Palmetto State Park, 268 acres, is a small, unique botanical area on the San Marcos River in the Post Oak-Savannah vegetational area. Camping, restrooms with hot showers, picnicking, and fishing are offered. To drive to the park, take US 183 east from Luling for 6 miles, or go west from Gonzales 13 miles. From US 183, the park can be reached from either FM 1586 or PR 11.

The park preserves swamps with extensive dwarf palmettos, an artesian well flowing with sulphur-laden water, an oxbow lake nearly one-half mile long, hardwood bottoms along the San Marcos River, thick understory vegetation, and open grassy areas, which altogether comprise a remarkable diversity of trees, shrubs, and wildfowers. Formerly, quaking bogs were present that helped make possible the unique flora. More than 500 species of plants have been identified in the park, with western and eastern species growing in close proximity. There are two self-guiding nature trails: one along the San Marcos River, and one in the swampy area near the artesian well. Pick up trail booklets at headquarters.

Approximately 39 species of birds nest in the park, including Wood Duck, Red-shouldered Hawk, Eastern Screech-Owl and Barred Owls, Prothonotary and Kentucky Warblers, Northern Parula, and Indigo and Painted Buntings. Swainson's Warbler has nested rarely.

Birds that winter include American Woodcock, Yellow-bellied Sapsucker, Brown Creeper, Brown Thrasher, Hermit Thrush, Golden-crowned Kinglet, Cedar Waxwing, Pine Siskin, and American Goldfinch. In addition, Savannah, Vesper, Lark, Dark-eyed Junco, Chipping, Field, Harris', White-crowned, White-throated, Fox, Lincoln's, and Song Sparrows can be expected in winter. Other wintering sparrows sometimes found are Grasshopper, Cassin's, Clay-colored, and Swamp. The park is excellent for migrants in spring.

In addition to the trails, the oxbow lake, river, and roads, a walk down PR 11 from the overlook to the village of Ottine will usually turn up most of the land birds present. Crested Caracara can usually be seen flying overhead in the open country surrounding the park. The Palmetto State Park Christmas Bird Count usually has the highest count of Crested Caracara and has had the high count for Black Vulture.

A bird checklist (1991) with 275 species is available at headquarters. The address is RR 5, Box 201, Gonzales, TX 78629, (830) 672-3266.

McKINNEY FALLS STATE PARK

McKinney Falls State Park, 640 acres, is at the southern city limit of Austin. The park offers a campground, restrooms with hot showers, picnic areas, a four-mile hike-and-bike trail, and a visitor's center.

To reach the park from Austin, drive south on US 183 past the intersection with SH 71, then proceed another four miles south on

US 183 to FM 812. Turn right (west) on Scenic Loop Road, and go about two miles to the park entrance. The park can also be reached south of Austin from I-35 by taking the William Cannon Drive exit. Drive east on William Cannon Drive 1.7 miles to a red light, angle right on William Cannon for 1.1 miles, turn right on Running Water, after a couple of blocks turn left on Colton-Bluff Springs Road, then stay on the paved road taking the left option at each intersection for 1.7 miles to the park entrance.

The park has been developed in such a way that the camping and picnic areas blend in with the various habitats to preserve most of them in a natural state. The soil and vegetation are a combination of Edwards Plateau and Blackland Prairie, but the birds are more representative of eastern Texas.

The wide variety of tall trees and underbrush along the creek, open grasslands, and large live oaks in the campground make the park an excellent location for migrating land birds.

Nesting birds include Eastern Screech-Owl, Barred Owl, Chuck-will's-widow, Canyon Wren, Great Crested Flycatcher, and White-eyed Vireo. Shorebirds and ducks can be found along the creek in fall, winter, and spring.

Common winter residents include Hermit Thrush, Brown Creeper, Golden-crowned and Ruby-crowned Kinglets, Fox, White-throated, Harris', Chipping, Lincoln's, and Vesper Sparrows. American Woodcock are uncommon in winter.

Some very rare records are Groove-billed Ani, Williamson's Sapsucker, Long-billed Thrasher, Green-tailed Towhee, and Reddish Egret.

A bird checklist (1988) with 223 species is available at headquarters. The address is 5805 McKinney Falls Parkway, Austin, TX 78744, (512) 243-1643.

6

Pineywoods

The Pineywoods region is approximately 9% of Texas. The western boundary of the region is a line from Texarkana through Tyler, Palestine, and west of Huntsville into Waller County. The southern boundary is a line extending eastward from just north of Houston to Beaumont and Orange. It is that part of Texas where, because of a combination of climate, soil, and moisture availability, the pine-hardwood forest of the southeastern United States reaches its southwestern limit.

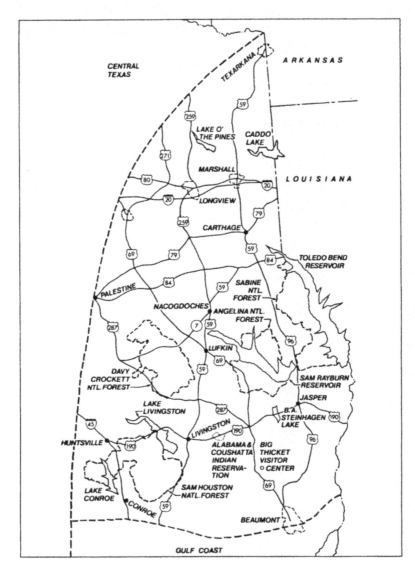

PINEYWOODS

The region consists of Tertiary and Quaternary deposits, with the former making up the northern two-thirds. The elevation ranges from 20 to 550 feet, with gently rolling to hilly terrain. There are many wide rivers, river bottoms, swamps, and bogs.

Loblolly, shortleaf, and longleaf pines are native. Slash pine has been introduced and is grown commercially. There are extensive hardwood forests of oak, beech, maple, magnolia, sweetgum, hickory, and other species mixed with the pines. Large bald cypress swamps are common. The Big Thicket in the southern portion of the region is a meeting ground for many vegetative types, now partially preserved as the Big Thicket National Preserve.

Nesting bird species unique to this region include Red-cockaded Woodpecker, Brown-headed Nuthatch, Prairie Warbler, and Bachman's Sparrow. Red-shouldered Hawk, Pileated Woodpecker, Pine Warbler, Louisiana Waterthrush, and Wood Thrush are common nesting species. Fourteen warbler species nest in the Pineywoods.

Tyler State Park has a bird checklist but is not included herein.

NORTHEAST TEXAS

The 24 counties in the northeast corner of the state are the province of the Northeast Texas Field Ornithologists. There are numerous large and small lakes (most with recreation opportunities), pine forests with extensive lumbering, and several large towns. The lakes provide wintering habitat for many waterfowl species and other water-seeking birds. Resident species of the pine and mixed forests include Red-headed, Red-bellied, Downy, Hairy, Northern Flicker, and Pileated Woodpeckers, and White-breasted and Brown-headed Nuthatches. Acadian Flycatcher and Wood Thrush are summer residents. Thirty-seven warbler species have been recorded, thirteen nest.

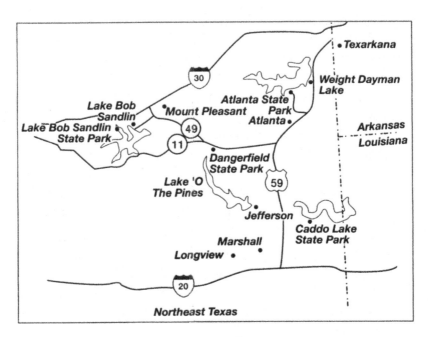

NORTHEAST TEXAS

A bird checklist for the twenty-four counties can be obtained by sending $1 to the Northeast Texas Field Ornithologists, RR 2, Box 117AB, Kilgore, TX 75662, plus a stamped, addressed 5½″ × 8½″ envelope.

RARE BIRD ALERT for Northeast Texas, (903) 234-2473.

Lake O' The Pines

Lake O' the Pines, 18,700 surface acres, is approximately 26 miles northwest of Marshall or 9 miles west of Jefferson. The primary purpose of this U.S. Army Corps of Engineers lake is flood control. Other benefits are domestic and industrial water supply, conservation of fish and wildlife, and recreation. There are at least twenty-nine developed areas with facilities for camping, picnicking, and boating on both the north and south shores of the lake.

This is an excellent location for wintering waterfowl, particularly diving ducks. Common Loon, Horned Grebe, Common Goldeneye, and Bonaparte's Gull are typical in winter. Red-throated and Yellow-billed Loons, Western Grebe, Oldsquaw and scoters have been recorded. This is one of the few spots where I have seen a Pacific Loon.

Good vantage points from which to scan the lake are the Dam Overlook and Lakeside Park at opposite ends of the dam, Johnson and Alley Creek Recreation Areas on the north shore, the SH 155 crossing at the western end of the lake, and Perry's Cove and Island View Marina on the south shore.

A regular occurrence in winter is the rafting of Common Goldeneye and Horned Grebe at dusk. Often several hundred of both species can be observed along with other ducks from the point at Alley Creek.

Nearer the middle of the lake, Black, White-winged and Surf Scoters and Oldsquaw have been observed. They are usually seen near the huge groups of Lesser Scaup. Recent Christmas Count data indicate at least 5% of the scaup are Greater Scaup.

From late November through February more than thirty wintering Bald Eagles are usually present. Purple Finch can be found in winter as well.

Often, birders come to this area to find species that specialize in the pines. One of these species is Brown-headed Nuthatch. The Lakeside Park in the middle of dam, which is on the east side of the lake, is one of the better places to find these birds. This is often a good place to find wintering Golden-crowned Kinglet. Great Black-backed Gull and Thayer's Gull have been recorded in this area also.

Another bird that is often sought in this area by visitors is the American Woodcock. The birds seem to prefer grassy fields where pines have been harvested recently or where the pines are just coming back. First or last light is the best time. American

Woodcock are easier to hear than to see well. Check the rare bird alert for current information.

Bachman's Sparrow have been found within a few miles of the dam. Go north of the dam overlook a few miles and turn east on a road going away from the lake, across from a landing that advertises the local Yacht Club. Within a few miles you should notice different sizes of pine trees, as this is an actively lumbered area. Stop along this stretch, listening for the birds' call. Early spring is usually the best time as the birds tend to be quite vocal then. The half-growth habitat is also excellent habitat in the summer for Prairie Warbler and Yellow-breasted Chat.

The address of the Reservoir Manager is P. O. Drawer "W", Jefferson, TX 75657, (903) 665-2336.

Wright Patman Lake

Wright Patman Lake, 20,300 acres, is about 10 miles south of Texarkana on US 59. This Army Corps of Engineers project was created for flood control on the Sulphur River, a tributary of the Red River. Other benefits are recreation, agriculture, forestry, and water supply. There are approximately 20 recreation areas along the lake, plus several natural areas offering a variety of facilities from boat ramps to cabins.

This lake attracts large numbers of Bonaparte's Gull. Rarities recorded include Black-headed, Little, and Laughing Gulls, and Black-legged Kittiwake. Sometimes, when the lake is discharging water, a thousand gulls can be within easy binocular range. When the gulls are on the water a scope is a must.

The address is Wright Patman Project Office, P. O. Box 1817, Texarkana, TX 75504-1817, (903) 838-8781.

Atlanta State Park

Atlanta State Park, 1,475 acres, is on the south shore of Wright Patman Lake. From Queen City, drive north on FM 96 6.5 miles to FM 1154, then north on FM 1154 1.6 miles to the park. The park offers camping, restrooms with hot showers, a hiking trail, picnicking, a boat ramp, fishing, and swimming.

The address is RR 1, Box 116, Atlanta, TX 75551, (903) 796-6476.

Caddo Lake

Caddo Lake, 26,800 surface acres, straddles the Texas-Louisiana border. By road, it is about 14 miles northeast of Marshall on SH 43. Turn east on FM 2198 to reach Caddo Lake State Park and the town of Uncertain. This is a fascinating area with large, picturesque bald cypress trees. Originally a natural lake, it is now maintained by a low dam. Fish Crow can be found here throughout the year. Thirteen warbler species nest regularly around Caddo Lake. Other nesting species are Anhinga, Mississippi Kite, Yellow-throated and Red-eyed Vireos, herons, egrets, and six flycatchers. Wood Stork are seen regularly during the summer, most often around the Carter's Lake area.

Caddo Lake State Park and Wildlife Management Area

Caddo Lake State Park, 480 acres, is on the south shore of Big Cypress Bayou, in Harrison County. Camping, cabins, screen shelters, restrooms with hot showers, picnicking, fishing, boat ramps, and a hiking trail are available. The park is a good base from which to explore the area. Canoes can be rented from a concession in the park. To see the real Caddo Lake, with its rich biological diversity, a motorized boat is recommended, preferably with a professional guide. It is easy to get lost as the boat channels are notoriously confusing. A map of the lake (available at most stores and restaurants in the area) and a compass are essential for exploring.

The birdlife of the park reflects the dominant woodland and riparian habitats within its borders. In spring and summer, Acadian Flycatcher, Wood Thrush, Northern Parula, Louisiana Waterthrush, Yellow-throated, Pine, Black-and-white, and Prothonotary Warblers are typical of the species to be found.

Most of the 7,000-acre Caddo Lake Wildlife Management Area is located in Marion County, on the north side of Big Cypress Bayou. Swainson's Warbler in spring and summer, and Rusty Blackbird in winter, have been reported regularly from a spot within the WMA. From FM 2198 drive north on SH 43 about 5.5 miles, then drive east on Johnson Road (CR 3416) approximately 2 miles. At the second dirt road on the right (an oak tree stands in the intersection), turn east (right) and continue about 0.6 mile and park at a small clearing on the left side of the road. A swampy area with many dead snags is ahead on the left. There is a yellow State Park and Wildlife Management Area sign on a tree on the right side of the road. A variety of woodland, riparian and swamp species are usually found in this general area.

A bird checklist is available at park headquarters. The park address is RR 2, Box 15, Karnack, TX 75661, (214) 679-3351.

Daingerfield State Park

Daingerfield State Park, 550 acres, is 2.4 miles east of Daingerfield on SH 11. This spot has cabins, camping, restrooms with hot showers, a boat ramp, picnicking, fishing, swimming, and hiking trails. During the last two weekends in September local birders meet here for hawk migration. Small groups of Broad-winged Hawk and American White Pelican migrate over the park. Osprey and Cooper's and Sharp-shinned Hawks are regular. A few Merlin, Peregrine Falcon, Bald Eagle, Mississippi Kite, and Wood Stork have been observed.

The park address is RR 1, Box 286-B, Daingerfield, TX, 75638, (903) 645-2921.

Lake Bob Sandlin

Lake Bob Sandlin, a project of the Titus County Fresh Water Supply District No. 1, was created to furnish water for domestic and industrial use. The lake is southwest of Mt. Pleasant or northwest of Pittsburgh.

There really are three lakes here, Lake Bob Sandlin, Cypress Springs Lake, and Lake Monticello. The fluctuating lake level often creates mud flats which make this one of the better areas in northeast Texas for attracting shorebirds. Viewing is especially good near the dam. Shorebird migration starts in July and continues until June, meaning something should be around nearly year-round. Common migrants include Spotted, Semipalmated, Western, Least, White-rumped (late spring), and Pectoral Sandpipers. There are 23 shorebird species on the area checklist.

During the winter this lake attracts several thousand Ring-billed Gull, a few Herring Gull, plus waterfowl. Pacific Loon and Black-legged Kittiwake are rarities that have been observed here. Also, numbers of Horned Grebe are usually easily found. This is one of the few places in northeast Texas with a small resident population of Mottled Duck.

There are several parks along the shoreline. The address is Titus County Fresh Water Supply District No. 1, P.O. Box 650, Mt. Pleasant, TX 75456-0659.

Lake Bob Sandlin State Park

Lake Bob Sandlin State Park, 640 acres, is located on the north shore of Lake Bob Sandlin. From Pittsburg drive west on SH 11 to SH 21, then north on SH 21 to the park; or from Mt. Pleasant drive southwest on SH 127 to SH 21, then south on SH 21 to the park.

Available are camping, restrooms with hot showers, picnicking, swimming, boat ramp, fishing, three miles of hiking trails, and a park store.

The address is RR 5, Box 224, Pittsburg, TX 75686, (903) 572-5531.

Henslow's Sparrow

Finding wintering Henslow's Sparrow in areas accessible to birders is very rare in Texas, however, there is a spot in Longview that has been reliable in recent years. From I-20 at the eastern edge of Longview, drive north on US 259 (Eastman Road) 2.7 miles to Cotton Street. Drive east (right) on Cotton Street 0.5 mile to Pine Crest Drive, turn north (left) on Pine Crest Drive and go to the dead end. Park and take the path through some trees. The path leads into a small field that is the Henslow's Sparrow location.

NACOGDOCHES

Nacogdoches, population 32,000, advertised as the oldest town in Texas, is near Sam Rayburn Reservoir, Angelina National Forest (20 miles to the south) and Davy Crockett National Forest (37 miles to the northwest). Each offers its own unique birding opportunities. Pecan Park, just south of the Stephen F. Austin State University campus, is the local mecca for migrating land birds.

Located in the approximate center of the Pineywoods, in what some Texans refer to as "Deep East Texas," Nacogdoches is an excellent base from which to start seeking out the specialty birds of the Pineywoods: Prairie Warbler, Pileated and Red-cockaded Woodpeckers, and Bachman's Sparrow.

Davy Crockett National Forest

Ratcliff Lake is in the Davy Crockett National Forest, 161,000 acres, about 37 miles southwest of Nacogdoches on SH 7. Nesting birds in the environs of the lake are Wood Duck, Common Yellowthroat, and an occasional Pied-billed Grebe.

In the mixed pine-hardwood forest adjacent to the lake, nesting birds include Barred Owl, Chuck-will's-widow, Broad-winged Hawk, Acadian Flycatcher, Summer Tanager, Red-eyed and Yellow-throated Vireos, Black-and-white, Kentucky, and Hooded Warblers, and with luck and persistence, Worm-eating and Swainson's Warblers, and Louisiana Waterthrush.

Northeast of the lake is an area of shortleaf and loblolly pines with resident Red-cockaded Woodpecker and Brown-headed Nuthatch. Areas cleared by lumbering or fire several years ago

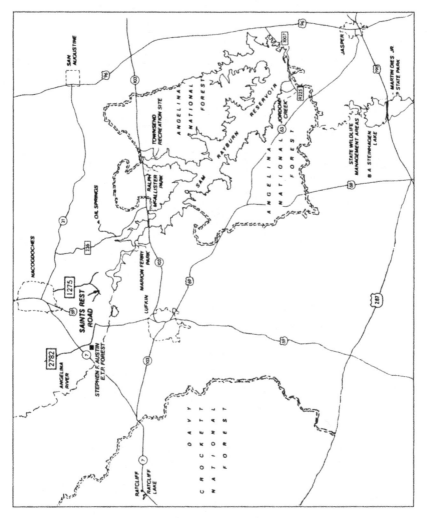

NACOGDOCHES

BROWN-HEADED NUTHATCH
(SHOWN IN COMMONLY OBSERVED POSITION)

with small, second-growth pines should be birded for Prairie War-bler, Yellow-breasted Chat, Indigo Bunting, and Blue Grosbeak.

Saint's Rest Road

Less than 10 miles south of Nacogdoches, Saint's Rest Road offers excellent birding in all seasons. From Loop 224 south of the city drive south on FM 1275 for 6.6 miles, then turn right (west) on a paved road marked "Saint's Rest Baptist Church." Drive 0.4 mile and turn left (south) on a good gravel road that follows Dorr Creek for 3 miles to a dead end at the Angelina River. Almost all Pineywoods forest birds can be found along this road in season. The road passes through several forest types, including extensive bottomland hardwoods. It is permitted to walk freely in areas marked with Angelina National Forest signs.

Nesting birds are Louisiana Waterthrush along Dorr Creek, Yellow-throated, Kentucky and Hooded Warblers in mixed woods, Prothonotary Warbler throughout the floodplain, and Swainson's Warbler in the thickets near the end of the road. Winter Wren, "Solitary" Vireo, Rusty Blackbird, and Purple Finch are seen regularly in winter. Spring migrants are also common in this area.

Stephen F. Austin Experimental Forest/Alazan Bayou Wildlife Management Area

The Stephen F. Austin Experimental Forest is located between Nacogdoches and Lufkin, west of US 59. To reach the entrance from Nacogdoches, drive south on US 59 about 6 miles to county road 628 (a dirt road), then 2.5 miles west on CR 628 to the gate (where CR 628 meets FM 2782). An alternate route is to drive southwest on SH 7 approximately 6.7 miles to FM 2782, then south on FM 2782, 2.5 miles to the gate. The southern boundary of the area is the Angelina River.

To enter the area, park at the gate and come in on foot (the gate will "soon" be moved to the headquarters area, which is where the trails start). The interpretive trail throughout the upland pine and mixed-forest will be handicapped accessible. This is a walk-in area only, open 24 hours a day. Motorized vehicles are not permitted past the gate.

There are "roads" throughout the forest that serve as excellent hiking access to all habitats. There are good stands of pines around the headquarters, mixed pine-hardwood along the main road, and side tracks to the left that offer access to tall and heavy river-bottom hardwoods along the Angelina River floodplain. Almost all East Texas warblers and other woodland birds are possible here in season. Breeding Wood Thrush and Yellow-throated Warbler can be found between the entrance and headquarters; Swainson's Warblers in tangles on the edge of the floodplain. The floodplain forest is one of the best local areas for resident White-breasted

Nuthatch. Woodpeckers are common and conspicuous, including large numbers of Red-headed Woodpeckers some winters.

Adjacent to the gate to the SFA Experimental Forest is Alazan Bayou Wildlife Management Area. This is a Type II State area, which means a non-game permit from the Texas Parks and Wildlife Department is required for entry. Song, Swamp, White-throated, Field, and Savannah Sparrows are abundant in winter, while most years LeConte's and White-crowned can be found, and some years a few Henslow's and Grasshopper Sparrows are in the drier grasslands adjacent to the Experimental Forest. This is also the best local area for wintering Northern Harrier and Sedge Wren, and some wet cold winters there are Rusty Black-bird. Purple Finch can turn up anywhere along the forest edge and hedgerows in winter. In spring large numbers of Dickcissel, Paint-ed and Indigo Buntings, Lincoln's Sparrow, Blue Grosbeak, Or-chard Oriole, Common Yellowthroat, and other migrants can be found. Some years migrant Bobolink occur in May. This is also a good area from which to observe kettles of Broad-winged Hawk and Mississippi Kite heading north in spring. There are mowed trails through the overgrown pastures. By walking to the south side of the fields and continuing into heavy floodplain forest, a good assortment of river-bottom nesting species such as Northern Parula, Prothonotary Warbler (abundant) and Swainson's Warbler (uncommon) can be encountered.

Sam Rayburn Reservoir

Sam Rayburn Reservoir, 114,500 surface acres at power pool level, is the largest lake completely within the state's bound-aries.The northern end of the lake is located about 20 miles south of Nacogdoches. The reservoir is about 50 miles long, north to south, with approximately 560 miles of shoreline.

Bald Eagle, Common Loon, Eared and Horned Grebes, ducks, and cormorants winter on the lake. Red-cockaded Woodpecker, Brown-headed Nuthatch, Prairie Warbler, and Bachman's Spar-row nest near the southern end of the lake in the Jordan Creek area of Angelina National Forest (153,000 acres). This area contains many pitcher plants and longleaf pines.

Marion Ferry Park, 12 miles east of Lufkin on SH 103, and 2 miles north on FM 1669, is one of the better places on the lake for shorebirds from July through November. It is also good for large wading birds and wintering waterfowl. Wood Stork and Roseate Spoonbill have been found in late summer.

Ralph McAllister Park and Townsend Recreation Site, just south of SH 103 and 2.3 miles west of FM 1277, on a northeast arm of the lake are two good locations for Red-headed Woodpecker and nesting warblers. These locations offer an excellent view of the lake for watching wintering ducks and spring and fall migrants.

HUNTSVILLE

Huntsville, population 29,000, is located on the western edge of the Pineywoods. It is within easy driving distance of Huntsville State Park, Sam Houston National Forest, Lake Livingston, and Lake Conroe.

Sam Houston Park, just west across Sam Houston Avenue from Sam Houston State University in downtown Huntsville, is an excellent location for land migrants: warblers, vireos, tanagers, flycatchers, thrushes, orioles, grosbeaks, and buntings. The peak of spring migration is from mid-April to mid-May.

There is a checklist of birds for Walker County available from the Division of Life Sciences, Geology and Geography, Sam Houston State University, Huntsville, TX 77341.

Huntsville State Park

Huntsville State Park, 2,083 acres of pines and hardwoods, is located 8 miles southeast of Huntsville on I-45. It has picnicking, camping, screen shelters, restrooms with hot showers, fishing in Lake Raven, 9 miles of hiking and nature trails, and a good representation of typical East Texas birds.

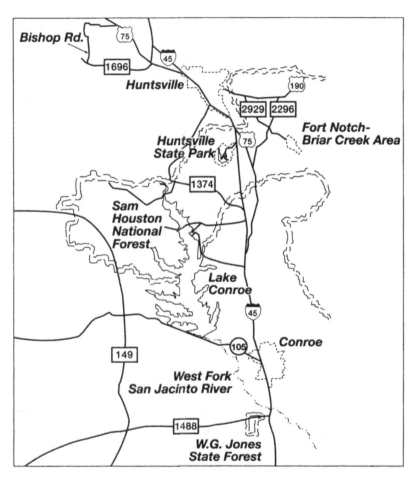

HUNTSVILLE

Summer is the most interesting bird season, with the many breeding birds in full song throughout the forest. Common nesting birds include Yellow-crowned Night-Heron, Pileated, Red-bellied, and Downy Woodpeckers, Great Crested and Acadian Flycatchers, Eastern Wood-Pewee, White-breasted and Brown-headed Nuthatches, Blue-gray Gnatcatcher, White-eyed, Yellow-throated, and Red-eyed Vireos, Indigo and Painted Buntings, and Chipping Sparrow. In addition, 12 warbler species have been

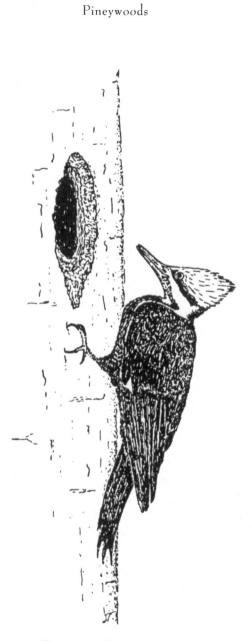

PILEATED WOODPECKER

recorded nesting in the park: Black-and-white, Prothonotary, Swainson's, Yellow-throated, Pine, Kentucky, and Hooded Warblers, American Redstart, Northern Parula, Louisiana Waterthrush, Common Yellowthroat, and Yellow-breasted Chat. Prairie Warblers are rare in summer.

In some winters the appearance of Red-breasted Nuthatch makes it possible to find three nuthatch species in the park. During incursion years, Pine Siskin and Evening Grosbeak can be present in very large numbers, along with the regular American Goldfinch and Purple Finch.

The creek bottoms along the trails and the large oaks are the most productive birding areas for nesting land birds and land migrants.

Lake Raven, 210 acres, is in the middle of the park and can be a good spot for shorebirds when the water is low and the mudflats are exposed. However, this is an infrequent occurrence.

The park is often very crowded on weekends, meaning birding is better at other times.

A bird checklist (1996) with 228 species is available at headquarters. The address is P.O. Box 508, Huntsville, TX 77342-0508, (409) 295-5644.

Bishop Road

Another area rich in birdlife in all seasons is along Bishop Road, a gravel road in northwestern Walker County. To reach the area, drive north on I-45 to Exit 123 (FM 1696), go west on FM 1696 to US 75, then right on US 75, 4.7 miles to Bishop Road. Turn left on the road that goes west, then south, ending up back at FM 1696. To return to US 75 and/or I-45, drive east on FM 1696.

Nesting species include Painted and Indigo Buntings, Blue Grosbeak, Pileated Woodpecker, and Summer Tanager. Some winter residents are Yellow-bellied Sapsucker, Northern Flicker, Eastern Bluebird, Orange-crowned and Yellow-rumped Warblers, White-breasted Nuthatch, and numerous sparrow species. Red-breasted Nuthatch are found some winters.

Lake Conroe

The dam area of Lake Conroe, 20,985 surface acres, offers good birding, especially in fall, winter, and spring. Permission to enter should be obtained from the San Jacinto River Authority personnel at the dam just north of SH 105, approximately 7 miles west of Conroe. Permission is readily granted Monday through Friday, 8 am to 5 pm.

By driving across the dam during fall, winter, or spring, large rafts of waterfowl can often be found just off the riprap. Look for Common Loon and Horned Grebe. Western Grebe, and Common and Red-breasted Mergansers are occasionally found in winter as well. The grassland below the dam is a good place for Savannah, LeConte's, and Grasshopper Sparrows. In migration check the rows of willows, which seem to be good migrant traps.

The upper portion of Lake Conroe in the Sam Houston National Forest has nesting warblers, including Swainson's and American Redstart. The area around Stubblefield Lake Recreation Area can be very rewarding. Look for Broad-winged Hawk and Anhinga in summer, and Bald Eagle in winter. There are Red-cockaded Woodpecker colonies in the national forest surrounding upper Lake Conroe.

Sam Houston National Forest

The Sam Houston National Forest, 158,411 acres, is south and east of Huntsville. Birds are comparable to those found in Huntsville State Park. The national forest contains the 100-mile Lone Star Hiking Trail, which extends from about the western edge of the forest northwest of Lake Conroe to the southeastern border just north of Cleveland.

One location for finding Red-cockaded Woodpecker is west of New Waverly on FM 1375. From Huntsville, drive south on I-45 to the Exit #103 (New Waverly). Drive west on FM 1375 and follow signs to the Sam Houston National Forest District Office on FM 1375. Go 2.3 miles beyond the office to an area where trees with nesting woodpeckers are marked with green paint bands. For information about specific locations, ask at the office or call the Forest Service at (409) 344-6205.

Red-cockaded Woodpecker colonies can also be found on FM 2929 about one mile south of US 190, just east of Huntsville. Early morning is the best time to be sure of success in locating this endangered woodpecker.

To the east of the intersection of FM 2929 and FM 2296 is the Four Notch-Briar Creek Area. Red-cockaded Woodpecker nest trees are generally marked at the base with green paint.

LAKE LIVINGSTON

Lake Livingston, 82,600 surface acres, is a Trinity River Authority impoundment surrounded by pine and hardwood forests approximately 26 miles east of Huntsville on US 190. Nesting species are comparable to those listed for Huntsville and Lake Conroe.

When the water is low and mudflats are exposed, from 10 to 20 migrating shorebird species can be found along the shoreline from mid-July through fall. They are best seen from a boat on the north end of the lake in the SH 19 area near Trinity, the Robb's Lake area just west of Sebastopol, and along FM 356.

In winter check from the two-mile US 190 causeway for Herring, Ring-billed, and Bonaparte's Gulls, Forster's and Caspian Terns, and waterfowl. It is possible to stop and park along the two-mile span. Also, in winter Double-crested Cormorant fly over the causeway, heading south in the morning to their feeding area, and north in the evening to the roosting area. Flights of more than 10,000 birds are not unusual. Rarities recorded include Black-headed Gull and Snow Bunting, both first records for Texas. Other rarities are Sabine's and California Gulls and Black-legged Kittiwake.

The area around the lake has experienced a great deal of development in recent years resulting in extensive habitat modification.

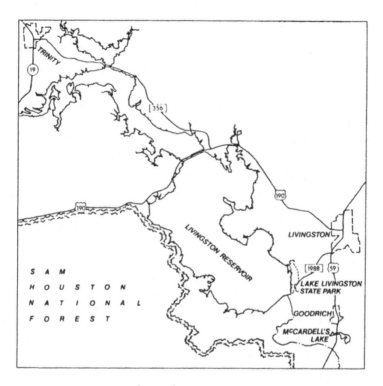

LAKE LIVINGSTON

Lake Livingston State Park

Lake Livingston State Park, 635 acres, is located near the southeast corner of the lake on FM 3216. The park has camping, picnicking, restrooms with hot showers, fishing, swimming, hiking, and boat ramps.

A bird checklist (1994) with 335 species is available at park headquarters. The checklist covers a four-county area and not only lists the birds but is also an excellent guide on bird finding in the area. The park address is RR 9, Box 1300, Livingston, TX 77351, (409) 365-2201.

McCardell's Lake

One highlight of the Pineywoods region is the exceptionally large nesting colony of wading birds at a natural oxbow swamp just east of US 59, eight miles south of Livingston, or one mile south of Goodrich. Between 5,000 and 10,000 birds nest in this swamp. Most are Cattle Egret, but Little Blue Heron, Black-crowned Night-Heron, Great Egret, Great Blue Heron, Snowy Egret, Tricolored Heron, Anhinga, White Ibis, Common Moorhen and Purple Gallinule nest also. There is a large nesting site at the extreme west end of the swamp that is visible from the highway. The swamp is north of the Trinity River and is called McCardell's Lake on county maps. American Alligators are also often seen here.

W. G. JONES STATE FOREST

W. G. Jones State Forest, 1,700 acres, is just south of Conroe. Red-cockaded Woodpecker and Brown-headed Nuthatch are permanent residents, along with many other Pineywoods species.

To reach the state forest, drive south from Conroe 4 miles on I-45. Turn west on FM 1488, and drive 1.5 miles to the entrance. Conroe is 39 miles north of Houston on I-45. The state forest is located on both sides of FM 1488 with picnicking facilities among the pines.

To find the Red-cockaded Woodpecker, look for mature pines with sap oozing around and below the woodpecker holes. These are the nest trees, and the birds are usually nearby. In general, the woodpeckers are easier to find in early morning. If you are unable to find them, the forest personnel often know where they can be located. Bachman's Sparrow has been recorded on a few occasions year-round.

MARTIN DIES, JR. STATE PARK

Martin Dies, Jr. State Park, 705 acres, preserves pine and river-bottom hardwoods along US 190 between Woodville and Jasper on the shores of B. A. Steinhagen Lake. This U.S. Army Corps of Engineers lake has 13,700 surface acres. The park is located about 3 miles north of the Upper Neches River Corridor of the Big Thicket National Preserve. The park has 3 units, with fishing, camping, screen shelters, restrooms with hot showers, hiking trails, picnicking, swimming, water skiing, and a boat ramp.

A bird checklist (1991) with 235 species is available at headquarters. The list describes birding locations for the park, the lake, and the surrounding area. The address is RR 4, Box 274, Jasper, TX 75951, (409) 384-5231.

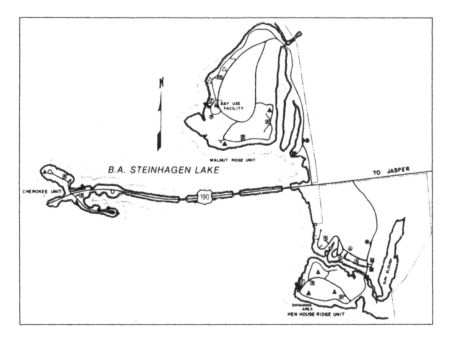

MARTIN DIES, JR. STATE PARK

Adjacent to and north of the park are two Wildlife Management Areas: Angelina-Neches Scientific Unit, 4,042 acres, and Dam B Wildlife Management Unit, 8,943 acres, which are managed by the Texas Parks and Wildlife Department with the cooperation of the U.S. Army Corps of Engineers. There are no trails or facilities and none are planned. Numerous heron rookeries are in the large stands of bald cypress, with Great Blue Heron, Great Egret, and Anhinga. To enter, a boat is needed to cross either the Angelina or Neches River. After doing so, it is possible to hike around and explore. Look for Pineywoods birds in the forested sections and waterfowl in winter along the lake.

There is a large rookery located in the middle of B.A. Steinhagen Lake just south of US 190. A scope is helpful if you are looking from the highway. There are usually 10,000-20,000 active nests in the spring. Cattle and Snowy Egrets, Little Blue and

ANHINGA

Tricolored Herons, White Ibis, Anhinga, and Yellow-crowned Night-Heron are the most common species.

BIG THICKET NATIONAL PRESERVE

Big Thicket National Preserve, 84,500 acres, the first preserve in the national park system, is managed in such a way that the unique mixture of ecosystems that occurs is protected. However, because of the vast energy resources concentrated here, the controlled extraction of minerals and other uses such as hunting (activities not usually allowed in a national park) are permitted.

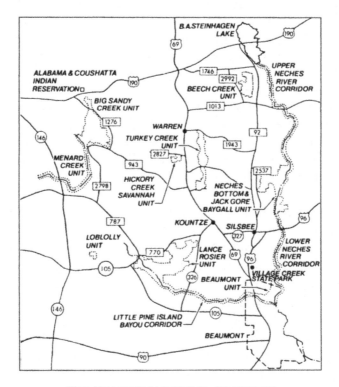

BIG THICKET NATIONAL PRESERVE

There are as many descriptions of the Big Thicket as there are describers, but the paragraph below from *Biological Survey of the East Texas Big Thicket Area* (1936) by H. B. Parks, V. L. Cory, et al., sums it up well:

The question now comes, is the Big Thicket to pass into legend as have the other areas, or is this area to be protected and made available to those who enjoy the study of animate nature; who enjoy the beauty of the primeval forest with its age old trees, its undergrowth of flowering shrubs, the delicately colored flowers and moss ground cover that bespeaks an age in making; who enjoy to study the wood warblers as high in the forest ceiling they call as they seek their food among the tree tops, or listen to the call of some large birds who far away are employed in nest building; who enjoy to seek out the mammals of such a place and become acquainted with them from the tiny shrew to the huge black bear; who enjoy a long quiet day in the thick shade along the banks of the creek attempting to lure from its water a selection of choice fish or enjoy in the fall of the year to garner the various kinds of fruits and nuts that grow within the Thicket, and as winter comes, per chance bring from among the numerous inhabitants of the Thicket a white-tail deer, as the prize of a long day's hunt.

I have visited the Big Thicket National Preserve many times to study its great diversity of plants and birds. The Big Thicket grows on a person; the more times I visit, the better I like it.

The Big Thicket has been divided into eight separate plant associations; six of these are in the Preserve. The Nature Conservancy has land holdings in the other two. The coming together of the hundreds of plants and other life forms from north, east, south, and west—"a biological crossroads"—is what makes the Big Thicket unique. The tall pines, about 20 different oaks, orchids, 4 carnivorous plants, climax forest with no understory vegetation, bald cypress-tupelo swamps, impenetrable tangles, wildflowers in all seasons, streams for canoeing, and much more, contribute to the diversity of the area.

A bird checklist (1996) with 235 species is available at the preserve headquarters, 3785 Milam Street, Beaumont (between College and Washington, just east of I-10); the Information Station on FM 420 (Turkey Creek Unit); or the North District Ranger Office in Woodville on US 287, 0.5 mile northwest of the US 69-287 junction. The Information Station is open 10 am to 4:30 pm daily, except Christmas and Tuesdays and Wednesdays in January and February. Nesting birds include Barred Owl, Red-shouldered Hawk, Pileated, Hairy, Downy, Red-bellied, and Red-headed Woodpeckers, White-eyed, Yellow-throated, and Red-eyed Vireos, and 13 species of warblers. Look for Black-and-white, Yellow-throated, Kentucky, and Hooded Warblers throughout. Prothonotary, Swainson's, Northern Parula, and American Redstart are found in the bottomlands, Louisiana Waterthrush along upland sandy bottom streams, Yellow-breasted Chat in beetle spots, Worm-eating Warbler in ti-ti thickets or acid bog-baygall wetlands, Common Yellowthroat in pitcher plant bogs, Prairie Warbler in longleaf pine-savannah areas, and Pine Warbler in upland forests. Brown-headed and White-breasted Nuthatches and Bachman's Sparrow can be common locally. Wintering species include American Woodcock, Purple Finch, American Goldfinch, and

HOODED WARBLER

woodland sparrows. Look in the uplands portion of the Big Sandy Creek Unit for Red-cockaded Woodpecker.

The preserve consists of eight land units and four river or stream corridor units located in Hardin, Polk, Tyler, Jasper, and Liberty counties. All units are open to the public. The Beaumont Unit and the Neches Bottom Unit are accessible only by boat.

The Turkey Creek Unit, 7,800 acres, has a visitor information station near the end of FM 420, 2.5 miles east of US 69. There are 3 trails totalling 12 miles. This unit contains the greatest concentration of plant diversity in the preserve, with magnificent stands of forest. Although probably not "virgin," the mature stands of bald cypress, sweetgum, and loblolly pine found in the southern portion of this unit between Village Creek and FM 420 are among the highlights of the Big Thicket National Preserve.

The Beech Creek Unit, 4,856 acres, has a short loop trail in a beech-magnolia-loblolly pine plant community. It is in this unit that so much forest was destroyed by pine bark beetles in the summer of 1975. One infestation covered more than 500 acres. Many beautiful magnolia and beech trees were destroyed in the effort to stop the spread of the infestation and in salvage operations to harvest the dead pines. Red-cockaded Woodpecker has been recorded in this unit.

The Hickory Creek Savannah Unit, 660 acres, has longleaf pine savannah forest and acid bog-baygall wetlands. Red-cockaded Woodpecker and Brown-headed Nuthatch have been reported in this unit. A one mile long loop trail leads through the savannah plant community.

The Lance Rosier Unit, 25,024 acres, is south and east of Saratoga. Some roads provide access, but there are no trails in this unit of palmetto flats and hardwoods. This is an excellent area for warblers.

The Loblolly Unit, 550 acres, a pine-hardwood forest, is north of Batson. Access is by road, and there are no trails.

The Beaumont Unit, 6,218 acres, is at the confluence of Pine Island Bayou and the Neches River. This unit is at the northern Beaumont city limits and is the wettest unit, with 80% bald cypress-tupelo swamps. It is subject to periodic flooding and saltwater intrusion, and is accessible by water only.

The Neches Bottom and Jack Gore Baygall Unit, 13,300 acres, is an ancient flood plain of the Neches River. Access to the Neches Bottom Unit is by boat. There are roads to the Jack Gore Baygall Unit, but there are no trails.

The Big Sandy Creek Unit, 14,300 acres, is mostly upland mixed pine-hardwood forest. Backcountry camping is permitted. A 6-mile hiking trail accesses the northern tip of the unit. Red-cockaded Woodpeckers are found in this unit.

There are four waterway corridor units:

Little Pine Island Bayou Corridor connects the Lance Rosier Unit to the Beaumont Unit.

Menard Creek Corridor connects the Big Sandy Creek Unit to the Trinity River.

Upper Neches River Corridor connects the B. A. Steinhagen Lake below the dam to the Neches Bottom and Jack Gore Baygall Unit.

Lower Neches River Corridor connects the Neches River and Jack Gore Baygall Unit to the Beaumont Unit.

There are no developed campgrounds in the preserve. Backcountry camping is allowed, by permit, in certain areas at certain times of the year. Picnicking is allowed where tables are provided, such as the Sundew Trail in the Hickory Creek Savannah Unit and Kirby Nature Trail at the southern end of the Turkey Creek Unit.

The address of the Preserve Superintendent is Big Thicket National Preserve, 3785 Milam Street, Beaumont, TX 77701, (409) 839-2689.

In addition to the national preserve, there are several other places in the immediate area well worth a visit. The Alabama-

Coushatta Indian Reservation on US 190 between Livingston and Woodville is open March through December. There are excellent stands of virgin forest, tours, displays, demonstrations, and a campground.

ROY E. LARSEN SANDYLAND SANCTUARY

The Roy E. Larsen Sandyland Sanctuary, 2,138 acres, owned and managed by The Nature Conservancy, preserves an excellent example of an Arid Sandyland ecosystem, an ecosystem not included in the Big Thicket National Preserve. The sanctuary is between Kountze and Silsbee on SH 327 bordering on and east of Village Creek. Guided hikes are conducted regularly. Contact the manager for the schedule at P. O. Box 909, Silsbee, TX 77656, (409) 385-4135.

JOHN K. KIRBY STATE FOREST

The John K. Kirby State Forest, 626 acres, is 2 miles south of Warren on US 69 and has a picnic area and self-guided nature trail.

VILLAGE CREEK STATE PARK

Village Creek State Park, 942 acres, is located between Beaumont and Silsbee east of Lumberton. To reach the park from US 96 in Lumberton drive east on East Chance Cut Off (there is a red light at this intersection), go 2 miles to the stop sign, turn right (south) on Village Creek Parkway and drive another 2 miles, then left (east) on Alma Drive and follow signs to the park. The park offers camping, picnicking, restrooms with hot showers, hiking, a boat ramp, and fishing. Birds should be typical East Texas species.

The address is P.O. Box 8575, Lumberton, TX 77657, (409) 755-7322.

7

Gulf Coast

The Gulf Coast region, about 6% of the state, includes the coastline from the Louisiana state line to just south of Corpus Christi. Inland it includes the coastal plains, which are bordered on the north by the Pineywoods and on the west by where the Quaternary deposits meet the Tertiary deposits approximately 100 miles from the coast.

Adjacent to the Gulf there are barrier islands, bays, estuaries, salt meadows, dunes, and marshes. Inland from the Gulf was originally tall-grass

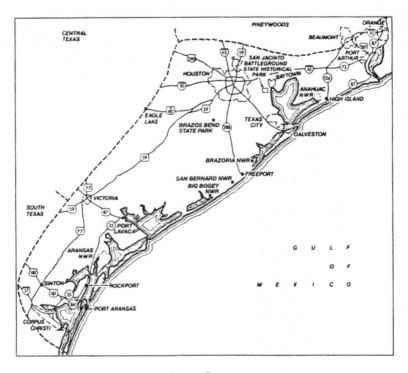

GULF COAST

prairie; now it is largely devoted to farming and ranching with several concentrations of heavy industry and urbanization. The elevation of the region increases very gradually northwestward from sea level to about 150 feet. Densely wooded sections of live oak and other species are found along the many slow-moving rivers, creeks, bayous, and sloughs, especially where the surface is elevated with adequate drainage, such as the Chenier Plain northeast of Sea Rim State Park, High Island, and Galveston Island.

The Texas Department of Transportation and Texas Parks and Wildlife Department are jointly sponsoring a project called "The Great Texas Coastal Birding Trail." The coast has been divided into three sections: the Upper Texas Coast, from Louisiana to

Freeport; the Central Texas Coast, from south of Freeport to south of Kingsville; and the Lower Texas Coast, from Kingsville to Mexico.

The Central Texas Coast Trail is complete. The Interpretative Map is available at Texas Department of Transportation Information Centers, the Texas Parks and Wildlife Department, 4200 Smith School Road, Austin, TX 78744-3291, or from the Chambers of Commerce of most larger cities included on the trail. There are 95 distinct birding sites, each marked with the trail logo and a unique site number. The interpretative map has information about birds expected at each site, best season to visit, plus information about food and lodging in the vicinity.

It is expected that the Birding Trail for the Upper Texas Coast will be complete in the Spring of 1998 and the Lower Texas Coast in early 1999.

As might be expected, many species nest along the coast that do not nest in other sections of the state. Among these are Mottled Duck, Willet, White-faced and White Ibises, Roseate Spoonbill, Brown and American White Pelicans, Reddish Egret, American Oystercatcher, Clapper Rail, Wilson's Plover, Laughing Gull, Gull-billed, Forster's, Royal, Sandwich, and Caspian Terns, Black Skimmer, Boat-tailed Grackle, and Seaside Sparrow. Greater Prairie-Chicken are unique inland nesters, but are in serious decline. Nesting species not unique to the region are White-tailed Hawk and White-tailed Kite. Herons, egrets, shorebirds, and waterfowl are very common most of the year. Sandhill Crane and Canada, Snow, and Greater White-fronted Geese winter on the inland prairies in large numbers. Aransas National Wildlife Refuge and vicinity is the wintering location for the wild flock of Whooping Cranes.

Bird checklists are available at Lake Texana State Park, P.O. Box 760, Edna, TX 77957-0760, and Matagorda Island, P.O. Box 117, Port O'Connor, TX 77982, locations not included below.

BEAUMONT

Beaumont, population 118,000, is near the southeast corner of Texas where the pineywoods meet the Gulf of Mexico and the Coastal Prairies. The near proximity of pine forests, salt marshes, freshwater marshes, extensive grasslands, irrigated rice farms, rivers, estuaries, and the gulf combine to make this one of the prime birding locations in the state for a variety of both species and habitats.

The Beaumont, Port Arthur, Orange area is known as the Golden Triangle. In this area chemical and petrochemical plants, oil production and refining, shipbuilding, sea ports, rice milling, farms, and ranches are common.

Fish Crow are permanent residents in the Golden Triangle area. They can be seen along I-10 between Beaumont and Orange. In Beaumont almost any crow seen or heard will be a Fish Crow except at the northernmost edge of the city. In Orange they are regularly seen on shopping center parking lots.

Some birding locations in the immediate vicinity of Beaumont are the Big Thicket National Preserve at the northern city limit, Tyrrell Park including the new cattail marsh wetlands area, Sabine Pass Battleground State Historical Park, Texas Point and Mc-Faddin National Wildlife Refuges, and Sea Rim State Park.

Sabine Pass Battleground State Historical Park

From Beaumont drive south on US 96-69-187 for 17 miles to Port Arthur, and turn right (south) on SH 87 to Sabine Pass. At the principal intersection in Sabine Pass go south on FM 3322 (South Gulfway Drive) 1.3 miles to the Sabine Pass Battleground State Historical Park. The park, 56 acres, has fishing, picnicking, restrooms, and soft drink machines. It commemorates the Civil War battle in which Richard W. Dowling, with a small Confederate force, repelled an attempted 1863 invasion of Texas by Union naval gunboats.

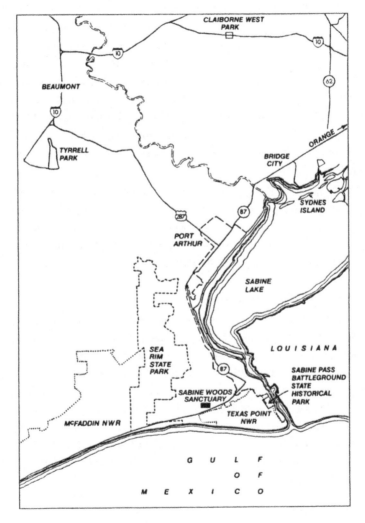

BEAUMONT/PORT ARTHUR/ORANGE

About a hundred yards north of the northern edge of the park is a stand of woods where Indigo and Painted Buntings, orioles, grosbeaks, warblers and vireos can be abundant during spring migration.

About 0.1 mile from the park entrance South Gulfway Drive, now Dowling Road, dead ends at the 7000 block of South 1st Avenue. Turn right and go 3.4 miles to the end of the road. Park and walk through the dilapidated gate on the shell road into the marsh. With a high tide the shell road may be flooded and impassible. After 100 yards the road turns right. Walk through the marsh to the gulf. This is a large, very accessible salt-water marsh. Most such areas in Texas are not very accessible. Rubber boots are recommended.

Permanent residents include Boat-tailed Grackle, Seaside Sparrow, Clapper Rail, Marsh Wren, White-faced Ibis, herons, egrets, etc. Least Bittern nest here. Many Whimbrel are recorded in spring migration as well as shorebirds and passerines. Nelson's Sharp-tailed Sparrow and Northern Harrier are winter residents.

Sabine Woods Sanctuary

Sabine Woods Sanctuary is owned and maintained by the Texas Ornithological Society. The sanctuary is four miles west of Sabine Pass on SH 87 on the right (north) side of the highway, adjacent to the field of satellite dish antennas. This is one of the best spring migration locations between the Louisiana border and High Island. Spring migrants found include essentially all of the migrating passerines from the eastern half of North America. Birdwise it is the same as the more popular High Island locations but much less crowded. In the spring look for parked cars near the gate as there is not a sign.

Tyrrell Park

Tyrrell Park, operated by the City of Beaumont, is west of downtown. There is a Garden Center, a golf course, picnicking, restrooms, and some good bird habitat. Drive west on I-10 to exit #849 (US 69 south), go south 0.9 mile to SH 124 (Fannett Road), turn right (west) for 1.1 miles to Tyrrell Park Road on the left, then 0.7 mile to the park entrance. Just past the entrance on the left is the Garden Center, a good birding spot for land birds. Also, check the woods both north and south of the fence around the Garden Center. There are usually a few American Woodcock in the woods just south of the fence in winter. Permanent residents in this general area are Red-shouldered Hawk, Barred Owl, Eastern Screech-Owl, Pileated, Red-bellied, and Red-headed Woodpeckers, Carolina Chickadee, and Tufted Titmouse.

Continue on the park road from the Garden Center to just past the golf course clubhouse where the road becomes a large circular drive. On the back side of the circle is a poorly marked trail leading through a wooded area that can be good in winter for White-throated Sparrow, Blue-gray Gnatcatcher, Orange-crowned Warbler, White-eyed Vireo, Downy Woodpecker, and with luck, Fox Sparrow and Brown Creeper. Rubber boots are recommended for Tyrrell Park birding.

On the east side of the circular drive there is a parking lot at the entrance to the Cattail Marsh Wetlands, a man-made marsh attracting many species of water birds, especially in winter. Levees criss-cross the area providing access to all sections.

Orange

Orange, population 23,000, is about 25 miles east of Beaumont. The Sabine River, the boundary between Texas and Louisiana, is also the eastern city limit of Orange. Orange County is surrounded on all sides but the north by the waters of the Sabine and Neches rivers and Lake Sabine.

Claiborne West Park, 435 acres, is 12 miles west of Orange on I-10. The park is operated by the Orange County Parks Board. Park hours are 7:30 am to 9 pm March through November; 7:30 am to 8 pm December through February. Picnicking, restrooms, and primitive camping are available. Cow Bayou dissects the park, with the recreation area on the west, and the nature preserve on the east. A pedestrian bridge connects the two areas. Pines, pine-hardwood understory, and hardwoods are the representative woody vegetation. Resident birds include Barred Owl, Pileated Woodpecker, Pine Warbler, Brown-headed Nuthatch, Fish Crow, and Wood Duck. In winter Yellow-bellied Sapsucker, Northern Flicker, Brown Thrasher, White-throated Sparrow, and Brown Creeper are common. The park office phone number is (409) 745-2255.

Bridge City—Sydnes Island

From Orange drive west on I-10 for 5 miles to exit #873 (SH 62). Turn south and go 4.2 miles to SH 87. Turn right (south) on SH 87 (Texas Avenue), continue through Bridge City 2.5 miles to Lake Street (second red light), turn left on Lake Street and go to the end of the road. The road becomes a gravel road and the Rainbow Bridges will be visible to the right. Along the way the wetland habitat makes for many birding opportunities. At the end of the road is Bailey's fish camp. The camp overlooks Sydnes Island, a very large heron, egret, cormorant and Roseate Spoonbill rookery in past years. The birds can still be seen in the area.

Back on SH 87 turn left to the Rainbow Bridges. Look for American Bittern, Yellow-crowned and Black-crowned Night-Herons, Neotropic Cormorant, Great and Snowy Egrets, Great Blue and Little Blue Herons, Boat-tailed Grackle, migrating warblers and shorebirds. Long-billed Curlew and American Avocet have been found.

McFADDIN AND TEXAS POINT NATIONAL WILDLIFE REFUGES

McFaddin and Texas Point National Wildlife Refuges, with 63,835 acres, are located on SH 87 southwest of Sabine Pass. The refuges provide wintering areas for great numbers of geese. Twenty-three duck species also winter with numbers up to 100,000. Hunting is allowed in the morning on certain days of the week during hunting season. Large portions of both refuges form estuarine environments not only for winter waterfowl but also for numerous other birds plus shrimp, crabs, and fish.

Both refuges are under the administration of the Refuge Manager at Anahuac National Refuge.

Texas Point National Wildlife Refuge is approximately 17 miles south of Port Arthur, adjacent to Sabine Pass and south of SH 87. There are no vehicular roads on the refuge. For a fee, shallow-water boats can be launched into Texas Bayou from a private boat launch located on the east side of the refuge. A cattle path leading from the refuge parking lot on SH 87 provides access by foot. Rubber boots are recommended as it is usually very muddy. The refuge is open during daylight hours seven days a week. The birds found here should be the same as those in Sea Rim State Park.

McFaddin National Wildlife Refuge is adjacent to and west of Sea Rim State Park. It includes 12 miles of beach along the Gulf of Mexico for swimming, fishing, camping, picnicking, beachcombing, and birding.

There are eight miles of interior roads on McFaddin NWR that provide access to inland lakes and waterways. The inland lakes are usually shallow and may be navigable only by canoe or shallow draft boats. Clam Lake Road is open to the 10-mile Cut Bridge every day from 6 am to sunset. The rest of the road system is open from 7:30 am to 3 pm, Monday through Friday, and is closed weekends and holidays.

The refuge probably has one of the densest populations of American Alligator in the state. Birds to be found are the same as in Sea Rim State Park.

For information check with the Refuge Manager at Anahuac NWR, P.O. Box 278, Anahuac, TX 77514, (409) 267-3337, or (409) 839-2680, or with the field headquarters at McFaddin NWR, P.O. Box 609, Sabine Pass, TX 77655, (409) 971-2909.

SEA RIM STATE PARK

Sea Rim State Park, 15,094 acres of beach and marshlands, is approximately 5 miles south of Texas Point National Wildlife Refuge. About 90% of this park is accessible only by boat. The park is divided into two units: the beach south of the highway and the marshlands to the north. The beach unit includes the headquarters, natural history interpretative center, camping on 3 miles of beach, trailer sites, and 2.2 miles of sea rim marsh, for which the park is named. The sea rim marsh is where marsh grasses extend into the surf, a fertile nursery ground for marine life. In addition, there is the Gambusia Trail, a boardwalk two feet above the marsh and 3,640 feet long, enabling one to observe the marsh life from above. A booklet is available at headquarters that explains the marsh ecology of the trail.

The marshlands unit north of the highway has a boat ramp, boat channels, canoe trails, and an air boat concession where canoes can be rented. In the marsh the Texas Parks and Wildlife Department has built six platforms at intervals for overnight camping, and four observation blinds for photography and observation. A canoe is the best way to see the birds of the marshlands. Most of the year, air boat rides are available for a fee allowing non-canoeists to see the marshlands; however, the noise of the air boat chases the birds away.

Seaside Sparrow, Boat-tailed Grackle, Clapper Rail, Great Blue Heron, Great, Snowy, and Cattle Egrets, White and White-faced Ibises, and Roseate Spoonbill are common year-round. Be on the lookout for Least Bittern in the spring and summer, and American Bittern and Nelson's Sharp-tailed Sparrow in fall, winter, and spring.

All migrants that are found elsewhere on the upper Texas coast should also be here. Thirty-seven warbler species have been recorded in the park.

The upper coast is of great importance to wintering geese and ducks. Numbers of more than 100,000 in winter are not uncom-

ROSEATE SPOONBILL

mon. Listed in order from abundant to rare are Snow Goose, Green-winged Teal, Lesser Scaup, Mottled Duck, Gadwall, Northern Pintail, American Wigeon, Northern Shoveler, Canvasback, Blue-winged Teal, Greater White-fronted Goose, Ring-necked Duck, Canada Goose, Mallard, Cinnamon Teal, Redhead, Red-breasted Merganser, Wood Duck, Greater Scaup, Common Goldeneye, Bufflehead, Oldsquaw, Surf, White-winged and Black Scoters, and Hooded and Common Mergansers.

Practically all ducks and geese that winter in Texas can be found at Sea Rim State Park, Texas Point NWR, and McFaddin NWR. The park checklist has 29 waterfowl species.

Other animals seen in the area include river otter, raccoon, nutria, muskrat, striped skunk, opossum, gray fox, bobcat, and an occasional mink. Small American Alligators are sometimes seen from the boardwalk; the larger ones are in the marshlands unit.

Fishing is permitted and certain sections of the park are open to duck hunting in season.

A bird checklist (1993) with 297 species is available at headquarters. The address is P.O. Box 1066, Sabine Pass, TX 77655, (409) 971-2559.

ANAHUAC NATIONAL WILDLIFE REFUGE

The 30,000-acre Anahuac National Wildlife Refuge is located on the north shore of East Bay, an arm of Galveston Bay 18 miles southeast of Anahuac. This refuge is maintained and managed primarily for migrating and wintering waterfowl, but with extensive coastal marsh and wet prairies, it also provides ideal habitat for many other birds and animals.

To reach the refuge from I-10, take Exit 812 (Hankamer), drive south on SH 61 2.1 miles to FM 562, and continue south on FM 562 8.3 miles to FM 1985. Turn east on FM 1985, and go about 4 miles to the refuge sign. Turn south and drive 3 miles to the entrance gate. Or, if approaching from the east, take SH 124 either north from High Island or south from Winnie to FM 1985, then drive west 10 miles to the refuge sign.

Common nesting birds include Black-crowned and Yellow-crowned Night-Herons, Mottled Duck, King and Clapper Rails, Least Bittern, Purple Gallinule, Common Moorhen, Least Tern, Green Heron, and Common Yellowthroat. Barn Owl and Marsh Wren are less common. Wood Stork is often a summer visitor.

On the refuge, I once saw King, Clapper, Virginia, Sora, Yellow, and Black Rails within a couple of hours. The presence of American Coot, Purple Gallinule and Common Moorhen means that all nine members of the rail family occurring regularly in the United States can be found here every year.

Snow, Canada, and Greater White-fronted Geese roost and loaf on the ponds from late September to March. A few Ross' Goose may be seen also. The geese flights at sunset as the birds are returning from feeding areas can be spectacular in late October and early November. Twenty-eight waterfowl species are on the refuge checklist; only six are considered rare. The best time to look for Fulvous Whistling-Duck on the refuge is in the fall. They are more easily found in rice fields on I-10 west of Winnie in spring, summer, and fall. Most of the wintering ducks have arrived on the refuge by the middle of November. Sedge Wren and Short-eared Owl winter in the coastal marsh.

In winter watch for Common Loon (on the bay), American White Pelican, Double-crested Cormorant, Bald and Golden Eagles, and Sprague's Pipit on the road.

Recommended places to look for migrating warblers, orioles, buntings, and grosbeaks in spring and fall are along the salt cedar hedgerow north of Teal Slough and the small grove of willows surrounding a pond near the entrance and along the road toward Shoveler Pond. The twelve miles of refuge roads are dikes, and using the vehicle as a blind while driving along these roads is an excellent way to view the marsh and ponds, particularly Shoveler Pond and Teal Slough. After heavy rains, some roads of the refuge may be closed to vehicular traffic.

Other animals that reside on the refuge include coyote, coyote-red wolf hybrids, river otter, mink, muskrat, bobcat, and swamp rabbit.

The Anahuac Public Hunting Area, located seven miles east of the main refuge on FM 1985, is closed to the public except during hunting season.

A bird checklist with 273 species is available at headquarters. Restroom facilities are at the refuge entrance and at two locations on East Galveston Bay. There is no drinking water on the refuge. The address is P.O. Box 278, Anahuac, TX 77514, (409) 267-3337, or (409) 839-2680.

CANDY CAIN ABSHIER STATE
WILDLIFE MANAGEMENT AREA

The Candy Cain Abshier State Wildlife Management Area, 204 acres, is located at Smith Point in Chambers County a few miles west of Anahuac National Wildlife Refuge. To reach the wildlife management area from I-10 take exit no. 812 (Hankamer/SH 61), drive south on SH 61 2.1 miles to FM 562, and take FM 562 south 8.3 miles to the intersection with FM 1985. Turn right on FM 562 (left on FM 1985 leads to Anahuac NWR) and drive 18 miles to Smith Point, then watch for signs to the wildlife management area. Smith Point juts deeply into Galveston Bay.

Smith Point is a wet prairie area with major stands of oak-hackberry mottes. Like the nearby High Island sanctuaries, CandyAbshier Wildlife Management Area is of major importance to passerine migrants in spring. In all seasons, the area is excellent for herons, egrets, gulls, terns, Brown Pelican, etc. It is perhaps best known for fall hawk watching. From early September through mid-October, Houston Audubon Society members monitor the site on a daily basis for migrating hawks. A 25-foot observation tower has been erected on the site. Often thousands of Broad-winged and Swainson's Hawks, hundreds of accipiters, as well as numerous kites, falcons, eagles, Osprey, vultures, etc., can be observed migrating south. May through September look for Magnificent Frigatebird over the bay. Wintering waterfowl are numerous at Smith Point. Check the surrounding marshes for herons, egrets, and shorebirds. Finally, this is one of the best areas on the upper coast to listen for Black Rail calling from April through June.

A colony of Eurasian Collared-Dove resides in the Smith Point area. This species is not officially accepted by the Texas Bird Records Committee, but a number of these birds are apparently spreading west from Florida.

HIGH ISLAND

High Island is 30 miles northeast of Galveston on SH 124, just north of SH 87. It has become the most popular place for bird seekers to visit for spring land bird migration. Mid-April to mid-May is usually the peak time. The town sits atop a salt dome, and thus has a slightly higher elevation than the surrounding coastal prairie, which results in the presence of several dense live oak groves, called "mottes." The migrants sometimes gather in these trees to rest and feed after crossing the Gulf of Mexico. Scarlet Tanager, Indigo Bunting, Rose-breasted Grosbeak, Gray Catbird, orioles, warblers, and vireos can be present in large numbers. Twenty to thirty warbler species in a day is not unusual, including Golden-winged, Blackpoll and Blue-winged Warblers. The timing of a "fall-out," the period during spring migration on the Texas coast when very large numbers of birds can be found, is very weather-dependent. The best time is after a cold front, especially if it was accompanied by rain. Other times a good variety of birds can be seen but numbers can be low. If possible, plan to spend a whole day to see all the migrants, because they can change from hour to hour. Several days is better; several visits for early and late migrants better yet.

There is no way to predict the best day, but whenever I get there on a Saturday, someone always says, "You should have been here on Thursday, it was fantastic."

Houston Audubon Society owns and manages four sanctuaries at High Island.

The first is Louis B. Smith Woods, 50+ acres, formerly called Boy Scout Woods. Driving north on SH 124, take the first right after the ball park (5th Street), and drive about two blocks to the wooded area on the right side of the road. The woods have a hummingbird garden, boardwalks, three ponds, and a photography blind. Check for photographic policies before setting up equipment. There is an entrance fee that also covers Smith Oaks, below. The only United States record of Greenish Elaenia was recorded here in 1984.

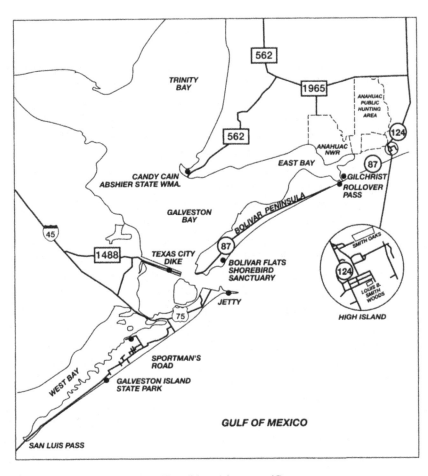

GALVESTON BAY/HIGH ISLAND/GALVESTON

The second sanctuary, Smith Oaks, 142+ acres, is reached by driving north on SH 124 past the Roadside Park at the north edge of town. Turn right, go one block, turn right again and go another block, then turn left on Winnie Street and drive to the parking lot at the end of the lane. This property includes trails, two large lakes (one with a rookery and observation tower), several board-walks in low areas, a drip pond in the forest for passerines, and a hummingbird garden. There is an entrance fee that also covers Louis B. Smith Sanctuary.

Here I have seen Black-throated Blue, Cape May and Cerulean Warblers and Black-billed Cuckoo, all difficult for me to find elsewhere in Texas. In the marshy area behind the woods Boat-tailed Grackle are sometimes present. This brown-eyed grackle is usually found in Texas near the coast from the Rockport area to Louisiana, increasing in numbers and expectancy south to north.

Eubanks Woods, 9.5 acres, and S.E. Gast Red Bay Sanctuary, 8.8 acres, are currently under development.

BOLIVAR PENINSULA

The town of Gilchrist is 8 miles south of High Island, or 20 miles north of the Bolivar ferry. There is a channel between the gulf and the bay called Rollover Pass. A short stop here to see what is on the bay side will usually turn up Reddish Egret, gulls, terns, and Black Skimmer. In migration there can be large numbers of American Avocet and Marbled Godwit. A scope is very helpful.

From Gilchrist, follow SH 87 south about 20 miles to Bolivar Flats. Along the way the road parallels the beach, with usually only sand dunes in between. There are many access roads to the beach, and it is possible to drive along the beach most of the way to see shorebirds and other species in the surf. Be sure the beach surface is safe for vehicles; following another vehicle's fresh tracks may help avoid getting stuck. In winter this sometimes results in finding all three scoter species (Black, White-winged, and Surf). Red-breasted Merganser, Eared Grebe, and Lesser Scaup are more likely. The trick is to find the birds close to the beach.

Bolivar Flats Shorebird Sanctuary

At the south end of Bolivar Peninsula, Loop 108 intersects SH 87 twice, north and south of the town of Port Bolivar. At the northern intersection, turn east on Rettilon Road and drive to the beach, then right to the vehicular barrier. This is Bolivar Flats Shorebird Sanctuary, 550 acres, owned by the State of Texas and leased to the Houston Audubon Society for management. The sanctuary is adjacent to 500–750 acres of mud flats, whose acreage fluctuates greatly with the tides. There are educational signs and an observation tower.

Here shorebirds, gulls, terns, egrets, and herons gather, sometimes in incredible numbers. Be on the lookout for rarities that turn up here from time to time, such as Great Black-backed, Lesser Black-backed, California, Glaucous and Kelp Gulls. Seaside Sparrow are permanent residents and Nelson's Sharp-tailed Sparrow winters in the spartina grass between the beach and the highway. Swallows are abundant migrants near the coast in spring and fall. The marsh areas near Port Bolivar should be checked for Clapper Rail year-round. Herons and egrets are permanent residents; both shorebird and land bird migrants are common.

Back on SH 87, take the free ferry to Galveston. From the ferry, watch among the abundant Laughing Gull for Bonaparte's Gull in winter and Magnificent Frigatebird in summer. One winter day I saw a Black-legged Kittiwake from the ferry.

GALVESTON

Galveston Island is about 30 miles long from northeast to southwest, and ranges from three-quarters of a mile to three miles wide. Galveston Bay is at the northern end, West Bay (a shallow estuary) to the west, and San Luis Pass at the southern tip. In between are an interesting historical city; a state park; countless freshwater, estuarine, and saltwater ponds and sloughs; coastal wetlands, oak mottes; prairies; the beach; and sand dunes—all providing extensive birding opportunities.

Herons, egrets, Roseate Spoonbill, White and White-faced Ibises, sandpipers and plovers, rails, gulls, terns, and waterfowl are present in all seasons. In summer watch for Magnificent Frigatebird flying up and down the shoreline along both the gulf and West Bay. Sandhill Crane are present in winter.

The number of warblers, tanagers, buntings, grosbeaks, thrushes, orioles, vireos, and other land birds in late April and early May can be unbelievable. These birds, which migrate both up the coast and over the Gulf of Mexico, make landfall in great concentrations along this bend in the Texas coast. The ideal time for migrant "fall-out" comes with the arrival of a cold front, especially when the front stalls and is accompanied by a rain storm.

Kempner Park is the favorite warbler park in the City of Galveston proper. It is located at Avenue O and 27th to 29th Streets. After checking the park, walk in the residential area surrounding the park and check the trees for migrants. Migrants in large numbers can be found south of the city on the drive to San Luis Pass if one is there at the proper time.

For several years a Peregrine Falcon has spent the winter at the retirement home at 23rd and Seawall Boulevard.

At the northern end of Galveston Island, a drive to the south jetty of the Galveston Ship Channel is always time well-spent. Drive north on Seawall Boulevard to the dead end, then turn right on Boddeker Road. Big Reef is on the left shortly after the turn between the jetty and the ship channel. There is a wooden pedestrian bridge leading to Big Reef. Also, the area can be scoped from Boddeker Road. East Beach is on the right and the jetty is at the end of the road. Big Reef, a 210-acre tidal delta, should be checked for Black Skimmer, Laughing, Ring-billed, and Herring Gulls, Sandwich, Gull-billed, Caspian, Royal, Least (summer), Forster's, Common, and Black Terns (migrants). Kelp Gull was recorded in January–April, 1996, and in late 1996 through early 1997. All species found at other beach locations in Texas should occur at Big Reef and/or East Beach. Walk the jetty, on which an occasional Purple Sandpiper has been found in winter. At the end of the jetty, watch for Common Loon, Masked Booby, jaegers, and Northern Gannet in winter. Peregrine Falcon migrate south in late September and early October. There is an admission fee if driving into the area. The toll booth is usually unmanned outside tourist season.

While in the Galveston area it is worthwhile to check the Texas City Dike, a jetty that juts five miles into Galveston Bay. To reach Texas City from Galveston, take I-45 toward Houston. Turn right on Loop 197, then right on FM 1764 to the dike. In winter there are usually Common Loon, Eared and Horned Grebes, and an occasional Pacific Loon, Red-throated Loon and Oldsquaw. Black-legged Kittiwake, and California and Lesser Black-backed Gulls have also been recorded in winter.

West Galveston Island

West Galveston Island is good for birding year-round. Shorebird migration is from the first week of July to the end of May. Thirty-six species of plovers and sandpipers have been recorded.

From 61st Street, drive west on FM 3005 (Seawall Blvd.) to 83rd Street, turn right and go to Stewart Road, then turn left. All roads off Stewart Road toward West Bay and between 99th Street and 11 Mile Road, as well as the ponds between Stewart Road and FM 3005, should be checked if time permits. A good bird location in all seasons is Sportsman's Road. Take 8 Mile Road, and turn left onto Sportsman's Road just before the dead end at West Bay. Extensive reeds, marshes, and backwater provide a haven for Reddish Egret (sometimes white phase), waterfowl, herons, egrets, rails, gulls, terns, sandpipers, and plovers. In winter, watch for Nelson's Sharp-tailed Sparrow in the grass. Least Bittern is rare in spring. An occasional American Oystercatcher, Red-breasted Merganser, Common Goldeneye, or a completely unexpected bird may be found in West Bay at the end of Sportsman's Road.

Laffite's Cove Nature Preserve, 10 acres, is well worth a visit. It is located on Stewart Road between 11 Mile and 12 Mile Road and is open daily sunrise to sunset. The preserve is owned by the City of Galveston and operated by the Laffite's Cove Nature Preserve. There is an interpretative trail through an oak hammock and a swamp with boardwalk.

Picnicking, fishing, and collecting are prohibited. Admission is free.

Galveston Island State Park

Galveston Island State Park, 1,950 acres, begins at 13 Mile Road where Stewart Road jogs to join FM 3005. The park consists of coastal wetlands, salt meadow or coastal prairie, and 1.6 miles of beach. The park offers campsites on the beach (with shade), restrooms with hot showers, picnicking, a bathhouse, a trailer camping area, screen shelters (inland), nature trails with bird blinds, an observation platform for viewing the marshes, and fishing areas.

Birds found nesting in the park include Least Bittern, Reddish Egret, Black-crowned Night-Heron, Roseate Spoonbill, Mottled Duck, White-tailed Kite, Clapper Rail, Purple Gallinule, Common Moorhen, American Oystercatcher, Wilson's Plover, Willet, Gull-billed, Caspian, Royal, Sandwich, Forster's, and Least Terns, Black Skimmer, Marsh Wren, and Seaside Sparrow. In winter look for Palm Warbler, LeConte's and Nelson's Sharp-tailed Sparrows, and Sedge Wren. Thirty-six warbler species have been recorded.

A bird checklist (1992) with 297 species is available at park headquarters. The habitat descriptions are very educational and useful. The park address is 14901 FM 3005, Galveston, TX 77554, (409) 737-1222.

San Luis Pass

San Luis Pass is at the southern tip of Galveston Island. A toll bridge connects Galveston Island with the mainland.

Pelagic birds such as Northern Gannet, Masked Booby, Black, White-winged, and Surf Scoters, and jaegers are possible at San Luis Pass in winter. Migrant and resident shorebirds, egrets, herons, Horned Grebe, gulls and terns are often found on the flats under and near the bridge, especially on the inland side. Winter visitors include Lesser and Great Black-backed Gulls (rare) and Burrowing Owl (occasional).

FREEPORT

The Freeport Christmas Count usually ranks among the top 10 in the nation in total species. The average found in the last five years has been 205 species with only one year below 200. The secret to finding this many species in a given area is, as always, a variety of habitats. The Freeport area has the gulf with beaches and jetties, oak and pine woodlands, salt marshes, coastal prairie, farmland, the Brazos River bottom, fresh-water ponds, urban areas, and estuarine bays.

The jetties at Surfside (north) and Quintana (south) along the ship channel near Freeport are good for getting out into the gulf. Some years a Purple Sandpiper has wintered on these jetties. The beach approaches to the jetties have gulls, terns, and shorebirds. Check the nearby marshes and ponds in spring and fall for Long-billed Curlew and Whimbrel. The vegetated dunes behind the beaches are good for land migrants as well, such as Clay-colored Sparrow and Bobolink.

The woods should be explored near the Lake Jackson-Clute area on SH 332 for Red-shouldered Hawk, Pileated Woodpecker, and other land birds. Many warblers winter or linger into December. For example, the following are the warblers recorded on at least one of the last five Freeport Christmas Counts: Tennessee, Orange-crowned, Nashville, Yellow, Yellow-rumped, Black-throated Green, Pine, Prairie, Palm, Black-and-white, American Redstart, Ovenbird, Northern Waterthrush, Common Yellowthroat, Wilson's, and Yellow-breasted Chat.

The Dow Chemical Company has set aside an area at the Plant A complex where Black Skimmer nest each spring. Check with the company for tour information. Peak nesting time is usually June and July.

BRAZORIA NATIONAL WILDLIFE REFUGE COMPLEX

The Brazoria National Wildlife Refuge Complex is made up of three large refuges in Brazoria and Matagorda Counties on the Gulf of Mexico north and south of Freeport. All have more or less the same general habitats: saline and non-saline prairies, mud flats, fresh and salt marsh, limited woodlands, ponds, lakes, and intermittent streams. The refuge complex is administered from one office at 1212 North Velasco, Suite 200, Angleton, TX 77515, (409) 849-6062.

The refuges provide habitat for wintering migratory waterfowl and other wildlife. Snow Goose is the most numerous with Greater White-fronted, Canada, and Ross' Geese present in lesser numbers. The refuge bird checklist reports 100,000 geese and 80,000 ducks (24 species) recorded in winter.

Birds that commonly nest on the refuges include Black-crowned Night-Heron, White Ibis, Roseate Spoonbill, Mottled Duck, White-tailed Kite, White-tailed Hawk, Clapper Rail, Wilson's Plover, Black-necked Stilt, Forster's and Least Terns, Black Skimmer, Horned Lark, Seaside Sparrow, and Boat-tailed Grackle. Less common are Least Bittern, Reddish Egret, Black and King Rails, and Purple Gallinule. Ten species of herons and egrets nest. The checklist has 30 migrant warblers and 14 winter sparrows. The coastal marshes are prime habitat for rails that occur regularly in Texas: Yellow, Black, Clapper, King, Virginia, and Sora. It is permissible to walk in the marshes at Brazoria and San Bernard NWRs to look for rails with bells attached to ropes, provided by refuge personnel. Be sure to check with the refuge office for current policy.

Hunting and fishing are permitted in some areas in proper season.

A bird checklist is available for Brazoria, San Bernard, and Big Boggy NWRs listing 278 species plus 20 accidentals.

BLACK-NECKED STILT

In April there is the Migration Celebration Birding Festival with speakers, trade shows, seminars, etc. Check with the refuge office for dates.

Brazoria National Wildlife Refuge, 43,388 acres, is open to the public on the first full weekend of each month and the third weekend from November through April. Public access is limited during the week. The Big Slough Auto Tour, over seven miles of gravel roads, passes through a variety of wildlife habitats. There are ten interpretative stops along the way. Access for organized groups at other times must be arranged with the refuge office in advance.

The entrance gate is about 15 miles east of Lake Jackson. From Lake Jackson take FM 2004 northeast about 5 miles to FM 523, then south on FM 523 about 6 miles. Turn left (northeast) on County Road 227 to the entrance on the right.

The largest flock of Black-crowned Night-Herons I have seen was on this refuge.

San Bernard National Wildlife Refuge, 27,414 acres, is about 12 miles west of Freeport. The refuge is open to visitors from daylight to dark, seven days per week to designated areas. From Freeport drive west on SH 36 about 9 miles, then left (south) on FM 2611 4.3 miles to FM 2918, turn left (east) on FM 2918 and drive 1 mile to County Road 306, then turn right (south) on County Road 306 and go one mile to the refuge entrance.

Big Boggy National Wildlife Refuge, 4,216 acres, is not usually open to the public, however, it is hoped to be open soon. Arrangements for organized groups can be made with the complex office. Hunting is allowed on the refuge in season. From Bay City drive south on SH 60 to FM 521 in Wadsworth, turn east on FM 521 for 2.9 miles to Chinquapin Road, turn right (south) on Chinquapin Road, and drive 7 miles to the refuge entrance on the right.

BAYTOWN NATURE CENTER

The Baytown Nature Center, 420 acres, is a peninsula surrounded by Burnet, Crystal, and Scott bays near the mouth of the San Jacinto River and located diagonally across the Houston Ship Channel from the San Jacinto Battleground-Monument State Historical Park. Formerly the Brownwood subdivision of Baytown, it was completely destroyed by Hurricane Alicia. The property was purchased by the city of Baytown and converted into a nature center. Over two hundred acres are brackish wetlands; the rest is mixed hardwoods and freshwater wetlands.

From Houston, take I-10 east across the San Jacinto River to exit no. 788 (Spur 330/Decker Drive/Baytown). If driving west on I-10 take exit no. 787, drive south on Spur 330 1.3 miles to Bayway Drive, turn right on Bayway Drive and go 1.3 miles to W. Shreck Street, then turn right again and drive to the Nature Center. A new entrance to the Nature Center is planned on Bayway Drive.

From San Jacinto Battleground-Monument State Historical Park, take the free ferry across the Ship Channel to Lynchburg Road, drive to the I-10 intersection, turn right at the stop sign, and drive south on Spur 330 as described above.

The Nature Center is a reliable inland location for Reddish Egret. Nesting species include Mottled Duck, Least Tern and all large Texas herons and egrets. Eastern Screech-Owls are residents in the live oaks that border the Ship Channel. Also, this is an excelllent location for Wood Stork in summer and early fall. Osprey should be present in fall, winter and spring. Shorebirds, gulls, and terns are present year-round.

SAN JACINTO BATTLEGROUND-
MONUMENT STATE HISTORICAL PARK

San Jacinto Battleground-Monument State Historical Park, 1,005 acres, has the San Jacinto Monument, a museum, and the Battleship Texas, which is what 99% of the visitors see when they visit the park. They are well worth a visit. However, there are also extensive marshes, the Houston Ship Channel, limited hedgerows, and woodlands, with many birding opportunities. The park is about 20 miles east of downtown Houston.

From Loop 610 drive east on SH 225 about 11 miles to SH 134, then north on SH 134 about 3 miles to the entrance on the right. From I-10 drive south on Lynchburg Road approximately 13 miles east from Loop 610.

The south end of the park usually has the greatest variety of birds. The Lynchburg Ferry area should be checked for species in the Houston Ship Channel.

Birds that can usually be found year-round include Neotropic Cormorant, Roseate Spoonbill, Red-shouldered Hawk, Mottled Duck, Clapper Rail, Common Yellowthroat, and Seaside Sparrow.

In May, Wood Stork usually make an appearance and stay until October, with the largest number in August. Other summer species are American White Pelican, Pied-billed Grebe, Least, Caspian, Royal, and Forster's Terns, Black Skimmer, and Reddish Egret. Osprey are present but easier to find in winter.

Least Bittern, White Ibis, Black-necked Stilt, Blue-winged Warbler, Yellow-breasted Chat, Orchard and Baltimore Orioles,

Black-bellied and Semipalmated Plovers, American Avocet, Willet, Sanderling, Dunlin, Long-billed and Short-billed Dowitchers, and many shorebirds have been recorded in migration. Some spend the winter as well.

Most waterfowl that are common in the area in winter occur here. This is one of the better spots in the area for wintering Hooded Merganser and Black-crowned Night-Heron. Marsh and Sedge Wrens are found in the marsh as winter residents.

A bird checklist (1994) with 191 species is available at headquarters. The address is 3523 SH 134, LaPorte, TX 77571, (281) 479-2431.

HOUSTON

Houston, population 1,700,000, the largest city in Texas, is located on the Gulf Coastal Plains approximately 50 miles from the Gulf of Mexico at the southern edge of the Pineywoods. In addition to the Port of Houston (the third largest in the nation) and the headquarters for the National Aeronautics and Space Administration, Houston is a financial, medical, educational, oil, petrochemical, manufacturing, and transportation center.

The City Parks and Recreation Department oversees some 250+ parks totaling some 7,000 acres. Most are highly developed, but some have extensive natural areas. Many of these parks, located on Buffalo, White Oak, and Braes bayous, have wooded areas with jogging trails, and can be good for migrants and wintering birds.

A Birder's Checklist of the Upper Texas Coast, 6th Edition, 1980, is available from the Ornithology Group, Houston Outdoor Nature Club, P.O. Box 270894, Houston, TX 77277-0894 for 25 cents plus stamped, addressed envelope. The checklist covers Brazoria, Chambers, Fort Bend, Galveston, Harris, and Jefferson counties.

TEXAS RARE BIRD ALERT/UPPER COAST RARE BIRD ALERT—A recording of sightings state-wide as well as the upper

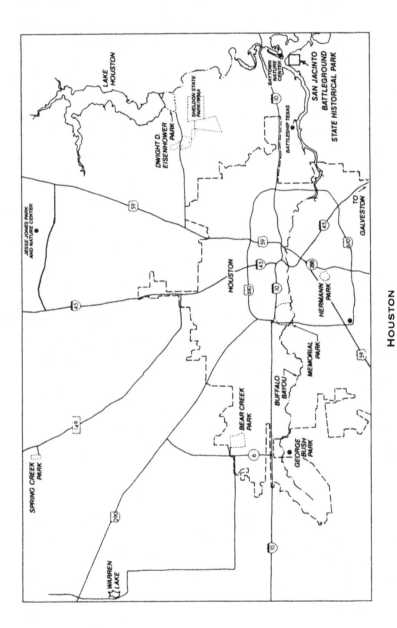

HOUSTON

Texas coast, (281) 992-2757, sponsored by the Houston Audubon Society.

Dwight D. Eisenhower Park

Dwight D. Eisenhower Park, operated by the City of Houston Parks and Recreation Department, is at the south end of Lake Houston. There are 632 land acres plus the surface of Lake Houston. To reach the park, drive north on US 59 about 9 miles beyond IH 10, then go east on Mt. Houston Road to Lake Houston Parkway. There is a sign on US 59 pointing to the park. It is about 12 miles to the park from Lake Houston Parkway. Camping, picnicking, restrooms, and fishing are offered. More than half of the park is undeveloped.

Nesting birds include Barred Owl, Yellow-throated, Hooded, and Swainson's Warblers, Orchard Oriole, Red-shouldered Hawk, Red-headed and Pileated Woodpeckers, and Eastern Bluebirds, as well as most of the birds found in Memorial Park. Belted Kingfisher can be found all year. White-tailed deer are also found in the park.

Sheldon Lake State Park/Wildlife Management Area

Sheldon Lake State Park/Wildlife Management Area, 2,502 acres, is a day-use area only. It is located adjacent to Dwight D. Eisenhower Park. There are numerous reservoirs that are excellent habitat for a variety of water birds inlcuding Anhinga, Purple Gallinule, Common Moorhen, herons, egrets, ducks and geese. There are about 20 tree-covered islands that provide nesting sites for herons and egrets. Grain is cultivated for wintering waterfowl.

The park offers picnicking, restrooms, a boat ramp, and fishing, and is headquarters for the State Urban Wildlife Biologist stationed in the Houston area.

A bird checklist (1994) with 209 species is available at headquarters. The address is 14320 Garrett Road, Houston, TX 77044, (281) 456-9350.

Jesse H. Jones Park and Nature Center

Jesse H. Jones Park and Nature Center, 225 acres, is a beautiful Harris County Park along Spring Creek dedicated to environmental education, wildlife conservation and passive recreation. From downtown Houston drive north on US 59 to FM 1960, turn west (left) on FM 1960 and drive 1.8 mile to Kenswick Drive, then go north on Kenswick Drive to the park.

There is a nature center, boardwalk, trails, and picnic and restroom facilities. Fishing is permitted in the creek. A unique feature is the boardwalk into a tupelo swamp, which provides an excellent opportunity to find Prothonotary Warbler and Acadian Flycatcher. I saw a Swainson's Warbler here on a short visit in April several years ago.

The park address is 20634 Kenswick Drive, Humble, TX 77338, (281) 446-8588.

Spring Creek Park

Spring Creek Park is located northwest of Tomball at the northern edge of Harris County. This county-run park of 114 acres is reached by driving north on IH 45 about 5.1 miles from its intersection with I-10 to FM 149 (West Mt. Houston Road and West Montgomery Road). Turn northwest on FM 149, and go about 22 miles to the town of Tomball. In summer, watch for Scissor-tailed Flycatcher and Eastern Kingbird along the way. About one mile north of the intersection with FM 2920, turn left (west) on Brown Road, and follow the signs to the park entrance.

Nesting birds in the woods along Spring Creek include Northern Parula, Hooded, Kentucky, and Swainson's Warblers, White-eyed and Red-eyed Vireos, Eastern Wood-Pewee, Pileated, Red-bellied, Red-headed, and Downy Woodpeckers, Wood Thrush, Great Crested Flycatcher, Summer Tanager, American Robin, and Inca Dove. Other species to look for in summer are Mississippi Kite, Belted Kingfisher, and Ruby-throated Hummingbird.

Wintering birds include Dark-eyed Junco, sparrows, Ruby-crowned Kinglet, Yellow-bellied Sapsucker, Brown Creeper, American Woodcock, and Red-tailed Hawk.

A playground, restrooms, and picnicking are available.

Hermann Park

Hermann Park is highly developed. The 398-acre park is about 4 miles south of downtown Houston on Main and/or Fannin Streets. There is a golf course, picnicking and, of particular interest, the Museum of Natural Science with the Burke Baker Planetarium, and the zoo. The zoo has one of the largest collections of cracids (curassows, guans, and chachalacas) and touracos anywhere, a large waterfowl pond, flamingos, and a tropical bird house. In the Tropical Bird House the visitor enters the flight area of more than 100 tropical bird species. It is well worth a visit. The duck pond in the park sometimes attracts wild ducks in winter along with the zoo residents. Black-crowned Night-Heron and Caspian Tern have been recorded; once a Masked Duck made an appearance. Black-bellied Whistling-Duck are common residents.

Memorial Park

Memorial Park, about 3.5 miles west of downtown on Memorial Drive, has 1,468 acres with a golf course, bridle path, arboretum, swimming, picnicking, and playgrounds. A large portion of the park is in its natural condition, especially the area from south of Memorial Drive to Buffalo Bayou, the southern boundary. Birding is best in the picnic area, the arboretum, and along the bayou. There are extensive loblolly pine groves in the park.

Nesting birds include Pine and Hooded Warblers, Inca Dove, Northern Parula, Barred Owl, Eastern Screech-Owl, Wood Thrush, Great Crested Flycatcher, American Robin, Acadian Flycatcher, White-eyed Vireo, Yellow-crowned Night-Heron, Summer Tanager, Common and Great-tailed Grackles, and Red-bellied, Downy, and Pileated Woodpeckers. I recorded a Swainson's

Warbler here one April day several years ago. Some years, Red-eyed Vireo and Northern Flicker are summer residents.

In winter look for White-throated Sparrow, Hermit Thrush, Brown Thrasher, Ruby-crowned Kinglet, "Solitary" Vireo, Brown Creeper, Sharp-shinned Hawk, Yellow-bellied Sapsucker, House and Winter Wrens, Yellow-rumped and Orange-crowned Warblers, American Goldfinch, and American Woodcock. Some winters there are Pine Siskin, Purple Finch, and Golden-crowned Kinglet.

Practically all land migrants expected in the area, warblers, vireos, tanagers, grosbeaks, for example, can be found in the picnic area during spring migation, especially April and May. The best birding is during migration fall-outs, when northers with rain force birds down.

Russ Pittman Park

Russ Pittman Park is located in Bellaire east of Loop 610 South. To reach the park from Loop 610 drive east on Evergreen (Evergreen is the sixth street south of Bellaire Street), a couple of long blocks to the light at Newcastle, then north on Newcastle along the four-acre park to a parking lot on the west side of the road.

The park is operated by the Friends of Bellaire Parks. There are picnic and playground facilities plus the Nature Discovery Center, which offers numerous children activities as well as adult programs. One such program is a spring lunchtime bird walk. Once over 65 species were found in one day. Feeders are provided for wintering hummingbirds with Ruby-throated, Black-chinned, Broad-tailed, Rufous, and Buff-bellied recorded. At least four of the species are present each winter.

The park address is 7112 Newcastle, Bellaire, TX 77042-0777, (713) 667-6550.

Bear Creek Park

Bear Creek Park, administered by Harris County, is on SH 6 about 2.5 miles north of I-10. SH 6 intersects I-10 about 17 miles west of downtown Houston. The park's 2,168 acres are about three-quarters undeveloped. There are three golf courses, camping, restrooms, picnicking, playgrounds, and a wildlife area.

Nesting birds include White-eyed, Yellow-throated, and Red-eyed Vireos, Northern Parula, and Swainson's, Kentucky, and Hooded Warblers. This is a favorable area for wintering sparrows. Red-shouldered Hawk is common. Both Golden-crowned Kinglet and Rusty Blackbird are often found in winter.

For information call the Parks Department at (281) 496-2177.

George Bush Park

George Bush Park, approximately 7,800 acres, is a Harris County Park with extensive wetlands, prairie, and riparian woodlands. The park is located south of I-10 along SH 6 about two miles south of Bear Creek. Facilities include playgrounds, a bridle path, picnicking, and restrooms. Look for migrating shorebirds in spring as well as passerines. White-tailed Hawk nest along the power line right-of-way adjacent to the shooting range.

For information call the Parks Department at (281) 496-2177.

Western Harris County and Eastern Waller County

Western Harris County is the area north of I-10, west of SH 6, and south of US 290. The former farmlands are steadily becoming suburbia, meaning it is necessary to bird west into eastern Waller County to find habitat formerly common in western Harris County.

The Hockley area is located on US 290 approximately 30 miles northwest of Loop 610. It is a favored wintering area for Bald Eagle, Canada, Snow, and Greater White-fronted Geese, Sandhill Crane, ducks, and sparrows. Ross' Goose is also found, but can be hard to distinguish from the abundant Snows without a telescope.

Warren Lake is reached by driving south from Hockley on Warren Ranch Road (the road with the large "UNITED SALT CORPORATION" sign on US 290). This large private lake is located about four miles south of US 290 on the east side of the road. Bald Eagle, geese, and other waterfowl are often present on the lake in winter. Park and bird from the road. A scope is very helpful. The same road north of Hockley will lead to the same birds. In addition, look for wintering sparrows along the county roads, especially in brushy areas. The most numerous are Savannah, Vesper, White-crowned, White-throated, Lincoln's, and Swamp Sparrows. Song, Fox, LeConte's, and Harris' Sparrows are usually present in smaller numbers. Some winters Grasshopper Sparrow is present as well. Watch overhead for Red-tailed, Red-shouldered, and Ferruginous Hawks in winter. Short-eared Owl can sometimes be found hunting over the fields at dawn and dusk in winter. Hudsonian Godwit are regular in early May in the field in any direction from the intersection of FM 529 (Clay Road) and Katy-Hockley Cutoff. Dickcissel are abundant at the same time. Permanent residents include White-tailed Hawk, Crested Caracara, Great Horned Owl, Barn Owl, King Rail, and Eastern Bluebird (more in winter). In late spring and summer look for Fulvous Whistling-Duck, (rice fields), White-tailed Kite, and the common Black-bellied Whistling-Duck. In fall and winter Groove-billed Ani, Ash-throated Flycatcher, Lapland Longspur, and Common Ground-Dove have been found. In October, rails, including Yellow Rail, are sometimes observed being flushed by rice combines.

BRAZOS BEND STATE PARK

Brazos Bend State Park, 4,897 acres, is on the Brazos River approximately 35 miles south of Houston.

To reach the park, drive southwest on US 59 to the City of Richmond, then go east on FM 762 about 19 miles to the park entrance. There are several habitats represented: wooded river bottom, grasslands, creeks, marsh, and lakes.

Attractions include camping, screen shelters, hiking trails, picnicking, restrooms with hot showers, and fishing. Twenty-three mammal species have been recorded in the park; white-tailed deer is the largest. American Alligator is found in the ponds. Most of the park has been preserved in a natural state.

Nesting birds include Purple Gallinule, Common Moorhen, Northern Parula, Acadian Flycatcher, Prothonotary, Hooded, and Swainson's Warblers, Anhinga, Eastern Kingbird, Red-shouldered Hawk, Barred Owl, Eastern Screech-Owl, Mottled and Wood Ducks, Black-bellied Whistling-Duck, Pileated Woodpecker, Red-eyed, White-eyed and Yellow-throated Vireos, and Painted and Indigo Buntings. American Redstart have also been found in summer and nest in small numbers.

Wintering birds include 24 species of waterfowl, Vermilion Flycatcher, American Woodcock, LeConte's, Swamp, Vesper, Fox, Song, Chipping, Field, and White-throated Sparrows.

Other birds that have been recorded at the park include Wood Stork, Tundra Swan, Greater Scaup, Masked Duck, White-tailed Kite, Golden and Bald Eagles, Black-billed Cuckoo, Ringed Kingfisher, Black and Say's Phoebes, Pyrrhuloxia, Rusty Blackbird, and Nelson's Sharp-tailed Sparrow.

A bird checklist (1990) with 274 species is available at headquarters. The address is 21901 FM 762, Needville, TX 77461, (409) 553-5101.

ATTWATER PRAIRIE CHICKEN NATIONAL WILDLIFE REFUGE

The Attwater Prairie Chicken National Wildlife Refuge, 8,000 acres, is located approximately 75 miles from the Gulf of Mexico on the tall-grass coastal plains near the town of Eagle Lake. The refuge is managed to preserve and restore habitat for Attwater's Prairie-Chicken, a subspecies of the Greater Prairie-Chicken. This subspecies has decreased from more than one million birds before 1900 to fewer than 50 in the wild in 1996 as the coastal prairies have been converted from native grasses to cropland, industrial, and urban use. In addition, prime prairie-chicken habitat has been replaced with the spread of introduced rose hedges and other shrubs. Formerly found on the coastal plains from Corpus Christi into Louisiana, the range of the prairie-chicken has been reduced now to only three Texas counties.

To reach the refuge, drive northeast 6 miles on FM 3013 from Eagle Lake, or go south from Sealy on SH 36 for 2 miles to FM 3013, then southwest 10 miles on FM 3013 to the refuge entrance. Sealy is approximately 48 miles west of Houston on I-10.

The best time to observe the chickens is when they are on their booming grounds, or "leks." The booming is part of the mating ritual of the chickens. Because of the low population, chances of seeing a prairie-chicken on the refuge are very slim. Portions of the refuge are open to the public from sunrise to sunset daily.

The San Bernard River is the eastern boundary of the refuge; there are extensive woodlands near the river. Most of the refuge is prairie, but management is focused toward providing the diversity of habitat necessary for the prairie-chickens. Many other coastal prairie wildlife species benefit from this program as well. Marsh habitat is also being developed on the refuge.

Some of the nesting birds of the refuge, in addition to the prairie-chickens, are Fulvous and Black-bellied Whistling-Ducks, White-tailed Hawk, Crested Caracara, King Rail, Common Moorhen, Black-necked Stilt, and Dickcissel.

Many birds spend the winter on the refuge. Christmas Bird Counts average over 160 species. Birds commonly found include geese, Northern Harrier, Sandhill Crane, American and Sprague's Pipits, and Brewer's Blackbird. Less common are American Bittern, Bald Eagle, Ferruginous Hawk, Long-billed Curlew, American Woodcock, Common Ground-Dove, Short-eared Owl, and Sedge Wren. Sixteen sparrow species have been found in winter.

Migrants include 23 warbler species, (mostly in the spring), along with 23 shorebird species. American Golden-Plover, Upland and Buff-breasted Sandpipers, and Hudsonian Godwit are common spring migrants.

A bird checklist (1996) containing 266 species for the refuge is available at headquarters. There is an exhibit of mounted local birds on display in the refuge office. The address is P.O. Box 519, Eagle Lake, TX 77434, (409) 234-3021. Limited picnicking facilities are available. Fires, camping, hunting, fishing, and canoeing are prohibited. Pets must be leashed.

EAGLE LAKE

The City of Eagle Lake, population 3,700, is known as "The Goose Hunting Capital of the World." Canada, Greater White-fronted, and Snow Geese are abundant in the area from October to March, with a few Ross' Goose usually present with the Snows. Look for the geese on the county roads around Eagle Lake. Fulvous Whistling-Duck nest in the rice fields of the area and are most easily found from April to September. If in the area when rice is being harvested and the combine is near the road, watch for rails flushing up in front of the combine.

Eagle Lake, 1,200 surface acres, is owned and operated by the Lower Colorado River Authority to supply irrigation water to area rice farmers. The lake is about two miles south of the City of Eagle Lake on FM 102. Wintering and migrating birds include American White Pelican, numerous waterfowl, egrets, herons, hawks (including Bald and Golden Eagles), roosting geese in uncountable numbers, rails, and land birds. Black-bellied Whistling-Duck are summer visitors and Roseate Spoonbill are frequently recorded.

My first organized field trip with the Travis Audubon Society was to this lake, and it remains one of my most memorable birding experiences. A Least Grebe, Fulvous Whistling-Ducks, and 18 other "life" birds were recorded on that first bird adventure with other bird seekers.

Permission to enter must be obtained from the Lower Colorado River Authority, Lakeside Water Division, 209 S. McCarty, Eagle Lake, TX 77434, (409) 234-7336.

PORT LAVACA

Port Lavaca, population 11,600, is located on the central Texas coast midway between Galveston and Corpus Christi. There is a wealth of very good birding locations in all directions from the city. Northeast is The Colorado River Outlet south of Bay City, the site of the Mad Island Marsh Christmas Bird Count; Matagorda Island is southeast; Aransas National Wildlife Refuge is south; and Lake Texana State Park is north. The Mad Island Marsh Christmas Bird Count has been in the top five counts for the nation from 1993 to 1996, with 197 species December 17, 1993; 205

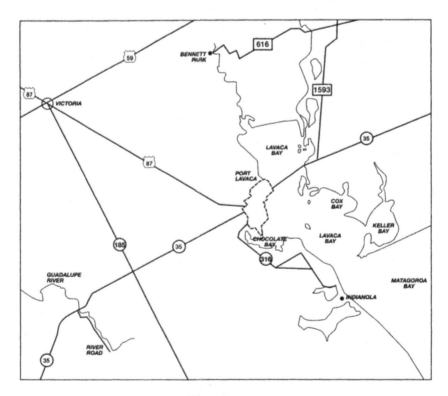

PORT LAVACA

species December 19, 1994; 209 species December 18, 1995; and 223 species December 23, 1996.

A stop at the Chamber of Commerce, 2300 SH 35 bypass, is recommended to pick up a bird checklist and brochures about birding Calhoun County. *"Finding Birds on the Central Texas Coast"* by Mark Elwonger, is an excellent guide for birding locations in the area with maps, directions, and other information. It is available from the author at 405 West Brazos, Victoria, TX 77901.

Lighthouse Beach Park at the west end of the causeway in Port Lavaca has a boardwalk that allows bird seekers the chance to look down into a marsh where shorebirds, wading birds, and especially Clapper Rail are found.

Indianola

Once the largest seaport in Texas, Indianola was twice destroyed by major hurricanes in the late 1800's and has never recovered. The site is currently used as a small residential and recreational area. In the spring, if there is time for only one location to visit in the area, this is a good selection.

To reach the area from Port Lavaca, travel south on SH 238. At the intersection with SH 316, take SH 316 straight to Indianola.

SH 316 is a very good site for Crested Caracara and Black-bellied Whistling-Duck year-round; Ross' Goose and Sandhill Crane during fall/winter; and Glossy Ibis, Fulvous Whistling-Duck, Hudsonian Godwit, Buff-breasted Sandpiper and thousands of shorebirds during spring, in association with rice-field farming activities. Yellow Rail might also be observed when farmers cut second-crop rice during October.

An excellent spot for spring migrants is along Zimmerman Road, which is accessed by turning left toward the Old Town Cemetery near the end of SH 316. The road is public, but the land bordering the road is private. Many Gulf-weary neotropical migrants follow the J-hook of Matagorda Island inland along the west bank of Lavaca Bay and eventually to Zimmerman Road.

The dense thorny shrubs serve as temporary habitat for them and many colorful birds can be observed in close proximity to the road. Marshes border the road and many water birds are present seasonally. Black Rails can occasionally be heard calling during spring and summer months in the small marsh near the cemetery. Horned Lark, Bewick's Wren, Curve-billed and Long-billed Thrashers, and Boat-tailed Grackle are resident.

After visiting Zimmerman Road, cross SH 316 and travel on Brighton Avenue, the paved road to Indianola. At the second bridge, listen for Black Rail during spring and summer mornings. Bird life is very diverse at this site within one mile of the bay and adjacent to coastal marshes. During May, over 25 species of birds might be observed in a 3-minute span just before sunrise.

Continue traveling on Brighton Avenue to the Bay. Turn right and drive to the end of the road for an overlook of the mouth to Powderhorn Lake. On the spoil ridge on the far side of the mouth, American Oystercatcher are normally common year-round.

Travel north along the bay-front road for a view of distant waterbirds. During the fall and winter check the large rafts of Lesser Scaup for Black, White-winged and/or Surf Scoters which are occasionally found with the scaups. Common Goldeneye and Bufflehead are common during winter. Brown Pelican is common year-round.

Bennett Park

Bennett Park is a primitive, wooded Jackson County park within a bend of Garcitas Creek. It is one of the better birding sites for songbirds in the county.

From Port Lavaca, drive northeast on SH 35 4.9 miles to FM 1593, north on FM 1593 9.6 miles to Lolita, then west on FM 616 8.7 miles to LaSalle. Look for CR 235 in LaSalle and turn right (north), at the dead end turn left, and after this county road makes a 90 degree right turn, take the first county road to the left, which will lead to the park. From Victoria, travel south on US 87 to Placedo, then turn left on FM 616. After crossing Garcitas Creek, look for road CR 235 in the community of LaSalle. From LaSalle follow directions above.

Many local residents fish, picnic and camp in the park. The area is remote and the road can be seasonally rough. Some visitors launch boats from cuts in the dirt bank and enjoy short boat trips.

With its location near the Gulf and directly north of Lavaca Bay, the park is at a good geographic location for funnelling and trapping incoming and outgoing neotropical migrants. The woodlands consist of typical river-bottom woods with an understory of dense shrubbery that contains both dwarf palmetto (*Sabal minor*) and juvenile Texas (*S. mexicana*) palms. The immature Texas palms are at the extreme north end of their range and are the only native Texas palm that reaches tree size.

Spring migrants can be abundant during the morning following April evening thunderstorms. Fall woodland migrants can be found from July through November. Large numbers of *Empidonax* flycatchers can normally be found in August and early September. Barred Owl and Pileated Woodpecker are resident.

Buffalo Lake Overlook

SH 35 southwest from Port Lavaca has several good birding opportunities. From Port Lavaca drive southwest on SH 35 about 10.5 miles to SH 185, then continue about 2 miles to a pull-off and observation platform located on the southeast side of the highway. Views can be obtained of a shallow freshwater lake that is being managed by the Texas Parks and Wildlife Department for water birds. During periods when open water exists, Wood Stork, Roseate Spoonbill and thousands of shorebirds use the site. When it is heavily vegetated, it serves as a roost site for millions of blackbirds. Waterfowl and other waterbirds can generally be observed flying over the site in early morning and late evening year-round. The Guadalupe River Delta supports large concentrations of swallows that are visible during early morning and late evening hours during September and October. Birding tours of the adjacent Guadalupe Delta Wildlife Management Area are normally given during April and October. Call the Texas Parks and Wildlife Department at (512) 576-0022 for information.

Old SH 35

Between the Victoria Barge Canal (just south of SH 185) and the Guadalupe River, watch for one of several sections of abandoned highway. The old highway can be accessed by vehicle or foot. It consists of an old paved road with a dense shrubby border surrounded by wetlands. Numerous brush-loving songbirds can be found during the appropriate season. Check under the numerous bridges along SH 35 for Cave Swallow roosting with hundreds of Cliff and Barn Swallows. They have been found at this site since 1995.

Guadalupe River Delta

Continue southwest on SH 35 to the Guadalupe River. From Tivoli the river is about 2.3 miles. Just south of the river turn southeast on River Road, just adjacent to and southeast of the Guadalupe River. River Road is a 4-mile gravel county road that parallels the south shore of the river. It is bordered by riparian woodlands on the left, marshes and salty prairies on the right, and a distant view of Hynes Bay at the end of the road.

The Texas Parks and Wildlife Department owns property for two miles on both sides of this road. The state-owned woodlands between the road and the river are normally open to the public for birdwatching and other non-consumptive activities during daylight hours year-round. Call the Texas Parks and Wildlife Department at (512) 576-0022 for current regulations.

Specialty birds for the area are: White-tailed Kite, White-tailed Hawk, Crested Caracara, Eastern Screech-Owl, and Golden-fronted Woodpecker, year-round; Couch's Kingbird, Vermilion Flycatcher, and Western Meadowlark during fall and winter; and numerous *Empidonax* flycatchers in the woodlands during August and early September.

The woodlands along the river serve as a migration corridor for spring and fall migrant passerines. A number of warbler species can be found on a short walk in the woods or by birding from the road bordering the woods. The river also serves as a migration corridor for raptors. Many vultures, accipiters, buteos, falcons and an occasional eagle can be observed during peak movements near the end of September and March.

Wood Stork roost in the marshes during the summer and can be observed flying to and from the roost during early morning and late evening hours. Thousands of geese, ducks, and other water-birds winter in the adjacent marshes. Brown Pelican and concentrations of gulls, terns, and shorebirds might be viewed at a distance from the end of the road during high-water events. Large numbers of swallows forage over the mosquito-infested marshes during early fall.

VICTORIA

Riverside Park is the best place to look for breeding and migrating songbirds in Victoria. Travel west on Red River Street from US 87 or US 77 in Victoria to reach the Nature Area in the park. At Vine Street, turn right and park in the RV park. Walk across the small bridge to the north on Vine Street to a gate to River Side Park Nature Area on the left. The gate leads to the mid-portion of a two-mile loop trail circling through medium-aged river-bottom woodlands consisting mostly of hackberry, cedar elm and green ash. It is noted for its Barred Owl, Great Crested Flycatcher (summer) and white-tailed deer.

The woodlands in the park are highly modified. The remnant patches of quality habitat serve as key sites to look for birds. Northern Parula and Brown-crested Flycatcher can be found here, along with Couch's Kingbird during appropriate seasons. A diverse assemblage of neotropical migrants can be observed passing through in spring and fall. Mississippi Kite roost in the park during migration. Green Kingfisher can regularly be found on the rocks in the river below the water treatment plant. Picnicking is available year-round and a visit to the Texas Zoo within the park can be an educational experience.

A more diverse portion of the nature trail can be accessed from the southwest corner of the nature area by walking the trail paralleling Red River Street to the golf course. This trail follows a river-bottom woodland at the edge of the golf course. It winds around an old river channel through a representative portion of what the river bottoms formerly looked like near Victoria.

Outside of the nature trails and within the highly developed park, other birding areas are along the river banks of Fox's Bend and Grover's Bend. Fox's Bend is located at the West end of Red River Street, and Grover's Bend is located to the north of the ball fields. Check the few areas that are not mowed by park staff for understory species and always be on the lookout for birds in the canopy of the pecan, cottonwood, and other shade trees.

GULF OF MEXICO

Finding birds in the Gulf of Mexico has not kept pace with land birding but is becoming increasingly popular. Before 1992 most pelagic birding consisted of tagging along on fishing excursions in the area of oil platforms, but not to areas past the Continental Shelf. In Texas the shelf is about 150 nautical miles at Sabine Pass and 45 nautical miles off of South Texas. Beginning in 1992, birding trips to deeper water began to yield species previously considered accidental. Since 1994, public trips on larger boats have been taken out of Port O'Connor and many have taken advantage of birding the "blue water" off Texas.

May through September are the prime birding months in this area. Regular summer species include Cory's and Audubon Shearwaters, Leach's and Band-rumped Storm-Petrels, Masked Booby, and Bridled and Sooty Terns. Audubon's Shearwater seem most common in August and September but are regular throughout the summer. Thirty to forty Band-rumped Storm-Petrels are often encountered in June and July; Leach's Storm-Petrel is regular but less common than the Band-rumped. Masked Booby is also commonly seen and often an individual will follow the boat for extended periods.

Rarities recorded are Black-capped Petrel, Greater Shearwater, and Red-billed Tropicbird. Arctic Tern is probable but has not been documented.

Non-bird species that have been found, along with bottle-nosed dolphins (common near shore), are sperm whale, pygmy sperm whale, pantropical spotted dolphins, Clymene dolphins, whale sharks, billfish (marlin), and several types of flying fish.

For information about future Texas Pelagic Trips contact Mark Elwonger, 405 W. Brazos, Victoria, TX 77901-5003; (email: maebird@aol.com); or Dwight Peake, 30 Lebrun Ct., Galveston, TX 77551-1566; (email: dpeake@phoenix.net).

ARANSAS NATIONAL WILDLIFE REFUGE

The Aransas National Wildlife Refuge is approximately 70 miles north of Corpus Christi or 7 miles southeast of Austwell. It is another "must" birding location in Texas. The refuge is the wintering ground for the natural wild flock of Whooping Crane, now about 158 birds, up from a low of 15 in 1941.

To reach the refuge, drive north from Rockport on SH 35 to FM 774. Turn right (east) and follow signs to the entrance. Lodging is available in Rockport, Refugio, or Port Lavaca, all about 35 miles distant. Camping is available at Goose Island State Park, 30 miles south of the refuge. RV facilities are available in Austwell, 7 miles north, as well as in Rockport and Port Lavaca. The refuge is open from sunrise to sunset.

In the Visitor Center there are excellent exhibits, and slide shows, plus literature that describes the history of the area and the wildlife found on the refuge. Particular emphasis is placed on the effort to save the Whooping Crane from extinction.

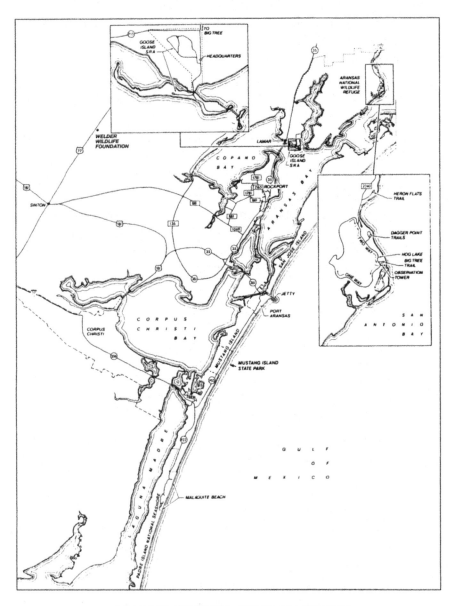

ARANSAS NATIONAL WILDLIFE REFUGE

The refuge, 54,829 acres, is on Blackjack Peninsula (once a barrier island) and incorporates many different habitats: wooded sand dunes, brushlands, oak mottes, grass meadows, cordgrass prairies, tidal marshes, freshwater ponds, and marine bays.

The refuge office also administers satellite refuge units, Matagorda Island NWR, Lamar Unit and Myrtle Foester Whitmiree Division. Matagorda Island consists of Matagorda Island NWR and Matagorda Island State Park and Wildlife Management Area. The island is cooperatively managed by the Texas Parks and Wildlife Department, U.S. Fish and Wildlife Service, and Texas General Land Office. It is accessible only by boat. For information, contact Matagorda Island State Park, South 16th and Maple Streets, P.O. Box 117, Port O'Connor, TX 77982-0117, (512) 983-2215.

Whooping Cranes usually begin arriving about the middle of October and stay until the first part of April. The wild flock of Whooping Cranes nests in Wood Buffalo National Park, Northwest Territories, Canada, some 2,500 miles northwest of Aransas NWR. They make this migration twice each year. In March the cranes begin their courtship dance. Count yourself lucky if you are fortunate enough to be a witness to this unique display.

An observation tower at the refuge gives an excellent overview of a tidal marsh. Roseate Spoonbill, herons, and egrets are usually present. Sometimes cranes can be seen from the tower, but most often at a great distance.

To get a better look at the cranes, take a boat up the Gulf Intracoastal Waterway and through the southeastern section of the refuge when the cranes are present. Several boat tours are available. Contact the Rockport-Fulton Chamber of Commerce, (512) 729-6445 or (800) 826-6441, for tour information. Many other birds can be seen from a boat trip. On my last trip I recorded 56 species from one of the boats.

Approximately 8,600 acres are open to the public and it is easy to spend a whole day. There is a 16-mile auto road, a loop along which it is not unusual to see 50 or more bird species, especially during migration or during the winter. The observation tower, sev-

WHOOPING CRANE

eral trails, a section of the bay, and a picnic area are along the loop. The Heron Flats Trail, 1.5 miles, offers a variety of habitats: thick undergrowth, trees, marshes, and perhaps a chance for rails and Groove-billed Ani. On the loop, look for Painted Bunting in spring and summer. Waterfowl and shorebirds can be seen in the bay from the road and on the freshwater ponds along the loop. Tree, Bank, Northern Rough-winged, Barn, and Cliff Swallows are common migrants.

Nesting birds of the refuge include Pauraque, White-tailed Hawk, Crested Caracara, Purple Gallinule, Common Moorhen, Wilson's Plover and Cassin's Sparrow.

In addition to birds, watch for American Alligator, white-tailed deer, collared peccary (javelina), armadillo and coyote. The interior of the refuge has a population of feral hogs, a cross between local wild domestic hogs and the introduced European boar.

While driving to or from the refuge, check at ponds and marshes for herons, egrets, rails, waterfowl, and shorebirds. Also, keep an eye on the fields for Greater White-fronted, Snow, and Canada Geese, and Sandhill Crane feeding in winter. White-tailed Hawk are usually found along SH 35 between Rockport and FM 774.

A bird checklist (1995) is available at the Visitor Center. The list has 392 species, including 37 waterfowl, 28 sandpipers, 42 warblers, and 29 sparrow species.

The refuge address is P.O. Box 100, Austwell, TX 77950, (512) 286-3559. No camping is allowed except to organized youth groups.

GOOSE ISLAND STATE PARK

Goose Island State Park, 314 acres, is approximately 12 miles northeast of Rockport at the southern tip of Lamar Peninsula. From Rockport, drive north on SH 35 to the north end of the Co-pano Bay causeway, turn east on PR 13, and follow signs to the entrance.

The park has a shell beach (Goose Island), marshes, meadows, and live oak groves. There are two campgrounds, one on the beach and one in the oaks, with picnicking, restrooms with hot showers, saltwater fishing, a boat ramp, and swimming.

The birding at this small park can be outstanding. Year-round resident birds include Reddish Egret, Black-crowned Night-Heron, Roseate Spoonbill, Clapper Rail, American Oystercatcher, Forster's, Royal, and Caspian Terns, Black Skimmer, and Seaside Sparrow.

Summer residents are Least Bittern, Black-bellied Whistling-Duck, and Gull-billed, Least, and Sandwich Terns. Neotropic Cormorant, Magnificent Frigatebird, and White-tailed Hawk are occasionally seen flying over.

In migration look for Sora and Virginia and King Rails in the marshes; warblers in the oaks (33 have been recorded); and shorebirds at the water's edge.

Some of the birds that winter in the area are Common Loon, American White Pelican, Common Goldeneye, and Red-breasted Merganser, along with about 12 other duck species. Blackjack Peninsula, the winter home of the Whooping Crane, is visible from the park and occasionally cranes can be seen from Goose Island.

The National Co-champion Live Oak is in the northern section of the park. The "Big Tree" is estimated to be more than 1,000 years old. After seeing the Big Tree, continue east to St. Charles Bay and check out the waterfowl and shorebirds from the drive along the bay. The pond at the corner of Bay Road and 4th Street, as well as the roads between the bay and the main section of the park where there are woods, marshes, ponds, etc. between the residences, can be very productive.

A bird checklist (1994) with 315 species is available at headquarters. The address is HC04, Box 105, Rockport, TX 78382, (512) 729-2858.

ROCKPORT

Rockport has been a "must" birding location in Texas since it was made famous by the late Connie Hagar. It is located on Live Oak Peninsula, 32 miles northeast of Corpus Christi on SH 35. Mrs. Hagar made twice-daily bird excursions on the peninsula for many years, and kept detailed records of her findings. Her checklist for the Central Coast, now out of print, lists 413 species (using current nomenclature) plus another 50 subspecies. A portion of Little Bay in the north section of Rockport has been set aside in her memory as the "Connie Hagar Wildlife Sanctuary."

Stop at the Chamber of Commerce to pick up a copy of *Birding in the Rockport-Fulton Area* ($2.00), a detailed guide to birding spots by Charles T. Clark. The Chamber of Commerce sponsors a Hummer/Bird Celebration in September. The address of the chamber is 404 Broadway, Rockport, TX 78382, (512) 729-6445 or (800) 826-6441.

Several boat tours leave from Rockport and/or Fulton for Whooping Cranes in season. Some are as follows: three from Rockport Harbor: Pisces, 49 passengers, phone (512) 729-7525 or (800) 245-9324; Lucky Day Charters, 93 passengers, phone (800) 782-2473 or (512) 729-4855; Pelican Tours, 65–70 passergers, phone (512) 729-8448; one from Sandollar Pavilion in Fulton: M.V. Skimmer, 40 passengers, phone (512) 729-9589 or (800) 338-4551. Contact the Chamber of Commerce for a complete list.

Live Oak Peninsula, roughly four miles by eight miles, offers a wide variety of bird habitats: live oak mottes with very large trees, grasslands, and freshwater ponds with marshes. Aransas Bay is on the east, Copano Bay on the west.

The drive north on Fulton Beach Road, then north on SH 35, then west on FM 1781, has been a very rewarding experience for me in all seasons. Near where FM 1781 turns south The Hummingbird Lodge and Educational Center is on the south side of the road. This is a bed and breakfast site that also offers birding tours, bird classes, dining, conferences, etc. Located on a 19-acre nature preserve, the center welcomes bird seekers. The wetlands and bayside of Redfish Point are across the road from the center, where wading birds, shorebirds, warbler fall-outs, hummingbirds, etc. can be seen. The center address is HCO 1, Box 245, 5652 FM 1781, Rockport, TX 78382, (512) 729-7555.

Other birding spots on Live Oak Peninsula include the 17-acre mitigation area on the east side of the new SH 35 bypass 3.5 miles south of FM 1069, where there are shorebirds, hawks, and warblers. In the Cape Valero subdivision, which is located on FM 1069 on the west edge of town, look for herons, egrets, etc. The boardwalk and demonstration garden on SH 35 north in Rockport is a nice spot for lunch and perhaps also to find some birds.

As is true in this section of the state, large concentrations of land birds in migration may occur anywhere on the peninsula. Mid-April to mid-May is the peak time. Franklin's Gull, Yellow-bellied Flycatcher, Veery, Gray-cheeked Thrush, and Philadelphia Vireo are regular migrants. In Little Bay, herons and egrets are common all year. In migration and winter there are usually Long-billed Curlew, Marbled Godwit, Snowy and Piping Plovers, Whimbrel (rare), Redhead, Canvasback, Red-breasted Merganser, and other waterfowl. Shorebirds can often be found at Rattlesnake Point on Copano Bay on the west side of Live Oak Peninsula. Construction at this site may alter accessibility.

Between Gregory and Bayside, FM 136 crosses the western edge of Copano Bay where there are extensive mud flats with many shorebird species. Wood Stork can be seen here in late summer, and numerous waterfowl in fall, winter, and spring. In the cultivated fields along FM 136 between Gregory and Bayside, and along FM 881 between Rockport and Sinton, look for wintering Sandhill Crane and Snow, Greater White-fronted, and Canada Geese. The inland ponds of the peninsula should be checked for Neotropic Cormorant, which are permanent residents.

MUSTANG ISLAND

Port Aransas

The town of Port Aransas is at the north end of Mustang Island where ocean-going vessels enter Corpus Christi Bay on their way to the Port of Corpus Christi. Brown Pelican, which nest on islands in the channel, can often be seen flying back and forth along the ship channel, especially on the north side near the town of Ingleside. They can also frequently be seen from the ferry that crosses the channel.

The jetties into the Gulf of Mexico at the mouth of the ship channel attract many fishermen, but they also provide an opportunity for the bird seeker to get a few hundred yards out into the gulf to see which pelagic or other birds are flying by. From this jetty, I have seen Magnificent Frigatebird, Masked Booby, and Peregrine Falcon, in addition to abundant terns, gulls, and shorebirds. Other reported rarities from the jetty include Sooty Tern, Brown Booby,

BROWN PELICAN

and Long-tailed, Parasitic, and Pomarine Jaegers. In winter Red-breasted Merganser, Bonaparte's Gull and Eared Grebe can sometimes be seen swimming very close to the jetty. Birding is excellent for shorebirds, gulls, and terns along the beach south of the jetty and on the drive between Port Aransas and the jetty.

It is possible to reach San Jose Island and the north jetty by boat for a fee. San Jose Island has much less human visitation than does Mustang Island. The boat leaves and returns from Woody's Boat Basin at least every two hours from 6:30 am to 6 pm daily. For exact information, call (512) 749-5252.

Port Aransas Park offers campsites with tables and electricity, restrooms with showers, and primitive camping on the beach. It is operated by Nueces County and is just south of the jetty on the beach.

The Port Aransas Bird Center is south of the ferry. Turn right at the first corner after getting off the ferry and follow the signs to the wastewater treatment plant. From the boardwalk look for alligators, Common Moorhen, waders, ducks, etc.

The Port Aransas Chamber of Commerce sponsors a Whooping Crane—Winter Bird Festival in February.

Probably the least-known bird habitat in Texas is the Gulf of Mexico. From Fishermen's Wharf, the Scat Cat, a fast fishing boat, makes regular trips some 50 miles into the Gulf for deep-sea fishing. Food and drinks are available aboard. Non-fishing bird seekers have been welcome at a reduced fee. Contact Box 387, Port Aransas, TX 78373, (512) 749-5448 for reservations. The trip usually lasts from 6:30 am to 6 pm. These trips do not reach the Continental Shelf.

From the Scat Cat, I have seen Cory's Shearwater, Masked Booby, Pomarine and Long-tailed Jaegers, and Magnificent Frigatebird. Birds found by others include Audubon's and Greater Shearwaters, Wilson's Storm-Petrel, Parasitic Jaeger, Northern Gannet, and Brown Booby. But on some trips no pelagic birds are seen. On such occasions seeing flying fish, Bottlenose and Dorado Dolphins, and the creatures the fishermen pull out of the water can make the trip worthwhile.

Mustang Island State Park

Mustang Island State Park, 3,704 acres, is 14 miles south of Port Aransas on PR 53. It has picnicking, swimming, camping, restrooms with hot showers, and beachcombing. The park has extensive sand dunes, mud flats, and 5 miles of frontage on both the Gulf of Mexico and Corpus Christi Bay. Birding should be the same as at the Padre Island National Seashore 13 miles south.

The park address is Box 326, Port Aransas, TX 78373, (512) 749-5246.

PADRE ISLAND NATIONAL SEASHORE

Padre Island National Seashore, 133,918 acres, is east of Corpus Christi between the Gulf of Mexico and the Laguna Madre. Approximately 80% of Padre Island is preserved in the national seashore.

To get there, drive east from Corpus Christi on SH 358 (Padre Island Drive) to Park Road 22. Cross the Kennedy Causeway, and continue south on Park Road 22 for about 13 miles to the seashore entrance. There is an entrance fee.

The Malaquite Beach complex has a Visitor's Center, an observation deck, a grocery and gift shop, restrooms, rinse-off showers, and changing rooms. The Visitor's Center has exhibits, brochures, maps, books, etc., and is open daily except January 1 and December 25. A boat ramp, camping, picnicking, and primitive camping are available.

Padre Island and Mustang Island (adjacent to and just north of Padre Island) are the longest of the Texas barrier islands. They act as a buffer against wind and wave action between the Gulf of Mexico and the mainland. Laguna Madre and Corpus Christi Bay are very shallow estuaries between the mainland and the islands. The bays are a nursery for many fish and other life forms. The gulf beach, sand dunes, and freshwater ponds of the islands, estuaries, and islands in the estuaries (both natural and man-made) each create a separate feeding, resting, and nesting habitat for the great variety of birds and other wildlife found in the area.

Nesting birds on or near the National Seashore include Royal, Sandwich, Gull-billed, Forster's, and Caspian Terns, a small flock of American White Pelican, eight heron and egret species, Snowy and Piping Plovers, Black-necked Stilt and Black Skimmer.

Land bird migration can be spectacular. There are 35 species of warblers on the checklist. Twenty-eight were recorded in two days one April at Packery Channel County Park, eight miles north of the seashore. I was birding in the area that day. Late September and early October is the best time for migrating Peregrine Falcon.

Shorebirds, gulls, and terns are abundant along the beach; waterfowl are plentiful on the inland ponds in fall, winter, and spring.

Some of the rarities that have been reported are Masked Duck, California, Lesser Black-backed, Glaucous, Great Black-backed, and Sabine's Gulls, Black-legged Kittiwake, and Brown and Black Noddies. My best record here was a Greater Flamingo on an island in Laguna Madre near the northern boundary of the National Seashore.

While the seashore is more than 80 miles long from north to south, only the northern 14 miles can be driven with a passenger car. Farther south, a 4-wheel-drive vehicle is needed.

A bird checklist (1990) with 329 species is available at the Visitor's Center, along with other literature about the area. The seashore address is 9405 South Padre Island Drive, Corpus Christi, TX 78418-5597, (512) 937-2621.

CORPUS CHRISTI

Corpus Christi, population 266,000, at the lower end of the Texas Coastal Bend, is a central location for good birding in all directions. The city has a major seaport, manufacturing, agriculture, water-oriented recreation, oil production, and petrochemical plants. Nearby are the Aransas National Wildlife Refuge, Padre Island National Seashore, Rockport, Kingsville, and the Welder Wildlife Foundation, all excellent for a wide variety of species.

Stop at the Corpus Christi Convention and Visitors Bureau, 1201 N. Shoreline Drive, and pick up a copy of "Birding in the Corpus Christi Area."

RARE BIRD ALERT FOR COASTAL BEND, (512) 265-0377.

Blucher Park, an in-town spot for spring passerine migrants, is three blocks south of the downtown courthouse between Carrizo, Blucher and Tancahua Streets. The entrance is on Carrizo.

Corpus Christi Botanical Gardens, 100 acres, 8500 South Staples (FM 2244), is owned and operated by the Corpus Christi Botanical Society, Inc., P.O. Box 81183, Corpus Christi, TX 78412. The undeveloped area is typical native mesquite brush with a variety of native woody plants, perhaps 30 species. There is a 12-acre pond with cattails and sedges. Birds recorded at the site include Least Grebe, Groove-billed Ani, Ash-throated Flycatcher, Couch's Kingbird, Verdin, Bewick's Wren, Long-billed and Curve-billed Thrashers, White-eyed Vireo, Pyrrhuloxia, and Olive and Cassin's Sparrows.

Oso Bay, also known as Cayo del Oso, is a very large inlet just south of Corpus Christi Bay between the City of Corpus Christi and the Corpus Christi Naval Air Station. With the extensive mud flats, some of the largest and most diverse concentrations of shorebirds in the state can be found here. Ennis Joslin Road follows the western shoreline of Oso Bay between Ocean Drive and Padre Island Drive (SH 358). At the junction of Ennis Joslin Road and Nile Drive, park at Hans A. Suter Wildlife Area. There is a boardwalk allowing the bird seeker to walk out into the marsh. Another good vantage spot for viewing the bay is from Ocean Drive at the western approach to the campus of Corpus Christi State University. Along with the many shorebirds, waterfowl and wading birds are also abundant in fall, winter, and spring. California Gull has been recorded here. Ruff and Jabiru are two special species I have seen at this spot.

Pollywog Ponds, a City of Corpus Christi wastewater facility, is a good location for Neotropic Cormorant, Anhinga, Least Grebe, Black-bellied Whistling-Duck, Groove-billed Ani, Great Kiskadee, and waterfowl. Also, this is a good spot for warblers during spring migration. From I-37 northwest of the city, take the Callicoate Road exit, go about one-fourth mile on Callicoate, then turn left (north) on Upriver Road. Upriver Road sometimes has White-winged Dove. After about one mile, where the road is near the interstate again, turn right on a dirt road, which is the entrance to the ponds. Water, tall trees, thick undergrowth, and reeds combine to create habitat for a variety of birds. This is an excellent spot to see how well insect repellent works. There are lots of mosquitoes; also fire ants, as is true of nearly all of the eastern part of the state.

"Birds of the Texas Coastal Bend, Abundance and Distribution," by John H. Rappole and Gene W. Blacklock, Texas A & M University Press, 1985, is highly recommended for persons interested in detailed records of all bird species of the area with comprehensive accounts of habitats and specific birding locations.

WELDER WILDLIFE FOUNDATION

The Rob and Bessie Welder Wildlife Foundation is approximately 8 miles north of Sinton, or 35 miles north of Corpus Christi, on US 77. With approximately 7,800 acres, the refuge preserves portions of both the Coastal Plains and South Texas.

The foundation is unique in many respects. It was established to be managed as a place where "wildlife could live, forage and propagate..." and "to provide the means and opportunity for research and education in wildlife, in conservation and in related fields." It is one of the largest privately-owned nature preserves of its type in existence. The foundation possesses an extensive natural history library, 2,500 bird study skins, 4,000 bird egg sets, a laboratory, living quarters for graduate students, facilities for overnight stays by school and professional groups, and classes for area students and teachers.

Habitats represented are extensive woodlands along 12 miles of the Aransas River, live oak-savannah and brushlands (chaparral) in the uplands, along with ponds, lakes, and marshes. The refuge has never been cultivated, but cattle graze under a carefully-managed program.

More than 1,300 plants, 55 mammals, 55 reptiles and amphibians, and 372 birds (96 of which nest or have nested) have been recorded on the refuge.

Typical South Texas nesting birds include Wild Turkey, Common Ground-Dove, Greater Roadrunner, Yellow-billed Cuckoo, Pauraque, Barn Owl, Golden-fronted and Ladder-backed Woodpeckers, Ash-throated Flycatcher, Painted Bunting, and Cassin's Sparrow.

Less common nesters are Brown-crested Flycatcher, Cactus Wren, Curve-billed Thrasher, Bell's Vireo, Pyrrhuloxia, Verdin, and Olive Sparrow.

Birds that nest near the ponds and lakes include Fulvous Whistling-Duck, Purple Gallinule, Least Grebe, Anhinga, and Black-necked Stilt.

Migration can be outstanding. Twenty-four hawks, 41 warblers, and 41 shorebirds are on the refuge checklist.

The refuge is open to the public at 3 pm each Thursday (holidays excluded) with tours and lectures to acquaint the visitor with the work of the foundation. Visits for organized groups of 15 or more can be arranged at other times by contacting the office in advance of the time of visit.

A bird checklist and other literature about the natural history of South Texas and the Coastal Bend are available at headquarters. The address is P.O. Drawer 1400, Sinton, TX 78387, (512) 364-2643.

8

South Texas

For the purposes of this book, South Texas is approximately 12% of the state. Its northern limit is the Balcones Escarpment from Del Rio to San Antonio, then southeast along the San Antonio and Guadalupe Rivers to near Goliad. The demarcation between Central Texas and South Texas (from San Antonio to Goliad) is gradual, wide, and indistinct. The boundary then proceeds south along the west limit of the Coastal Plains to near Kingsville, then east to the Gulf. The Rio Grande forms the southern and western boundaries.

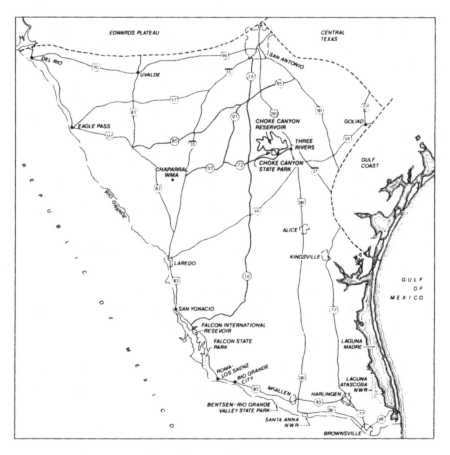

SOUTH TEXAS

Also called the South Texas Plains, Rio Grande Plains, Tamaulipan Brushlands, or Mesquite Grasslands, the area is mostly level or slightly rolling hills. Quaternary and Tertiary deposits predominate with sandy and loamy soils. The western portion is quite arid. Parks and/or refuges are rare except on the eastern and southern perimeters. The major drainage is the Nueces River plus the tributaries of the Rio Grande.

The dominant vegetation on natural sites consists of head-high shrubs and extensive grasslands. The shrubs represent many species, nearly all of which seem to have thorns. Collared peccary (javelina), coyote, white-tailed deer and western diamondback rattlesnake are common throughout. Most of the region consists of large ranches.

Nesting birds of the region include Least Grebe, Black-bellied Whistling-Duck, Long-billed and Curve-billed Thrashers, Harris' Hawk, Crested Caracara, White-winged Dove, Common Ground-Dove, Golden-fronted Woodpecker, Chihuahuan Raven, Cactus Wren, Pyrrhuloxia, Black-throated and Cassin's Sparrows, Scaled Quail, Pauraque, Lesser Nighthawk, Wild Turkey, Greater Roadrunner, Bronzed Cowbird, Ash-throated and Brown-crested Flycatchers, and Verdin.

Hawks and sparrows are very common throughout the region in winter.

Birding locations with checklists not described in this chapter are Goliad State Historical Park, near Goliad on the San Antonio River, and Lake Corpus Christi State Park on the Nueces River near Mathis.

The extreme southern portion is the Lower Rio Grande Valley, a subregion with many public parks and refuges that are all excellent birding locations.

SAN ANTONIO

San Antonio, population 991,000, is astride the Balcones Escarpment near the meeting point for three of the regions presented in this book. The Edwards Plateau is west and north, Central Texas (Blackland Prairies and Post Oak Savannah) is east, and South Texas is south. This diversity of habitats means lots of birds.

A checklist of Bexar County birds (1995) with 425 species can be obtained from the San Antonio Audubon Society, c/o Georgina Swartz, 3006 Belvoir, San Antonio, TX 78230, for 40 cents plus addressed, stamped envelope. Envelope must accommodate the 4″ × 7″, 20-page checklist.

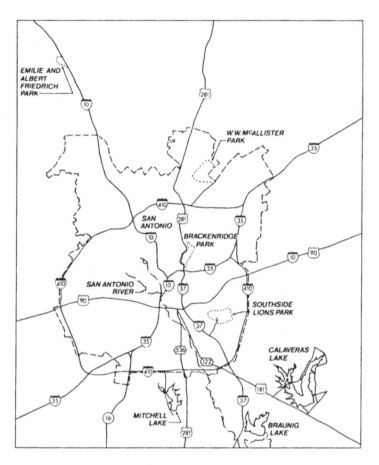

SAN ANTONIO

RARE BIRD ALERT, (210) 308-6788, operated by San Antonio Audubon Society.

Mitchell Lake Wetlands

Mitchell Lake, 660 surface acres, is one of three large lakes favored by local birders for migrating shorebirds, waterfowl in winter, and visiting herons and egrets in late summer and fall. The lake was formerly part of the sewage disposal system for the city. To reach the lake from the south section of Loop 410, drive south on Moursund Boulevard between SH 16 and US 281. From there, it is about 0.6 mile to the entrance. Birders are authorized to proceed where the sign says, "Authorized Vehicles Only." The lake and surrounding acreage is owned by San Antonio Water System and the gate has a combination lock. The current number may be obtained by calling (210) 308-6788 (allowing at least a day in advance) or by contacting a member of the San Antonio Audubon Society.

Migrating and wintering birds include American White Pelican, Double-crested and Neotropic Cormorants, Little Blue and Tricolored Herons, Mallard, Gadwall, Northern Pintail, Green-winged, Blue-winged and Cinnamon Teals, American Wigeon, Redhead, Ring-necked Duck, Canvasback, Lesser Scaup, and Ruddy Duck. March, April, July, and August are the most favorable months for migrating shorebirds. There are 40 shorebirds and 18 gulls and terns on the local checklist. Wilson's and Mountain Plovers, Whimbrel, Red Knot, Ruff, Red-necked Phalarope, Parasitic Jaeger, California and Sabine's Gulls, and Royal Tern have been recorded at San Antonio lakes. Sooty Tern has been blown in by a hurricane. Over 265 species have been found at this location.

Calaveras Lake

Calaveras Lake, 3,450 surface acres, is operated by the City Public Service Board of San Antonio. It is located 15 miles southeast of San Antonio and has 3,450 surface acres. Drive southeast from Loop 410 on US 181 for approximately 8.5 miles. Turn left on Loop 1604 to the sign leading to the picnic area. There is an entrance fee, which is also good for same-day entry to Braunig Lake. About one mile before Loop 1604, two roads lead to the lake on the south side of the dam. Here the lake shore has not been cleared. There is high grass for sparrows in winter, trees for perching birds, and the possibility of approaching close to the lake without flushing the water birds. One road is Kilowatt Road, and the other is Adkins-Elmendorf Road. Both are good for overlooking the lake with a minimum of competition from fishermen, picnickers, and other visitors.

Red-throated and Pacific Loons have been recorded in winter. The brushy sections around the lake are nesting habitat for South Texas birds: White-winged Dove, Curve-billed and Long-billed Thrashers, Pyrrhuloxia, Black-throated Sparrow, Lesser Nighthawk, Brown-crested Flycatcher, Common Ground-Dove, Golden-fronted Woodpecker, Verdin, Cactus Wren, and Bronzed Cowbird.

Braunig Lake

Braunig Lake, 1,350 surface acres, is operated by the City Public Service Board of San Antonio to provide cooling water for a power plant. The lake is 15 miles southeast of downtown on I-37. Access to Braunig and Calaveras Lakes is controlled by the San Antonio River Authority. The principal access is for fishing, but there are tables for picnickers. The entrance fee is also good for same day entry to Calaveras Lake. The bird life is much the same for all three lakes, although some species might be found at one and not the others.

Emilie and Albert Friedrich Park

Emilie and Albert Friedrich Park is 232 acres of typical Edwards Plateau (Hill Country) habitat preserved in a near-natural state by the San Antonio Department of Parks and Recreation. To reach the park, drive about 12 miles north of Loop 410 on I-10. Take the Camp Bullis exit, and turn left under I-10 at the underpass. Then drive north on the west side access road one mile to the sign "Friedrich Wilderness Park." Turn left, drive one-half mile to a dead end, and turn right to the entrance.

Located in the northwest section of Bexar County, the park provides the nearest location to the city for nesting Golden-cheeked-Warbler. There are seven trails within the park, each exemplifying a different habitat or feature of the park. All but one of the trails branch off the Main Loop Trail.

The nesting sites of the Golden-cheeked Warbler are usually where mature Ashe junipers are present. Ask at headquarters about recent sightings of the warbler as well as other notable sightings.

Other nesting species include Ash-throated Flycatcher, Bewick's Wren, Painted Bunting, Bullock's Oriole, Black-chinned Hummingbird, Verdin, Bell's Vireo, Yellow-breasted Chat, Orchard Oriole, and Lesser Goldfinch.

A brochure is available at headquarters listing some of the animals of the area, a list of "Hill Country" plants in the park, and archeological highlights.

The park is open from 9 am to 5 pm Wednesday through Sunday, with no admission after 4 pm.

Jack Judson Nature Trail

The Jack Judson Nature Trail is located within the Olmos Flood Basin along Hondondo and Olmos Creeks. The trail is rich in native trees and shrubs within the ten-acre area. Visitors should obtain permission from the Alamo Heights Police Department, (512) 822-3321, before entering the trails. There is a field trip here every weekend, including a monthly Beginner's Bird Walk.

Drive north on Broadway for two blocks past the intersection with US 81 Business (Austin Highway). Turn left on Ogden Lane, continue past two stop signs and turn left on Greely. Take the first right to the Nature Trail parking lot on the left.

Birds that nest include Inca Dove, Chuck-will's-widow, Great Crested Flycatcher, Carolina Wren, White-eyed Vireo, and House Finch.

During spring and fall, the Nature Trail can be a good location for migrating land birds, warblers, vireos, tanagers, thrushes, and grosbeaks.

In winter look for Northern Flicker, Brown Creeper, Blue-gray Gnatcatcher, "Solitary" Vireo, Brewer's Blackbird, Common Grackle, Spotted Towhee, Fox and Song Sparrows. Also, watch for these less common birds: Red-breasted Nuthatch, Winter Wren, Black-and-white Warbler, Purple Finch, and Pine Siskin.

Southside Lions Park

Southside Lions Park, 500 acres, is along Salado Creek in the southeast section of the city. Take I-37 south about three miles beyond IH 10 to the Pecan Valley Drive exit. Turn east on Pecan Valley Drive, and drive about two miles to the park.

A lake in the park is the wintering area for Northern Shoveler and other waterfowl. The bottomland along Salado Creek has the typical land birds of the area as permanent residents: Northern Cardinal, Carolina Chickadee, and Tufted Titmouse. Eastern Bluebird have been found nesting recently. In the mesquite shrub, about one-quarter of the park, look for typical South Texas birds such as Long-billed Thrasher and Cactus Wren. In winter, watch for Harris' and Vesper Sparrows.

W. W. McAllister Park

W. W. McAllister Park, 856 acres, operated by the San Antonio Department of Parks and Recreation, is north of the airport in the northern part of the city. From Loop 410 drive north on US 281 3.2 miles to Bitters Road, turn right (east) on Bitters Road to the junction with Starcrest, and continue straight ahead on Starcrest (Bitters Road veers to the right). At Jones-Maltsberger (0.9 mile from US 281), turn left (north) and drive 0.8 mile to the entrance on the right.

The park has a wide variety of habitats: extensive live oak groves, mesquite grasslands, and prairies. There is a large campground, as well as picnic areas and playgrounds.

When there is water in the lake, look for shorebirds during July, August, April, and May, and ducks in winter. Golden-crowned Kinglet and American Woodcock have been recorded here in winter. This is a good place for wintering sparrows.

The park is subject to large crowds on weekends; other times are better for birding.

Brackenridge Park

Brackenridge Park, 343 acres, is located on the San Antonio River about two miles north of downtown. It includes a large zoo, concessions, a golf course, picnicking, a playground, and the Sunken Gardens. From downtown, take either North St. Mary's or Broadway to the park. The zoo has approximately 700 bird species from around the world, including a male and female Whooping Crane.

The F. C. Hixon Tropical Bird House has a free-flying area in the center surrounded by 14 dioramas. Each diorama represents a specific habitat from a different part of the world. The scenes are changed periodically. The African Flight Cage features many birds from Africa in a large enclosed area. Visitors can enter and view the birds from within the cage.

Also, there is a large collection of waterbirds from around the world. These are joined in summer by Wood Duck and Black-bellied Whistling-Duck, and in winter by wild wintering ducks. Yellow-crowned Night-Heron nest regularly in the park.

The woodlands of the park can be very good for land birds during migration.

The San Antonio Botanical Center is just east of the park at 555 Funston Place. Wood Duck and Black-bellied Whistling-Duck can be found on the lake in summer. Plant communities from several Texas vegetational areas have been constructed here, making this a worthwhile stop whether there are any birds or not.

DEL RIO

Del Rio, population 30,000, is on the Rio Grande at the convergence of three major vegetational areas, the Chihuahuan Desert, the South Texas Plains, and the Edwards Plateau. Nearby is the Amistad Reservoir, an additional bird habitat. Most of the area is devoted to ranching. ALWAYS OBTAIN PERMISSION BEFORE ENTERING PRIVATE PROPERTY. If birding in the area during deer season, bright clothing is highly recommended.

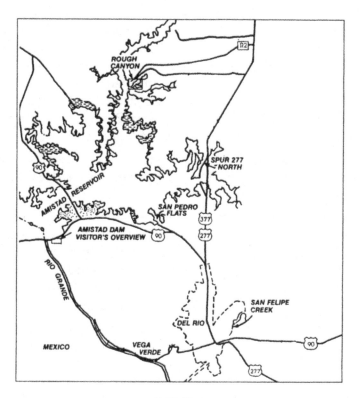

DEL RIO

Amistad National Recreation Area

Amistad National Recreation Area on the United States side of Amistad Reservoir offers marinas, boat ramps, swimming, fishing, hunting, picnicking, and camping. The reservoir, owned by the United States and Mexico, has 64,900 surface acres at conservation pool level. Watch for rattlesnakes on land and water moccasins in the water. Both are common, as are non-poisonous and beneficial snakes. Birding opportunities abound, not only on the water and the shoreline, but in the dry uplands surrounding the lake as well.

San Pedro Flats is on a southeast arm of the lake at the end of Spur 454. Spur 454 is 2.5 miles west of the intersection of US 90 and US 277-377 north of Del Rio. Permanent residents include Green Kingfisher, Cactus, Rock, and Canyon Wrens, Harris' Hawk, Chihuahuan Raven, Black-tailed Gnatcatcher, Olive Sparrow, Pyrrhuloxia, Verdin, and Scaled Quail. In summer look for Black-necked Stilt, Snowy Egret, Black-capped Vireo, Lesser Nighthawk, and Hooded Oriole. Say's Phoebe, Sage Thrasher, Green-tailed and Canyon Towhees are found in winter.

Migrants include American White Pelican, White-faced Ibis, Snowy Plover, Forster's Tern, and White-tailed and Mississippi Kites.

Spur 277 North is reached by driving north on US 277-377. Six miles from the US 90 intersection, turn right (south) after crossing the bridge and drive back to the lake. Here, bird along the park roads or hike along the lakeshore. Curve-billed Thrasher and Black-throated Sparrow are present year-round. In winter Cinnamon Teal and Lark Bunting have been recorded.

Rough Canyon is on the Devils River Arm of the lake. Drive 11 miles north on US 277-377 from the intersection with US 90 west, then left (west) on Recreation Road No. 2 for 6 miles to the marina where there are boat ramps, picnic tables and a Ranger Station. Black-tailed and Blue-gray Gnatcatchers, Canyon Wren, Osprey, Vermilion Flycatcher, and Fox Sparrow have been recorded.

Amistad Dam Visitor's Overview is 3 miles south of US 90 on Spur 349. Spur 349 is 7.6 miles west of the intersection of US 90 and US 277-377 north of the city. A Ringed Kingfisher is sometimes perched on the power plant railings or nearby. There are restrooms at the visitor's center near the dam.

San Felipe Creek

San Felipe Creek is created by San Felipe Springs, which has a daily flow of about 90 million gallons. From the downtown intersection of US 90 (Avenue F) and US 277 drive east on US 90 (Gibbs Avenue) one mile to San Felipe Springs Road. Turn north, then west off the pavement onto the dirt road before reaching the spring pumphouse. Park north of the dirt road. The gate is open from 7 am to 5:30 pm. Permission to bird the area north of the dirt road must be obtained from the golf course manager at the pro shop. Hike along the dirt road, cross the bridge, and bird north along the west side of the creek. Birds found year-round include Green Kingfisher, Great Kiskadee, Black Phoebe, Long-billed Thrasher, and Lesser Goldfinch. Brown-crested Flycatcher have been found in summer. Look for Marsh Wren and Brewer's Sparrow in winter. Another bird location along the creek is south of US 277. From the intersection of US 90 and US 277 downtown, drive south on US 277 about one mile to De La Rosa, go southwest two blocks, and park at the Nutrition Center, 1105 De La Rosa. Hike north to the paved walk along the creek.

Vega Verde

From the downtown intersection of US 90 east (Gibbs Avenue) and US 277-377, drive two blocks north on US 90 (Avenue F), turn left (west) on Second Street, go about 1 mile to St. Peter Street, turn south on St. Peter to Cienegas Road, then drive west about 1.5 miles to the ranch pond at the dam. Waterfowl (wild and domestic) are found in winter. Also, Neotropic Cormorant are common.

From the pond continue on Cienegas Road, cross the dam and turn south. Follow the pavement on Cienegas Road west to the River Road, about two miles from the pond. Before reaching the intersection, stop and scan the ponds on both sides of the road. Summer residents include Black-bellied Whistling-Duck and Groove-billed Ani. The River Road extends north about seven miles. To go further, park off the road, and walk up to the road along the railroad tracks. Couch's Kingbird have been recorded.

CHAPARRAL WILDLIFE MANAGEMENT AREA

Chaparral Wildlife Management Area, 15,200 acres, is located in Dimmit and LaSalle Counties, 8 miles west of Artesia Wells on FM 133. Artesia Wells is on I-35 about 103 miles south of San Antonio, or 52 miles north of Laredo. All visitors should check in at the office or campground for brochures, maps, and other infor-

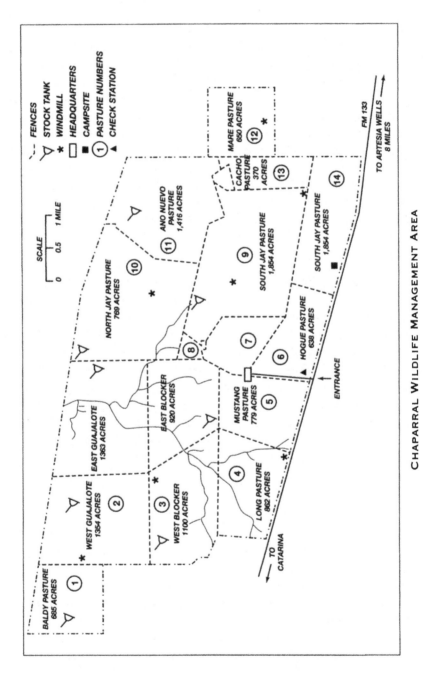

CHAPARRAL WILDLIFE MANAGEMENT AREA

mation. The office is generally open 8 am to 5 pm, Monday through Friday. Information kiosks are under construction near both entrances, for use when the office is closed.

Camping facilities are located 1.5 miles east of the main entrance. Picnic tables and restrooms with showers are available, but there is no water or electrical hookups. The campground entrance should be used for access whenever the main gate is closed.

The area is typical South Texas brush, dominated by mesquite, cactus, granjeno, blackbrush, whitebrush, and guayacan. Principal objectives of the area are research, land-use and game management, public hunting, and non-consumptive recreational use such as hiking and birding. There is an 8.5-mile driving trail, a 2-mile hiking trail, and a shorter hiking trail near the office. A detailed guide for each trail is available. All visitors, especially hikers, should be sure to carry water with them. Potable water is available at the office and campground. Hikers should also be aware that this is western diamondback rattlesnake country.

For entry, visitors must have either an Annual Public Hunting Permit, a Limited Use Permit, or a Texas Conservation Passsport (Silver or Gold). The area is not open for birding or other activities during any scheduled public hunts, i.e., the period from September 1st to March 31st. For entry during this period, call ahead to verify accessibility.

Nesting bird species include Harris' Hawk, Common Ground-Dove, Groove-bill Ani, Pauraque, Long-billed Thrasher, Verdin, Cactus Wren, Pyrrhuloxia, Painted Bunting, Olive, Black-throated and Cassin's Sparrows, and Bronzed Cowbird. The area checklist has over 180 species, including 10 warbler species and 14 sparrow species.

The address is P.O. Box 115, Artesia Wells, TX 78001, (830) 676-3413.

CHOKE CANYON STATE PARK

Choke Canyon State Park, 1,485 acres in the developed section of the park, is located 4.2 miles west of Three Rivers on SH 72. Three Rivers is about 70 miles south of San Antonio and 60 miles northwest of Corpus Christi. The park is in two non-contiguous units along the south shore of Choke Canyon Reservoir, 26,100 surface acres, on the Frio River. The reservoir was created to supply municipal water to the City of Corpus Christi. Camping, picnicking, boat ramps, fishing, a swimming pool with bathhouse, playgrounds, and concessions are available. Along the west shore is the James E. Daugherty Wildlife Management Area, 8,700 acres, where public hunting is conducted on a permit-only basis. FM 99 crosses the western portion of the reservoir where herons, egrets, cormorants, waterfowl in winter, etc., can be found.

The area below the dam along the river is a good area for a variety of birdlife, including Green Kingfisher.

In fall and winter the stands of flowering tree tobacco that surround the lake should be checked for hummingbirds: Rufous, Anna's, Black-chinned, Buff-bellied, and Broad-tailed have been recorded in recent years. Most have been found at the Calliham Unit but a few have been seen at the South Shore Unit.

The lands surrounding the reservoir are typical South Texas brushlands, where Greater Roadrunner, Verdin, Long-billed Thrasher, Cactus Wren, Black-throated Sparrow, Common Ground-Dove, collared peccary (javelina), and rattlesnakes are common.

A bird checklist (1994) with 243 species is available at both unit headquarters. The park address is Box 1548, Three Rivers, TX 78071, (512) 786-3538.

LAREDO

Lake Casa Blanca International State Park

Lake Casa Blanca International State Park, 525 acres, is located at the eastern edge of Laredo at the south end of Lake Casa Blanca. To reach the park from Laredo drive east on US 59 to the airport. Just east of the airport, drive north on Loop 20 to the park entrance.

The park offers picnicking, camping, restrooms with hot showers, swimming, fishing, a boat ramp, playgrounds, and a park store.

The habitats represented are typical South Texas upland brush, plus the lake and the cultural areas.

Franklin's Gull (January and sometimes in spring migration), Eared and Pied-billed Grebes (winter), Brown Pelican, (February), Audubon's Oriole (January) and Sage Thrasher have been recorded at the park. So far as is known there has been no regular birding at the park but from the few records available there should be the possibility of tropical species, such as Altamira Oriole, Great Kiskadee, and Olive Sparrow, xeric species like Pyrrhuloxia and Chihuahuan Raven, plus numerous ducks in winter, herons, egrets, gulls, terns and shorebirds on or near the lake.

The address is P.O. Box 1844, Laredo, TX 78044, (956) 725-3826.

Laredo Junior College

Laredo Junior College is located in the southwest section of Laredo adjacent to the Rio Grande. From downtown drive west on Washingon Street to the college. The following species have been recorded in the riparian habitat: White-collared Seedeater, Audubon's Oriole, Altamira Oriole, Great Kiskadee, Olive Sparrow, Green and Ringed Kingfishers, and Brewer's Sparrow. There is an excellent opportunity for systematic birding here.

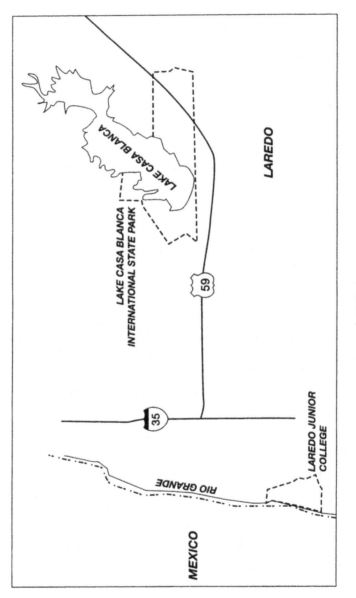

KINGSVILLE

Kingsville, population 28,000, is on US 77 about 40 miles southwest of Corpus Christi. The headquarters for the King Ranch, said to be the largest privately-owned ranch in the world with more than 800,000 acres, is located here as well as Texas A&M University–Kingsville. The close proximity of Baffin Bay and its estuaries, Cayo del Grullo and Laguna Salada, many fresh water ponds (except in prolonged drought), city and county parks, and woodlands and pastures on the large ranches combine to create abundant birding opportunities.

Species near the northern limit of their nesting range include White-tailed Hawk, Green Jay, Great Kiskadee, Brown-crested Flycatcher, Audubon's Oriole, and Buff-bellied Hummingbird. Other nesting species are Black-chinned and Ruby-throated Hummingbirds, Common Ground-Dove, and Hooded Oriole.

On the 1995 Christmas Bird Count 153 species were recorded including Least Grebe, Fulvous Whistling-Duck, Groove-billed Ani, Couch's Kingbird, Long-billed Thrasher, Olive Sparrow, and a Rufous-morph Red-tailed Hawk. Worthy of mention are 12 Rufous Hummingbirds, 226 Green Jays, 97 Great Kiskadees, 28 Vermilion Flycatchers, and over 1,500 Bronzed Cowbirds.

GREEN JAY

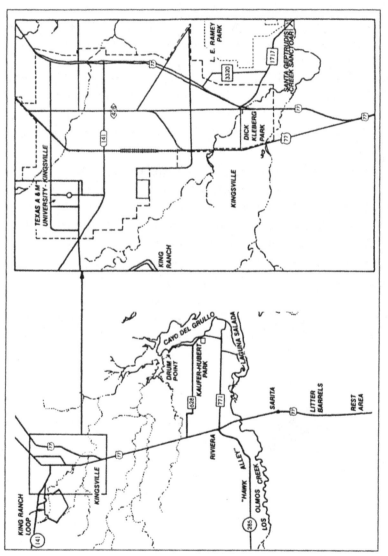

KINGSVILLE

King Ranch

To reach the King Ranch drive 2.5 miles west of the city on SH 141. Several hundred yards inside the entrance a sign will indicate a left turn to the ranch's tourism office. Make arrangements there for a variety of guided tours. Tours for bird seekers are offered also; call (512) 592-8055 for information.

Texas A&M University–Kingsville

The university is in the northwest part of the city. From US 77 Business drive west on Santa Gertrudis Blvd. to the campus or west on SH 141, then north on University Blvd. The Caesar Kleberg Wildlife Institute and the J. E. Conner Museum are located here. The museum has a collection of bird study skins and some natural history exhibits. The campus is a good spring migrant location. Birds that nest on campus include Hooded Oriole, Western King-bird, and White-winged Dove. Look for the oriole in the tall palms. Cave Swallows nest under the verandahs of several buildings.

Dick Kleberg Park

Dick Kleberg Park, another good spring migrant location, is at the south edge of the city between US 77 and US 77 Business and can be reach from either highway. Permanent residents are Pyrrhuloxia, and Golden-fronted and Ladder-backed Woodpeckers. In winter watch for Vermilion Flycatcher (regular), Cave Swallow (sometimes) and Couch's Kingbird (occasional).

L. E. Ramey Park

From US 77 drive east on either Gen. Cavazos or FM 1717, turn onto FM 3320 and follow the signs. Drive behind the tennis courts to the brush lining the old runways. This is on the back side of the golf course where there is a large pond. The ponds of the golf course can have Least and American Bitterns, Sora, Mottled Duck, and other waterfowl. In the mesquite, watch for Groove-billed Ani, Lesser Nighthawk, and Great Horned Owl.

Santa Gertrudis Creek Sanctuary

Near the south end of the city, drive left (east) from US 77 on FM 1717 where there is an excellent cattail marsh about one mile southeast of the city. Formed by wastewater discharge, the marsh can be birded by walking 100 yards or so along the levee on the east side of the road. There is a viewing platform about 75 yards down the levee. In winter look for Swamp Sparrow, Marsh Wren, Least and Eared Grebes, rails, ducks and wading birds. A Ringed Kingfisher was here from early November, 1996, to January, 1997.

Drum Point

For shorebirds, herons, egrets, and wintering ducks drive south on US 77 about 12 miles to FM 628, then east to county road 2250 (King's Inn Seafood Restaurant is just past this county road), and drive north on 2250 about one mile where it veers to the west. Continue about 0.7 mile to county road 1132, turn north and drive to the bluff. Below the bluff the pavement soon ends, and the caliche road can be very slick and perhaps impassable when wet. If there immediately after a rain be very careful. Continue on this road to Drum Point. All fishermen of the area know where Drum Point is if these directions are too involved. It is usually worth the trouble to get there. Wilson's Plover and Least Tern nest here, nearly all Texas herons and egrets are present most of the year, and waterfowl winter in large numbers. Thousands of Lesser Scaup, hundreds of Bufflehead, and other waterfowl species in smaller numbers have been recorded. There are often as many as a half-dozen or more white-morph Reddish Egret present in late summer. Shorebirds are found in large numbers in migration and wintering, and since shorebirds are either going south or north on the Texas coast all year they can be expected most any time. Rarities found here include White-winged Scoter and Oldsquaw.

Kaufer-Hubert Park

Kaufer-Hubert Park is about one mile south of where FM 628 turns southeast and Vattmann Creek empties into Baffin Bay.

Shorebirds and wading birds can gather in profusion. Trailer hookups are available for campers.

Riviera, Vattmann

All farm and ranch ponds in the area, and there are many, should be checked for rarities. On ponds in and near Riviera, 16 miles south of Kingsville on US 77, a Garganey was found in the spring of 1985 and a Masked Duck in the early 1990's. Another rarity is the Gray Hawk, which has been seen near Riviera and also near Ricardo, most recently during fall and winter, 1996. Buff-breasted Sandpiper have been found in large numbers on freshwater just south of Vattmann. Vattmann is on FM 628 east of US 77. South of Vattmann at the end of FM 2510 is Laguna Salada, another bird spot where Eurasian Wigeon was found in January, 1988.

Sprague's Pipit have been found more or less regularly in winter along FM 772 north of Vattmann. From Vattmann drive north, then west, then north again. When the road turns west again, the Sprague's Pipit area has been reached. Look for fields where grass has been baled, as other areas will likely be unproductive. The pipits are usually abundant and landowners have allowed birders to enter. PLEASE RESPECT PRIVATE PROPERTY AND ASK PERMISSION BEFORE ENTERING.

US 77 South, Sarita, SH 285

Resident hawks are Harris' and White-tailed as well as a few Red-tailed and Crested Caracara. All can usually be seen on US 77 south of the city.

In late winter some of the ranchers sometimes conduct controlled burns to discourage invading plants and to encourage grass. This brings White-tailed Hawks and other raptors to the site by the dozens looking for easy prey; a rare sight indeed.

Wintering hawks, in addition to those cited, include White-tailed Kite, Merlin and occasionally Ferruginous Hawk.

SH 285, west of Riviera, is called "Hawk Alley" by local birders. Thousands of Broad-winged Hawks, and hundreds of Mississippi Kites and Swainson's Hawks have been sighted along this road in fall migration, mid-September to mid-October.

There are several worthwhile bird stops on US 77 south of Riviera. Los Olmos Creek is two miles south of Riviera. About 0.3 mile south of the creek there is a historical marker where Hooded Orioles nest in palms. The ponds north of the courthouse in Sarita are usually productive. Turn right at the flashing yellow light, drive to the courthouse and turn right again. About 1.7 miles south of Sarita there is a large Cave Swallow colony under a cattle run bridge. Most of the nests are under the northbound lane. South 1 more mile there is a litter barrel; another 0.5 mile another litter barrel; then 3 miles to a large rest area with picnic and restroom facilities; finally another 0.5 mile to a large rest stop on the west side of the highway. Birds recorded at these locations include Lesser Goldfinch, Summer Tanager, Eastern Bluebird, Ferruginous Pygmy-Owl, Tropical Parula, Clay-colored Robin, Buff-bellied Hummingbird, and Curve-billed Thrasher. This is also close to where some Aplomado Falcon have been released.

Checklists of the birds of Kleberg (1994), Brooks (1994), and Kenedy (1996) counties, Texas, are available from Paul C. Palmer, 615 S. Wanda, Kingsville, TX 78363 for 25 cents each plus stamped, addressed business-sized envelope. They can also be picked up at the Conner Museum on the Texas A&I University campus. A checklist for Jim Wells County is in preparation.

ALICE

Alice is 45 miles west of Corpus Christi in the heart of the South Texas Plains. A favorite birding spot locally is Lake Alice. The lake is north of the city at the end of North Texas Boulevard. From US 281 north of the city turn east on FM 3376 (Commerce Road), go 1.5 miles to North Texas Boulevard, turn north (left), and drive 0.5 mile to the lake. From the intersection of SH 44 and

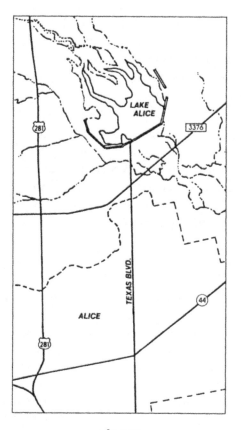

ALICE

North Texas Boulevard, drive north on North Texas Boulevard about 2.7 miles to the lake.

The lake, about 90 acres, is operated by the City of Alice for municipal water supply. Camping is allowed but there are no facilities. There is unrestricted public access. It is a popular spot for fishermen.

For birds, park at one of the parking areas and walk the dike or shoreline. Only pedestrian traffic is allowed beyond the parking areas. In general, the west side of the lake is more productive for birds.

Permanent residents include Great Kiskadee, Groove-billed Ani, Least Grebe, Black-bellied Whistling-Duck, Long-billed Thrasher, Green Jay, and Olive Sparrow. Winter residents are Sandhill Crane, Sprague's Pipit (in grass pastures), Say's Phoebe, geese, and ducks. Audubon's Oriole, Wood Stork, and Roseate Spoonbill are seen from time to time.

In migration large concentrations of Couch's, Western, and Eastern Kingbirds are recorded, as well as warblers and shorebirds. A very rare visitor was a Snail Kite in 1977, the only fully-accepted record of this species ever in Texas. Over 90 species have been recorded here in one day on at least two occasions, once in spring, and once in fall.

LOWER RIO GRANDE VALLEY

The Lower Rio Grande Valley, a subregion of South Texas, is generally considered to be the part of Texas that was formerly the flood plain of the Rio Grande. The river has changed courses several times as it nears the Gulf, leaving resacas (oxbows) and alluvial deposits that are very fertile. The area has been almost completely cleared for agriculture. Citrus and vegetables are the principal crops, with much of the land irrigated from the river. The traditional valley is an irregular line from just north of Mission to just south of Raymondville but birdwise could be considered to include the lands adjacent to the river up to and including the International Falcon Reservoir. The vegetation is the same as the South Plains, except for a few Mexican species that reach their northern limit along the Rio Grande. These plants include Montezuma bald cypress, Texas palmetto (also called sabal palm), ebony, and others.

Before being cleared, the Valley was composed of dense brush, a small portion of which is preserved at Santa Ana National Wildlife Refuge, Bentsen-Rio Grande Valley State Park, and a few other locations.

RARE BIRD ALERT for the Rio Grande Valley, (956) 969-2731.

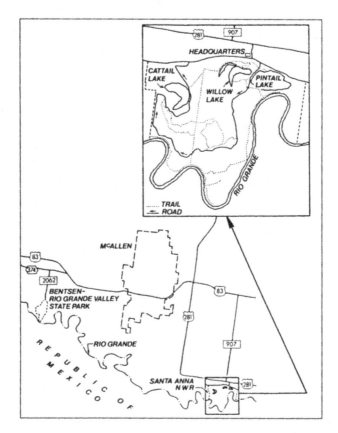

LOWER RIO GRANDE VALLEY

Some of the nesting species include Plain Chachalaca, White-tipped Dove, Groove-billed Ani, Buff-bellied Hummingbird, Green and Ringed Kingfishers, Couch's Kingbird, Great Kiskadee, Green Jay, Audubon's and Altamira Orioles, and Olive Sparrow.

White-collared Seedeater were once more common in the Valley than they are now, but they have been found in recent years in winter behind the library in Zapata, along the river at Chapeno Falls (just south of Falcon Dam), and in the village of San Ygnacio, which is 14 miles northwest of Zapata on US 83. They also breed in the area but are very difficult to find.

SANTA ANA NATIONAL WILDLIFE REFUGE

Referred to as the "Gem of the National Wildlife Refuge System," Santa Ana NWR is generally considered one of the "must" places to look for birds in Texas and, indeed, the nation. The refuge is located on the Rio Grande between the flood control levee of the International Boundary and Water Commission and the river between McAllen and Brownsville.

To reach the refuge from McAllen, drive 6 miles east on US 83 to Alamo, and turn south on FM 907 to US 281. Go east 0.5 mile to the entrance sign.

Santa Ana NWR contains 2,088 acres preserving a remnant of the native subtropical vegetation that made up much of the Lower Valley before the land was cleared for farming and development. There is a one-way loop road through the refuge and a dozen or more trails that crisscross around the lakes, woodlands, and thick brush that comprise the refuge. The river is the southern boundary. Plan to walk some trails and the edges of some of the lakes to realize the maximum number of bird possibilities available. Currently, driving through the refuge is limited from late November to the end of April. When driving is limited a tram may be available. Foot access is allowed seven days per week, sunrise to sunset. Check at the Visitor Center for policy at time of visit. Due to heavy visitation, recorded bird calls are prohibited.

Visitors should stop at the Visitor's Center for information on recent sightings and to pick up a checklist, a map, and other information. Visitor Center hours are 8 am to 4:30 pm Monday through Friday, 9 am to 4:30 pm Saturday, Sunday, and Holidays. The refuge is closed Thanksgiving, Christmas, and New Day Year's.

Trail A is paved (handicapped access) from the trailhead south of the Visitor's Center to Willow Lake. This trail can be very productive, with Least Grebe, Purple Gallinule, Common Moorhen,

Ringed Kingfisher, Black-necked Stilt, numerous duck species in winter at the lake, plus whatever surprises the refuge has to offer. The woodlands on the way to the lake and the cattail marshes surrounding the lake provide additional habitats.

Many Mexican species may be found that are near their northern limit. Of course, the same can be said for the other birding locations in the Lower Valley, such as Bentsen-Rio Grande Valley State Park, Anzalduas County Park south of Mission, Laguna-Atascosa NWR, and the Falcon Dam area.

Nesting birds include Least Bittern, Black-bellied Whistling-Duck, Hook-billed Kite (not usually easy to find), Harris' Hawk, Purple Gallinule, White-winged Dove, Barn and Elf Owls, Pauraque, Great Kiskadee, Brown-crested Flycatcher, Long-billed Thrasher, Tropical Parula, and Bronzed Cowbird.

Masked Duck, Gray Hawk (nest rarely), Northern Jacana, Red-billed Pigeon, Rose-throated Becard, Northern Beardless-Tyrannulet, Clay-colored Robin, Rufous-backed Robin, and Yellow-green Vireo have been recorded but are not usually easy to find. A Crane Hawk visited from December, 1987, to April, 1988, which I had the good fortune to see. It was the first-ever record for the United States.

Many migrants funnel up and down the southern tip of Texas. Their concentrations at the refuge can be spectacular. Broad-winged Hawks have been reported in the thousands. Forty-three warbler species, most in migration, are on the refuge checklist. Accidentals from Mexico include Gray-crowned Yellowthroat, Golden-crowned Warbler, and Blue Bunting.

A walk among the tall trees around the clearing south of the levee (site of the old headquarters) can be a very good introduction to the land birds of the refuge. Altamira Oriole, Green Jay, Plain Chachalaca, and White-tipped Dove should be easy to find. The red flowers surrounding the clearing attract hummingbirds.

I have many fond memories of birding experiences at Santa Ana NWR. With no diary of all my trips, I don't know exactly how

ALTAMIRA ORIOLE

many times I have been there, but the first time was April, 1966, and I have birded there many times since. Masked Duck, Northern Jacana, Hook-billed Kite, Gray Hawk, Northern Beardless-Tyrannulet, Yellow-green Vireo, Tropical Parula, Crane Hawk and Buff-bellied Hummingbird come to mind as some of the highlights.

In particular I remember the Hook-billed Kite. The plan was for a one-day trip—to leave Austin early, see the bird, and return late. On the way there was car trouble, which cost us two or three hours, but eventually the car was made whole again, and we were on our way. The grapevine said the birds came to a certain grove of trees just west of the refuge and so shouldn't be hard to see, but no one passed this information on to the birds.

We stayed all afternoon until nearly dark. Then the word was that they were very easy to see first thing in the morning. So with not even a toothbrush for an overnight stay, it was decided we should give the kites a chance in the morning, and we spent the night. Sure enough, about 7 a.m. the kites made their appearance and were duly recorded on our lists. With their bulky body and rounded wings, they looked nothing like a White-tailed Kite or Mississippi Kite. Satisfied we had recorded a very rare bird in Texas, we returned to Austin, 300 miles north.

There is a chance to see not only many unique bird species but also the other animals and plants that were common in the Lower Valley before the land was cleared. The refuge brochure states that more than 450 species of plants and 29 species of mammals have been recorded.

A bird checklist (1995) is available at the visitor's center with 388 species plus 11 hypothetical species, a great number for only 2,080 acres.

To contact the Refuge Manager, write Route 2, Box 202-A, Alamo, TX 78516 or call (512) 787-3079. Picnicking and camping are not allowed on the refuge.

LOWER RIO GRANDE VALLEY NATIONAL WILDLIFE REFUGE

At the time of writing, the refuge has 65,000 acres in over 100 tracts. The refuge may eventually contain as much as 132,500 acres in Starr, Hidalgo, Cameron, and Willacy counties, depending on availability of funds. The plan is to preserve portions of 11 different habitat types reflecting the natural diversity of the area. More than 100 unique vertebrate species occur in the region that are endangered, threatened, or at the periphery of their range.

To visit, permission must be obtained from the refuge manager. The tract at La Sal Vieja west of Raymondville and one just east of Santa Ana NWR can be birded from public roads. The address is the same as that of Santa Ana National Wildlife Refuge.

BENTSEN–RIO GRANDE VALLEY STATE PARK

Bentsen–Rio Grande Valley State Park, 588 acres, is located about 20 miles up the Rio Grande from Santa Ana NWR. To reach the park drive west from Mission for 5 miles on US 83 to Loop 374. Continue west 1.5 miles to FM 2062, then turn south to the park. The park has camping, picnicking, fishing, hiking, and restrooms with hot showers.

The park bird list is very similar to that of the Santa Ana NWR, but some species have been easier for me to find at Bentsen than at Santa Ana. These include Red-billed Pigeon and Barn and Elf Owls. In summer Groove-billed Ani are very common. Hook-billed Kite are permanent residents but are not always easy to find. Blue Bunting, both male and female, have been recorded but are very rare. Other rarities found here include Roadside Hawk, Masked Tityra, and Ruddy Quail-Dove.

An advantage of Bentsen over Santa Ana is that you can camp and do some night and early morning birding. A favorite activity of some observers is to drive or walk the park roads after dark to look for Pauraque on the road and to listen and look for owls.

The practice of playing cassette tapes to attract owls at night may be overdone at this park. Because of heavy birding pressure, especially in winter, birders are cautioned about excessive harassment of the birds.

The Singing Chaparral Trail, which starts just south of the headquarters, will acquaint the visitor with the vegetation of the Lower Valley, especially if one of the brochures available at headquarters is taken along. A longer hiking trail in the park leads through dense trees from the loop road south to the Rio Grande.

The bird checklist (1991), with 291 species recorded within the park and adjoining land, is available at headquarters. There is also a list of reptiles and amphibians with 28 species. The address is P.O. Box 988, Mission, TX 78572, (512) 585-1107.

SANTA MARGARITA RANCH

The Santa Margarita Ranch has been one of the best places in the United States to find the Brown Jay, a bird which has been regular north of Mexico for only a couple of decades. The ranch is located on the Rio Grande off old US 83 between Falcon Dam and Roma-Los Saenz. Approximately 8 miles north of Roma-Los Saenz (or 6 miles south of Falcon Dam), the old highway jogs west from US 83. There are three gravel roads that lead from the old highway toward the river; take the middle one at the top of the hill, and drive to the ranch where there are several houses. This is private property, and a fee is charged for entry. Stop at the houses until someone comes out to collect the fee. Drive straight toward the river, park at the top of the bluff, and walk to the river.

Though the jays are sometimes seen at other locations, this site has been a very reliable one. They are usually found along the river below the bluff. In addition to Brown Jay, Santa Margarita Ranch is also an excellent place for most of the other Valley specialties, including Hook-billed Kite, Green and Ringed Kingfishers, Olive Sparrow, Green Jay, and Great Kiskadee.

SALINEÑO

Salineño is a small village between US 83 and the Rio Grande. Watch for the highway sign on US 83 about 1.2 miles north of the entrance to Santa Margarita Ranch. Drive south 2 miles to the village, then follow the main road straight through town to the river and park. There is a trail upriver (west) where Audubon's Oriole and Brown Jay have been sighted. Watch also for the Hook-billed Kite. There is a private trailer area where some "Snowbirds," as northerners who spend the winter in the valley are sometimes called, feed birds. Visitors are welcome in the trailer area from November to March 15th when residents are present. Please sign the register. Birders should respect the privacy of these folks, but by standing a good distance away an observer can sometimes see

Brown and Green Jays, and Altamira and Audubon's Orioles at the feeders. Muscovy Duck has been sighted along the river but is not expected regularly.

FALCON DAM

Falcon Dam spans the Rio Grande to form International Falcon Reservoir. It is owned jointly by the United States and Mexico and is operated by the International Boundary and Water Commission for power generation, flood control, municipal and irrigation water supply, and recreation. The lake has 87,210 surface acres at conservation storage level.

The most popular birding location is the area just below and east of the dam on the Texas side. Take the paved road to the left (south) off the road to the dam to the parking lot overlooking the spillway. It is about a one-mile hike downriver from the parking lot at the dam to where birds can be expected. It can be very hot

FALCON RESERVOIR AREA

here any time of the year, therefore, taking water on this walk is recommended. This is one of the best places in the United States to find three kingfisher species: Ringed, Belted, and Green; sometimes all three are present at the same time. If all three are not found here try Chapeno Falls, Salineño, Santa Margarita Ranch, and/or Fronton, all immediately south along US 83.

In addition to kingfishers, other birds to look for on this hike include Brown Jay, Northern Beardless-Tyrannulet, White-collared Seedeater, and Ferruginous Pygmy-Owl (a very rare species in Texas, especially in areas accessible to the public). A stray Rufous-capped Warbler was recorded here in 1973, the first United States record. In addition, most of the specialities of the Lower Valley occur in these woods, including Altamira and Audubon's Orioles, Great Kiskadee, Green Jay, and Olive Sparrow.

Chapeno Falls is reached by driving south from Falcon Heights. Brown Jay, Red-billed Pigeon, and White-collared Seedeater have been found there recently.

FALCON STATE PARK

Falcon State Park, 572 acres, is located on the Rio Grande just off US 83, 29 miles northwest of Rio Grande City or 25 miles southeast of Zapata. The park includes about 4 miles of shoreline on International Falcon Reservoir and offers camping, screen shelters, picnicking, fishing, trails, a boat ramp, swimming, and restrooms with hot showers.

In the park most of the birds are those expected in the semi-desert portion of the South Texas region: Scaled Quail, Inca Dove, Greater Roadrunner, Ash-throated Flycatcher, Black-throated Sparrow, Pyrrhuloxia, Verdin, Curve-billed Thrasher, Cactus Wren, and Chihuahuan Raven.

Look for Crested Caracara, Harris' Hawk, and White-tailed Kite in the open country north of the park and the river. Neotropic Cormorant and Vermilion Flycatcher are found along the river and reservoir. The reservoir attracts many species not otherwise expect-

CRESTED CARACARA

ed in this xeric environment; for example, there are 24 waterfowl, 19 shorebirds, and 17 gulls and terns on the park checklist. Ring-billed Gulls are very common in winter. Least Terns nest. The dawn calls of the ready-to-migrate Common Loon in late winter seem totally out of place in the desert-like surroundings.

This is rattlesnake country, so walk carefully, especially at night.

A bird checklist (1996) with 290 species, which includes the area below the dam, is available at park headquarters. The park address is P.O. Box 2, Falcon Heights, TX 78545, (956) 848-5327.

LAGUNA ATASCOSA NATIONAL
WILDLIFE REFUGE

Laguna Atascosa National Wildlife Refuge, 45,190 acres, is about 25 miles east of Harlingen on Laguna Madre. From Harlingen drive east on FM 106 to the intersection with FM 1847. Continue east on the county road to the refuge entrance. From north of Harlingen, go east on FM 508 until it joins FM 106. From Brownsville, drive north on FM 1847 to the intersection with FM 106, then east on the county road.

The Visitor Center is open daily from 10 am to 4 pm October through April; 10 am to 4 pm weekends in May; and is closed June through September. The refuge administrative office is open weekdays year-round from 8 am to 4:30 pm. The refuge tour roads are open daily from sunrise to sunset.

The refuge is typical coastal prairie, with grass and cacti in the low places and thick brush on the higher ground. Practically all of the brush seems to have thorns. For contrast, there are 7,000 acres of ponds and marshes as well as about 12 miles of shoreline frontage on Laguna Madre. Each offers different animal and plant habitats.

Canada, Snow, and Greater White-fronted Geese and Sandhill Crane are plentiful in winter and should be looked for in cultivated fields along the roads leading to the refuge as well as within its boundaries. Check among the Snow Geese carefully for an occasional Ross' Goose.

Laguna Madre, Laguna Atascosa, and the ponds of the refuge support about two dozen species of ducks. Black-bellied Whistling-Duck and Mottled Duck are regular nesters. Blue-winged Teal are uncommon in spring and summer. Masked Duck has occurred but is not expected. Large numbers of Redhead winter on Laguna Madre.

The Bayside Tour, a 15-mile, one-way drive through the southern section of the refuge, leads through marshlands, ponds, sever-

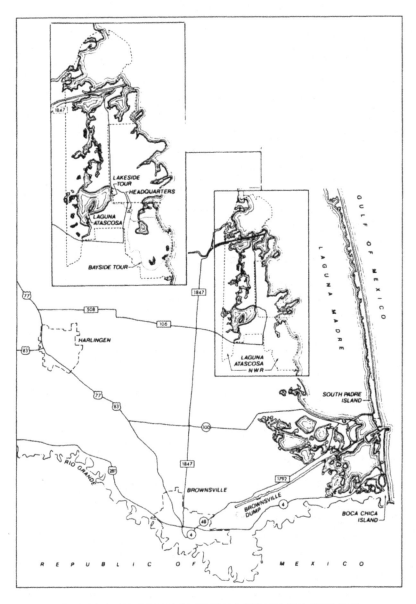

LAGUNA ATASCOSA NATIONAL WILDLIFE REFUGE

al miles of Laguna Madre, and through the dry uplands on the west side. Shorebirds, waterfowl, herons, and egrets, including the Reddish Egret, are plentiful in the marshlands. A White-cheeked Pintail spent the winter of 1978–79 on one of the inland ponds.

Most of the specialty species of the Lower Valley can be found, such as Harris' Hawk, Pauraque, Brown-crested Flycatcher, Bronzed Cowbird, Olive Sparrow, Couch's Kingbird, Great Kiskadee, Groove-billed Ani, Plain Chachalaca, Green Jay, and Long-billed Thrasher.

In spring, listen and look for Varied Bunting and Botteri's Sparrow in the open brush country along the west side of the Bayside Tour. Both nest regularly on the refuge. Other regular nesters include the Crested Caracara, White-tailed Kite, Cassin's Sparrow, and Lesser Nighthawk. Nesting species of the marshes and Laguna Madre are Wilson's Plover, Black-necked Stilt, Least Grebe, King Rail, Common Moorhen, and occasionally Purple Gallinule. Nesting in the dry uplands are Cactus Wren, Curve-billed Thrasher, Verdin, and occasionally Chihauhuan Raven and Black-throated Sparrow.

PLAIN CHACHALACA

Laguna Atascosa NWR is also a great place to be during spring migration. Many species stop here to feed and rest on their journey north: Baltimore Oriole, Blue Grosbeak, Indigo Bunting, and Rose-breasted Grosbeak. Seven vireo species and 35 warbler species have been recorded in spring. Two of the warblers, Common Yellowthroat and Yellow-breasted Chat, nest.

The 1.5-mile Lakeside Tour leads to Laguna Atascosa, the 3,100-acre lake that gives the refuge its name. In addition to waterfowl there is usually a Western Grebe or two on Laguna Atascosa in winter.

I remember a field trip in November when it was cold, raining, and muddy. We tallied 93 species in about 6 hours, mostly without getting out of the car. This is the only place in Texas I have seen a wild long-tailed weasel. In August, 1985, I and ten other birders saw a vagrant Red-faced Warbler at the picnic area near headquarters.

The first United States record of an Orange-billed Nightingale-Thrush was recorded at the refuge in April, 1996.

Captive-raised Aplomado Falcon have been released on the refuge in an effort to restore them to their historic range. Occasionally one is seen.

A bird checklist (1992) is available at headquarters with 391 species. The current count is 402 species. The address of the Refuge Manager is P.O. Box 450, Rio Hondo, TX 78583, (956) 748-3607. There is no camping on the refuge.

BROWNSVILLE

Birds of the Valley can be found in all directions from Brownsville. Red-crowned Parrot and Green Parakeet are permanent residents in substantial numbers at times. In the city in winter, watch for strays from Mexico: Clay-colored Robin and Golden-crowned Warbler, for example, which make an appearance occasionally. For several years, Tropical Kingbird has been seen and heard. Check the rare bird alert for current information about rarities. The surrounding area has many resacas replenished by rainfall and periodic floods. Hurricanes, which strike the Lower Valley from time to time, often with torrential rain, are another water source. In addition to the resacas, hurricane water collects in numerous low places and will sometimes remain for several years. This casual water attracts wintering and migrating waterfowl and shorebirds and, from the south, an occasional Masked Duck and Northern Jacana.

Boca Chica is on the Gulf of Mexico about 25 miles east of Brownsville on SH 4. After reaching the end of SH 4, a drive south along the beach will lead to the mouth of the Rio Grande. Laughing, Ring-billed, and Herring Gulls, Sanderling, Black-bellied, Snowy, and Piping Plovers, and Ruddy Turnstone are regulars along the beach in winter. Watch for migrating hawks such as Merlin and Peregrine Falcon.

A drive north from the end of SH 4 will lead to the mouth of the Brownsville ship channel. The stone jetty is sometimes worth checking, especially in winter. One winter a Purple Sandpiper was found.

Rarities that have been found in winter include Lesser Black-backed, Thayer's, and Glaucous Gulls, and Northern Gannet. In summer Wilson's Plover, and Least, Sandwich, Royal, and Caspian Terns are common.

South Padre Island is reached by driving northeast from Brownsville on SH 48 about 23 miles to Port Isabel, then east over the causeway to the island. Drive north on PR 100 and then on the beach for the same birds listed previously. Here the white phase of the Reddish Egret is often found.

Port Isabel can be reached from Harlingen by driving south on US 77-83 for 6 miles, then east on SH 100 for 24 miles.

The Brownsville dump has been an excellent location for years for Tamaulipas Crow, November through March, along with Chihuahuan Raven and the numerous Great-tailed Grackle. The dump is just south of the Port of Brownsville on FM 511, 1.5 miles north of SH 4, or 0.5 mile south of SH 48. The Tamaulipas Crow numbers have declined in recent years and they now are far outnumbered by the ravens and grackles. Listen for the nasal Fish Crow-like sound of the Tamaulipas Crow.

Sabal Palm Sanctuary is owned and maintained by the National Audubon Society to protect a small relict stand of Sabal palm, (*Sabal mexicana*), once much more widespread along the Rio Grande. To reach the sanctuary from Brownsville, drive east on SH 4 or SH 48 to FM 511, drive south on FM 511 until it becomes FM 3068, continue south to dead end at FM 1419, then drive west on FM 1419 about 0.7 mile to the first road south, which leads to the sanctuary. Rare winter visitors in the past have included Crimson-collared Grosbeak and Gray-crowned Yellowthroat. Buff-bellied Hummingbirds are usually at feeders provided.

A Checklist of Texas Birds

This appendix is the official list of all bird species accepted for Texas by the Texas Bird Records Committee (TBRC) of the Texas Ornithological Society. The list totals 606 species as of July 14, 1997, two are extinct and one is extirpated.

The numbers change continuously: new birds keep showing up and review of past records is an ongoing project. I have added nesting symbols (* or **) for the species I believe nest in Texas or have nested in the past.

Following the Accepted List is the Presumptive List, an additional 13 species lacking full acceptance by the committee or presently under review by the committee.

To be considered a fully accepted species on the Texas list at least one of the following is required:

1. An extant specimen identified by a recognized authority together with convincing evidence that the specimen was obtained within Texas.
2. One or more photographs that clearly demonstrate definitive characters with convincing evidence that the photographs were taken within Texas.
3. A tape recording of a bird vocalization that clearly demonstrates definitive characters with convincing evidence that the recording was made within Texas.

In addition to 1, 2, or 3 above, the record itself must be reviewed and accepted by the TBRC. At time of writing, the Saltmarsh Sharp-tailed Sparrow has been accepted, however, it is apparently still under review.

The English and scientific names and sequence follow the Check-list of North American Birds, Sixth Edition, 1983, American Ornithologists' Union, as amended through the Forty-first Supplement, 1997. This supplement was released at the time this manuscript was going to press. A diligent effort has been made to accurately reflect the many changes. Of interest to Texans are the movement of the American Vultures from the order Falconiformess (Diurnal Birds of Prey) to the order Ciconiformes (Herons, Ibises, Storks, and Allies), changing the sequence of several families, genera, and species, raising several subfamilies to family rank, and the splitting of the Solitary Vireo into three species (Blue-headed Vireo, Cassin's Vireo, and Plumbeous Vireo), and the splitting of the Plain Titmouse into two species (Juniper Titmouse [Texas] and Oak Titmouse [western United States]).

The following symbols are used:

(E) Extinct

(e) Extirpated

(A) The committee requests details of future records

(I) Introduced

(u) Uncertain origin

(*) Has nested since 1930, more or less

(**) No nest record since 1930, more or less

The committee requests as many details as possible, such as time, place, observers, photographs, recordings, etc., for all species with the symbol (A). Please send to Texas Bird Records Committee, c/o Dr. Keith A. Arnold, Department of Wildlife and Fisheries Sciences, Texas A&M University, College Station, TX 77843, or Gregory W. Lasley, 305 Loganberry Court, Austin, TX 78745-6527.

ACCEPTED TEXAS SPECIES

Order GAVIIFORMES: Loons
Family GAVIIDAE: Loons
Red-throated Loon (A)
Gavia stellata
Pacific Loon
Gavia pacifica
Common Loon
Gavia immer
Yellow-billed Loon (A)
Gavia adamsii

Order PODICIPEDIFORMES: Grebes
Family PODICIPEDIDAE: Grebes
Least Grebe*
Tachybaptus dominicus
Pied-billed Grebe*
Podilymbus podiceps
Horned Grebe
Podiceps auritus
Red-necked Grebe (A)
Podiceps grisegena
Eared Grebe*
Podiceps nigricollis
Western Grebe
Aechmophorus occidentalis
Clark's Grebe
Aechmophorus clarkii

Order PROCELLARIIFORMES: Tube-nosed Swimmers
Family DIOMEDEIDAE: Albatrosses
Yellow-nosed Albatross (A)
Thalassarche chlororhynchos

Family PROCELLARIIDAE: Shearwaters and Petrels
White-chinned Petrel (A)
Procellaria aequinoctialis

Cory's Shearwater
Calonectris diomedea

Greater Shearwater (A)
Puffinus gravis

Sooty Shearwater (A)
Puffinus griseus

Manx Shearwater (A)
Puffinus puffinus

Audubon's Shearwater (A)
Puffinus lherminieri

Family HYDROBATIDAE: Storm-Petrels

Wilson's Storm-Petrel (A)
Oceanites oceanicus

Leach's Storm-Petrel (A)
Oceanodroma leucorhoa

Band-rumped Storm-Petrel (A)
Oceanodroma castro

Order PELECANIFORMES: Totipalmate Swimmers

Family PHAETHONTIDAE: Tropicbirds

Red-billed Tropicbird (A)
Phaethon aethereus

Family SULIDAE: Boobies and Gannets

Masked Booby
Sula dactylatra

Blue-footed Booby (A)
Sula nebouxii

Brown Booby (A)
Sula leucogaster

Red-footed Booby (A)
Sula sula

Northern Gannet
Morus bassanus

Family PELECANIDAE: Pelicans

American White Pelican*
Pelecanus erythrorhynchos

Brown Pelican*
Pelecanus occidentalis

Family PHALACROCORACIDAE: Cormorants

Double-crested Cormorant*
Phalacrocorax auritus

Neotropic Cormorant*
Phalacrocorax brasilianus

Family ANHINGIDAE: Darters

Anhinga*
Anhinga anhinga

Family FREGATIDAE: Frigatebirds

Magnificent Frigatebird*
Fregata magnificens

Order CICONIIFORMES: Herons, Ibises, Storks and Allies

Family ARDEIDAE: Bitterns and Herons

Tribe BOTAURINI: Bitterns

American Bittern*
Botaurus lentiginosus

Least Bittern*
Ixobrychus exilis

Tribe ARDEINI: Typical Herons

Great Blue Heron*
Ardea herodias

Great Egret*
Ardea alba

Snowy Egret*
Egretta thula

Little Blue Heron*
Egretta caerulea

Tricolored Heron*
Egretta tricolor

Reddish Egret*
Egretta rufescens

Cattle Egret*
Bubulcus ibis

Green Heron*
Butorides virescens

Tribe NYCTICORACINI: Night-Herons

Black-crowned Night-Heron*
Nycticorax nycticorax

Yellow-crowned Night-Heron*
Nyctanassa violacea

Family THRESKIORNITHIDAE: Ibises and Spoonbills

Subfamily THRESKIORNITHINAE: Ibises

White Ibis*
Eudocimus albus

Glossy Ibis
Plegadis falcinellus

White-faced Ibis*
Plegadis chihi

Subfamily PLATALEINAE: Spoonbills

Roseate Spoonbill*
Ajaia ajaja

Family CICONIIDAE: Storks

Tribe LEPTOPTILINI: Jabiru, etc.

Jabiru (A)
Jabiru mycteria

Tribe MYCTERIINI: Wood Storks

Wood Stork*
Mycteria americana

Family CATHARTIDAE: American Vultures

Black Vulture*
Coragyps atratus

Turkey Vulture*
Cathartes aura

Order PHOENICOPTERIFORMES: Flamingos

Family PHOENICOPTERIDAE: Flamingos

Greater Flamingo (A)
Phoenicopterus ruber

Order ANSERIFORMES: Screamers, Swans, Geese and Ducks

Family ANATIDAE: Swans, Geese and Ducks

Subfamily ANSERINAE: Whistling-Ducks, Swans and Geese

Tribe DENDROCYGNINI: Whistling-Ducks

Fulvous Whistling-Duck*
Dendrocygna bicolor

Black-bellied Whistling-Duck*
Dendrocygna autumnalis

Tribe CYGNINI: Swans

Tundra Swan
Cygnus columbianus

Trumpeter Swan (A)
Cygnus buccinator

Tribe ANSERINI: Geese

Greater White-fronted Goose
Anser albifrons

Snow Goose
Chen caerulescens

Ross' Goose
Chen rossii

Brant (A)
Branta bernicla

Canada Goose
Branta canadensis

Subfamily ANATINAE:

Tribe CAIRININI: Muscovy Ducks and Allies

Muscovy Duck
Cairina moschata

Wood Duck*
Aix sponsa

Tribe ANATINI: Dabbling Ducks

Green-winged Teal
Anas crecca

American Black Duck (A)
Anas rubripes

Mottled Duck*
Anas fulvigula

Mallard*
Anas platyrhynchos

White-cheeked Pintail (A)
Anas bahamensis

Northern Pintail*
Anas acuta

Garganey (A)

Anas querquedula
Blue-winged Teal*
Anas discors
Cinnamon Teal*
Anas cyanoptera
Northern Shoveler*
Anas clypeata
Gadwall*
Anas strepera
Eurasian Wigeon (A)
Anas penelope
American Wigeon
Anas americana

Tribe AYTHYINI: Pochards and Allies

Canvasback
Aythya valisineria
Redhead*
Aythya americana
Ring-necked Duck
Aythya collaris
Greater Scaup
Aythya marila
Lesser Scaup
Aythya affinis

Tribe MERGINI: Eiders, Scoters, Mergansers and Allies

Harlequin Duck (A)
Histrionicus histrionicus
Oldsquaw
Clangula hyemalis
Black Scoter
Melanitta nigra
Surf Scoter
Melanitta perspicillata
White-winged Scoter
Melanitta fusca
Common Goldeneye
Bucephala clangula
Barrow's Goldeneye (A)
Bucephala islandica

Bufflehead
Bucephala albeola
Hooded Merganser*
Lophodytes cucullatus
Common Merganser
Mergus merganser
Red-breasted Merganser
Mergus serrator

Tribe OXYURINI: Stiff-tailed Ducks
Masked Duck* (A)
Nomonyx dominicus
Ruddy Duck*
Oxyura jamaicensis

Order FALCONIFORMES: Diurnal Birds of Prey

Family ACCIPITRIDAE: Kites, Eagles, Hawks and Allies.

Subfamily PANDIONINAE: Ospreys
Osprey*
Pandion haliaetus

Subfamily ACCIPITRINAE: Kites, Eagles Hawks and Allies
Hook-billed Kite*
Chondrohierax uncinatus
Swallow-tailed Kite*
Elanoides forticatus
White-tailed Kite*
Elanus leucurus
Snail Kite (A)
Rostrhamus sociabilis
Mississippi Kite*
Ictinia mississippiensis
Bald Eagle*
Haliaeetus leucocephalus
Northern Harrier*
Circus cyaneus
Sharp-shinned Hawk*
Accipiter striatus
Cooper's Hawk*
Accipiter cooperii

Northern Goshawk (A)
Accipiter gentilis
Crane Hawk (A)
Geranospiza caerulescens
Gray Hawk*
Asturina nitida
Common Black-Hawk*
Buteogallus anthracinus
Harris' Hawk*
Parabuteo unicinctus
Roadside Hawk (A)
Buteo magnirostris
Red-shouldered Hawk*
Buteo lineatus
Broad-winged Hawk*
Buteo platypterus
Short-tailed Hawk (A)
Buteo brachyurus
Swainson's Hawk*
Buteo swainsoni
White-tailed Hawk*
Buteo albicaudatus
Zone-tailed Hawk*
Buteo albonotatus
Red-tailed Hawk*
Buteo jamaicensis
Ferruginous Hawk*
Buteo regalis
Rough-legged Hawk
Buteo lagopus
Golden Eagle*
Aquila chrysaetos

Family FALCONIDAE: Caracaras and Falcons

Subfamily CARACARINAE: Caracaras
Crested Caracara*
Caracara plancus
Subfamily MICRASTURINAE: Forest-Falcons
Collared Forest-Falcon (A)
Micrastur semitorquatus

Subfamily FALCONINAE: True Falcons

Tribe FALCONINI: True Falcons

American Kestrel*
Falco sparverius

Merlin
Falco columbarius

Aplomado Falcon*
Falco femoralis

Prairie Falcon*
Falco mexicanus

Peregrine Falcon*
Falco peregrinus

Order GALLIFORMES: Gallinaceous Birds

Family CRACIDAE: Curassows and Guans

Plain Chachalaca*
Ortalis vetula

Family PHASIANIDAE: Partridges, Grouse, Turkeys and Quail

Subfamily PHASIANINAE: Partridges and Pheasants

Tribe PHASIANINI: Pheasants

Ring-necked Pheasant* (I)
Phasianus colchicus

Subfamily TETRAONINAE: Grouse

Greater Prairie-Chicken*
Tympanuchus cupido

Lesser Prairie-Chicken*
Tympanuchus pallidicinctus

Subfamily MELEAGRIDINAE: Turkeys

Wild Turkey*
Meleagris gallopavo

Family ODONTOPHORIDAE: Quail

Montezuma Quail*
Cyrtonyx montezumae

Northern Bobwhite*
Colinus virginianus

Scaled Quail*
Callipepla squamata

Gambel's Quail*
Callipepla gambelii

Order GRUIFORMES; Cranes, Rails and Allies
Family RALLIDAE: Rails, Gallinules and Coots

Subfamily RALLINAE: Rails, Gallinules and Coots
Yellow Rail
Coturnicops noveboracensis
Black Rail*
Laterallus jamaicensis
Clapper Rail*
Rallus longirostris
King Rail*
Rallus elegans
Virginia Rail
Rallus limicola
Sora
Porzana carolina
Paint-billed Crake (A)
Neocrex erythrops
Spotted Rail (A)
Pardirallus maculatus
Purple Gallinule*
Porphyrula martinica
Common Moorhen*
Gallinula chloropus
American Coot*
Fulica americana

Family GRUIDAE: Cranes

Subfamily GRUINAE: Typical Cranes
Sandhill Crane
Grus canadensis
Whooping Crane**
Grus americana

Order CHARADRIIFORMES: Shorebirds, Gulls, Auks and Allies
Family BURHINIDAE: Thick-knees

Double-striped Thick-knee (A)
Burhinus bistriatus

Family CHARADRIIDAE: Plovers and Lapwings

Subfamily CHARADRIINAE: Plovers

Black-bellied Plover
Pluvialis squatarola

American Golden-Plover
Pluvialis dominica

Collared Plover (A)
Charadrius collaris

Snowy Plover*
Charadrius alexandrinus

Wilson's Plover*
Charadrius wilsonia

Semipalmated Plover
Charadrius semipalmatus

Piping Plover
Charadrius melodus

Killdeer*
Charadrius vociferus

Mountain Plover*
Charadrius montanus

Family HAEMATOPODIDAE: Oystercatchers

American Oystercatcher*
Haematopus palliatus

Family RECURVIROSTRIDAE: Stilts and Avocets

Black-necked Stilt*
Himantopus mexicanus

American Avocet*
Recurvirostra americana

Family JACANIDAE: Jacanas

Northern Jacana* (A)
Jacana spinosa

Family SCOLOPACIDAE: Sandpipers, Phalaropes and Allies

Subfamily SCOLOPACINAE: Sandpipers and Allies

Tribe TRINGINI: Tringine Sandpipers

Greater Yellowlegs
Tringa melanoleuca

Lesser Yellowlegs
Tringa flavipes

Solitary Sandpiper
Tringa solitaria
Willet*
Catoptrophorus semipalmatus
Wandering Tattler (A)
Heteroscelus incanus
Spotted Sandpiper*
Actitus macularia

Tribe NUMENIINI: Curlews

Upland Sandpiper*
Bartramia longicauda
Eskimo Curlew (A)
Numenius borealis
Whimbrel
Numenius phaeopus
Long-billed Curlew*
Numenius americanus

Tribe LIMOSINI: Godwits

Hudsonian Godwit
Limosa haemastica
Marbled Godwit
Limosa fedoa

Tribe ARENARIINI: Turnstones

Ruddy Turnstone
Arenaria interpres

Tribe CALIDRIDINI: Calidridine Sandpipers

Surfbird (A)
Aphriza virgata
Red Knot
Calidris canutus
Sanderling
Calidris alba
Semipalmated Sandpiper
Calidris pusilla
Western Sandpiper
Calidris mauri
Red-necked Stint
Calidris ruficollis

Least Sandpiper
Calidris minutilla

White-rumped Sandpiper
Calidris fuscicollis

Baird's Sandpiper
Calidris bairdii

Pectoral Sandpiper
Calidris melanotos

Sharp-tailed Sandpiper (A)
Calidris acuminata

Purple Sandpiper (A)
Calidris maritima

Dunlin
Calidris alpina

Curlew Sandpiper (A)
Calidris ferruginea

Stilt Sandpiper
Calidris himantopus

Buff-breasted Sandpiper
Tryngites subruficollis

Ruff (A)
Philomachus pugnax

Tribe LIMNODROMINI: Dowitchers

Short-billed Dowitcher
Limnodromus griseus

Long-billed Dowitcher
Limnodromus scolopaceus

Tribe GALLINAGININI: Snipe

Common Snipe
Gallinago gallinago

Tribe SCOLOPACINI: Woodcocks

American Woodcock*
Scolopax minor

Subfamily PHALAROPODINAE: Phalaropes

Wilson's Phalarope*
Phalaropus tricolor

Red-necked Phalarope
Phalaropus lobatus
Red Phalarope (A)
Phalaropus fulicaria

Family LARIDAE: Skuas, Gulls, Terns and Skimmers

Subfamily STERCORARIINAE: Skuas and Jaegers

Pomarine Jaeger
Stercorarius pomarinus
Parasitic Jaeger
Stercorarius parasiticus
Long-tailed Jaeger (A)
Stercorarius longicaudus

Subfamily LARINAE: Gulls

Laughing Gull*
Larus atricilla
Franklin's Gull
Larus pipixcan
Little Gull (A)
Larus minutus
Black-headed Gull (A)
Larus ridibundus
Bonaparte's Gull
Larus philadelphia
Heermann's Gull (A)
Larus heermanni
Mew Gull (A)
Larus canus
Ring-billed Gull
Larus delawarensis
California Gull (A)
Larus californicus
Herring Gull
Larus argentatus
Thayer's Gull (A)
Larus thayeri
Iceland Gull (A)
Larus glaucoides
Lesser Black-backed Gull (A)
Larus fuscus

Slaty-backed Gull (A)
Larus schistisagus

Western Gull (A)
Larus occidentalis

Kelp Gull (A)
Larus dominicanus

Glaucous Gull (A)
Larus hyperboreus

Great Black-backed Gull (A)
Larus marinus

Black-legged Kittiwake (A)
Rissa tridactyla

Sabine's Gull (A)
Xema sabini

Subfamily STERNINAE: Terns

Gull-billed Tern*
Sterna nilotica

Caspian Tern*
Sterna caspia

Royal Tern*
Sterna maxima

Elegant Tern (A)
Sterna elegans

Sandwich Tern*
Sterna sandvicensis

Common Tern**
Sterna hirundo

Forster's Tern*
Sterna forsteri

Least Tern*
Sterna antillarum

Bridled Tern (A)
Sterna anaethetus

Sooty Tern*
Sterna fuscata

Black Tern
Chlidonias niger

Brown Noddy (A)
Anous stolidus

Black Noddy (A)
Anous minutus

Subfamily RYNCHOPINAE: Skimmers
Black Skimmer*
Rynchops niger

Order COLUMBIFORMES: Sandgrouse, Pigeons and Doves
Family COLUMBIDAE: Pigeons and Doves

Rock Dove* (I)
Columba livia

Red-billed Pigeon*
Columba flavirostris

Band-tailed Pigeon*
Columba fasciata

White-winged Dove*
Zenaida asiatica

Mourning Dove*
Zenaida macroura

Passenger Pigeon (E)
Ectopistes migratorius

Inca Dove*
Columbina inca

Common Ground-Dove*
Columbina passerina

Ruddy Ground-Dove (A)
Columbina talpacoti

White-tipped Dove*
Leptotila verreauxi

Ruddy Quail-Dove (A)
Geotrygon montana

Order PSITTACIFORMES: Parrots and Allies
Family PSITTACIDAE: Lories, Macaws and Parrots

Subfamily ARINAE: New World Parakeets, Macaws and Parrots
Monk Parakeet* (I)
Myiopsitta monachus

Carolina Parakeet (E)
Conuropsis carolinensis

Green Parakeet* (u)
Aratinga holochlora
Red-crowned Parrot* (u)
Amazona viridigenalis

Order CUCULIFORMES: Cuckoos and Allies

Family CUCULIDAE: Roadrunners and Anis

Subfamily COCCYZINAE: New World Cuckoos

Black-billed Cuckoo
Coccyzus erythropthalmus
Yellow-billed Cuckoo*
Coccyzus americanus
Mangrove Cuckoo (A)
Coccyzus minor

Subfamily NEOMORPHINAE: Ground-Cuckoos and Roadrunners

Greater Roadrunner*
Geococcyx californianus

Subfamily CROTOPHAGINAE: Anis

Groove-billed Ani*
Crotophaga sulcirostris

Order STRIGIFORMES: Owls

Family TYTONIDAE: Barn Owls

Barn Owl*
Tyto alba

Family STRIGIDAE: Typical Owls

Flammulated Owl*
Otus flammeolus
Eastern Screech-Owl*
Otus asio
Western Screech-Owl*
Otus kennicottii
Great Horned Owl*
Bubo virginianus
Snowy Owl (A)
Nyctea scandiaca
Northern Pygmy-Owl (A)
Glaucidium gnoma

Ferruginous Pygmy-Owl*
Glaucidium brasilianum
Elf Owl*
Micrathene whitneyi
Burrowing Owl*
Speotyto cunicularia
Mottled Owl (A)
Ciccaba virgata
Spotted Owl*
Strix occidentalis
Barred Owl*
Strix varia
Long-eared Owl*
Asio otus
Stygian Owl
Asio stygius
Short-eared Owl
Asio flammeus
Northern Saw-whet Owl* (A)
Aegolius acadicus

Order CAPRIMULGIFORMES: Goatsuckers, Oilbirds and Allies
Family CAPRIMULGIDAE: Goatsuckers

Subfamily CHORDEILINAE: Nighthawks
Lesser Nighthawk*
Chordeiles acutipennis
Common Nighthawk*
Chordeiles minor

Subfamily CAPRIMULGINAE: Nightjars
Pauraque*
Nyctidromus albicollis
Common Poorwill*
Phalaenoptilus nuttallii
Chuck-will's-widow*
Caprimulgus carolinensis
Whip-poor-will*
Caprimulgus vociferus

Order APODIFORMES: Swifts and Hummingbirds
Family APODIDAE: Swifts

Subfamily CYPSELOIDINAE: Cypseloidine Swifts
White-collared Swift (A)
Streptoprocne zonaris

Subfamily CHAETURINAE: Chaeturine Swifts
Chimney Swift*
Chaetura pelagica

Subfamily APODINAE: Apodine Swifts
White-throated Swift*
Aeronautes saxatalis

Family TROCHILIDAE: Hummingbirds

Green Violet-ear (A)
Colibri thalassinus

Green-breasted Mango (A)
Anthracothorax prevostii

Broad-billed Hummingbird* (A)
Cynanthus latirostris

White-eared Hummingbird (A)
Hylocharis leucotis

Buff-bellied Hummingbird*
Amazilia yucatanensis

Violet-crowned Hummingbird (A)
Amazilia violiceps

Blue-throated Hummingbird*
Lampornis clemenciae

Magnificent Hummingbird*
Eugenes fulgens

Lucifer Hummingbird*
Calothorax lucifer

Ruby-throated Hummingbird*
Archilochus colubris

Black-chinned Hummingbird*
Archilochus alexandri

Anna's Hummingbird*
Calypte anna

Costa's Hummingbird (A)
Calypte costae

Calliope Hummingbird
Stellula calliope
Broad-tailed Hummingbird*
Selasphorus platycercus
Rufous Hummingbird
Selasphorus rufus
Allen's Hummingbird (A)
Selasphorus sasin

Order TROGONIFORMES: Trogons
Family TROGONIDAE: Trogons
Elegant Trogon (A)
Trogon elegans

Order CORACIIFORMES: Kingfishers and Allies
Family ALCEDINIDAE: Kingfishers
Subfamily CERYLINAE: Typical Kingfishers
Ringed Kingfisher*
Ceryle torquata
Belted Kingfisher*
Ceryle alcyon
Green Kingfisher*
Chloroceryle americana

Order PICIFORMES: Puffbirds, Toucans, Woodpeckers and Allies
Family PICIDAE: Woodpeckers and Allies
Subfamily PICINAE: Woodpeckers
Lewis' Woodpecker (A)
Melanerpes lewis
Red-headed Woodpecker*
Melanerpes erythrocephalus
Acorn Woodpecker*
Melanerpes formicivorus
Golden-fronted Woodpecker*
Melanerpes aurifrons
Red-bellied Woodpecker*
Melanerpes carolinus
Yellow-bellied Sapsucker
Sphyrapicus varius

Red-naped Sapsucker
Sphyrapicus nuchalis

Williamson's Sapsucker
Sphyrapicus thyroideus

Ladder-backed Woodpecker*
Picoides scalaris

Downy Woodpecker*
Picoides pubescens

Hairy Woodpecker*
Picoides villosus

Red-cockaded Woodpecker*
Picoides borealis

Northern Flicker*
Colaptes auratus

Pileated Woodpecker*
Dryocopus pileatus

Ivory-billed Woodpecker** (e)
Campephilus principalis

Order PASSERIFORMES: Passerine Birds

Family TYRANNIDAE: Tyrant Flycatchers

Subfamily ELAENIINAE: Tyrannunlets, Elaenias and Allies

Northern Beardless-Tyrannulet*
Camptostoma imberbe

Greenish Elaenia (A)
Myiopagis viridicata

Subfamily FLUVICOLINAE: Fluvicoline Flycatchers

Tufted Flycatcher (A)
Mitrephanes phaeocercus

Olive-sided Flycatcher*
Contopus cooperi

Greater Pewee (A)
Contopus pertinax

Western Wood-Pewee*
Contopus sordidulus

Eastern Wood-Pewee*
Contopus virens

Yellow-bellied Flycatcher
Empidonax flaviventris

Acadian Flycatcher*
Empidonax virescens

Alder Flycatcher
Empidonax alnorum

Willow Flycatcher
Empidonax traillii

Least Flycatcher
Empidonax minimus

Hammond's Flycatcher
Empidonax hammondii

Dusky Flycatcher
Empidonax oberholseri

Gray Flycatcher*
Empidonax wrightii

Cordilleran Flycatcher*
Empidonax occidentalis

Black Phoebe*
Sayornis nigricans

Eastern Phoebe*
Sayornis phoebe

Say's Phoebe*
Sayornis saya

Vermilion Flycatcher*
Pyrocephalus rubinus

Subfamily TYRANNINAE: Tyrannine Flycatchers

Dusky-capped Flycatcher (A)
Myiarchus tuberculifer

Ash-throated Flycatcher*
Myiarchus cinerascens

Great Crested Flycatcher*
Myiarchus crinitus

Brown-crested Flycatcher*
Myiarchus tyrannulus

Great Kiskadee*
Pitangus sulphuratus

Sulphur-bellied Flycatcher* (A)
Myiodynastes luteiventris

Tropical Kingbird (A)
Tyrannus melancholicus

Couch's Kingbird*
Tyrannus couchii
Cassin's Kingbird*
Tyrannus vociferans
Thick-billed Kingbird (A)
Tyrannus crassirostris
Western Kingbird*
Tyrannus verticalis
Eastern Kingbird*
Tyrannus tyrannus
Gray Kingbird* (A)
Tyrannus dominicensis
Scissor-tailed Flycatcher*
Tyrannus forficatus
Fork-tailed Flycatcher (A)
Tyrannus savana
incertae sedis
Rose-throated Becard* (A)
Pachyramphus aglaiae
Masked Tityra (A)
Tityra semifasciata

Family LANIIDAE: Shrikes

Subfamily LANIINAE:Typical Shrikes
Northern Shrike
Lanius excubitor
Loggerhead Shrike*
Lanius ludovicianus

Family VIREONIDAE: Vireos

Subfamily VIREONINAE: Typical Vireos
White-eyed Vireo*
Vireo griseus
Bell's Vireo*
Vireo bellii
Black-capped Vireo*
Vireo atricapillus
Gray Vireo*
Vireo vicinior

Blue-headed Vireo*
Vireo solitarius

Cassin's Vireo
Vireo cassinii

Plumbeous Vireo
Vireo plumbeus

Yellow-throated Vireo*
Vireo flavifrons

Hutton's Vireo*
Vireo huttoni

Warbling Vireo*
Vireo gilvus

Philadelphia Vireo
Vireo philadelphicus

Red-eyed Vireo*
Vireo olivaceus

Yellow-green Vireo* (A)
Vireo flavoviridis

Black-whiskered Vireo (A)
Vireo altiloquus

Yucatan Vireo (A)
Vireo magister

Family CORVIDAE: Jays, Magpies and Crows

Steller's Jay*
Cyanocitta stelleri

Blue Jay*
Cyanocitta cristata

Green Jay*
Cyanocorax yncas

Brown Jay*
Cyanocorax morio

Western Scrub-Jay*
Aphelocoma californica

Mexican Jay*
Aphelocoma ultramarina

Pinyon Jay
Gymnorhinus cyanocephalus

Clark's Nutcracker (A)
Nucifraga columbiana

Black-billed Magpie (A)
Pica pica
American Crow*
Corvus brachyrhynchos
Tamaulipas Crow
Corvus imparatus
Fish Crow*
Corvus ossifragus
Chihuahuan Raven*
Corvus cryptoleucus
Common Raven*
Corvus corax

Family ALAUDIDAE: Larks

Horned Lark*
Eremophila alpestris

Family HIRUNDINIDAE: Swallows

Subfamily HIRUNDININAE:Typical Swallows
Purple Martin*
Progne subis
Gray-breasted Martin (A)
Progne chalybea
Tree Swallow**
Tachycineta bicolor
Violet-green Swallow*
Tachycineta thalassina
Northern Rough-winged Swallow*
Stelgidopteryx serripennis
Bank Swallow*
Riparia riparia
Barn Swallow*
Hirundo rustica
Cliff Swallow*
Petrochelidon pyrrhonota
Cave Swallow*
Petrochelidon fulva

Family PARIDAE: Titmice

Carolina Chickadee*
Poecile carolinensis

A Checklist of Texas Birds

Black-capped Chickadee (A)
Poecile atricapillus
Mountain Chickadee*
Poecile gambeli
Juniper Titmouse*
Baeolophus ridgwayi
Tufted Titmouse*
Baeolophus bicolor

Family REMIZIDAE: Penduline Tits and Verdins
Verdin*
Auriparus flaviceps

Family AEGITHALIDAE: Long-tailed Tits and Bushtits
Bushtit*
Psaltriparus minimus

Family SITTIDAE: Nuthatches

Subfamily SITTINAE: Typical Nuthatches
Red-breasted Nuthatch
Sitta canadensis
White-breasted Nuthatch*
Sitta carolinensis
Pygmy Nuthatch*
Sitta pygmaea
Brown-headed Nuthatch*
Sitta pusilla

Family CERTHIIDAE: Creepers

Subfamily CERTHIINAE: Typical Creepers
Brown Creeper*
Certhia americana

Family TROGLODYTIDAE: Wrens
Cactus Wren*
Campylorhynchus brunneicapillus
Rock Wren*
Salpinctes obsoletus
Canyon Wren*
Catherpes mexicanus
Carolina Wren*
Thryothorus ludovicianus

Bewick's Wren*
Thryomanes bewickii
House Wren*
Troglodytes aedon
Winter Wren
Troglodytes troglodytes
Sedge Wren
Cistothorus platensis
Marsh Wren*
Cistothorus palustris

Family CINCLIDAE: Dippers

American Dipper (A)
Cinclus mexicanus

Family REGULIDAE: Kinglets

Golden-crowned Kinglet
Regulus satrapa
Ruby-crowned Kinglet
Regulus calendula

Family SYLVIIDAE: Gnatcatchers and Allies

Tribe POLIOPTILINI: Gnatcatchers
Blue-gray Gnatcatcher*
Polioptila caerulea
Black-tailed Gnatcatcher*
Polioptila melanura

Family TURDIDAE: Solitaires, Thrushes and Allies

Northern Wheatear (A)
Oenanthe oenanthe
Eastern Bluebird*
Sialia sialis
Western Bluebird*
Sialia mexicana
Mountain Bluebird
Sialia currucoides
Townsend's Solitaire
Myadestes townsendi
Orange-billed Nightingale-Thrush
Catharus aurantiirostris

Veery
  Catharus fuscescens
Gray-cheeked Thrush
  Catharus minimus
Swainson's Thrush
  Catharus ustulatus
Hermit Thrush*
  Catharus guttatus
Wood Thrush*
  Hylocichla mustelina
Clay-colored Robin* (A)
  Turdus grayi
White-throated Robin (A)
  Turdus assimilis
Rufous-backed Robin (A)
  Turdus rufopalliatus
American Robin*
  Turdus migratorius
Varied Thrush (A)
  Ixoreus naevius
Aztec Thrush (A)
  Ridgwayia pinicola

Family MIMIDAE: Mockingbirds, Thrashers, etc.

Gray Catbird*
  Dumetella carolinensis
Black Catbird (A)
  Melanoptila glabrirostris
Northern Mockingbird*
  Mimus polyglottos
Sage Thrasher
  Oreoscoptes montanus
Brown Thrasher*
  Toxostoma rufum
Long-billed Thrasher*
  Toxostoma longirostre
Curve-billed Thrasher*
  Toxostoma curvirostre
Crissal Thrasher*
  Toxostoma crissale

Family STURNIDAE: Starlings and Allies
Subfamily STURNINAE:
European Starling* (I)
Sturnus vulgaris

Family MOTACILLIDAE: Wagtails and Pipits
American Pipit
Anthus rubescens
Sprague's Pipit
Anthus spragueii

Family BOMBYCILLIDAE: Waxwings
Bohemian Waxwing (A)
Bombycilla garrulus
Cedar Waxwing
Bombycilla cedrorum

Family PTILOGONATIDAE: Silky-flycatchers
Gray Silky-flycatcher (A)
Ptilogonys cinereus
Phainopepla*
Phainopepla nitens

Family PEUCEDRAMIDAE:
Olive Warbler (A)
Peucedramus taeniatus

Family PARULIDAE: Wood-Warblers
Blue-winged Warbler
Vermivora pinus
Golden-winged Warbler
Vermivora chrysoptera
Tennessee Warbler
Vermivora peregrina
Orange-crowned Warbler
Vermivora celata
Nashville Warbler
Vermivora ruficapilla
Virginia's Warbler*
Vermivora virginiae
Colima Warbler*
Vermivora crissalis

Lucy's Warbler*
Vermivoras luciae
Northern Parula*
Parula americana
Tropical Parula*
Parula pitiayumi
Yellow Warbler*
Dendroica petechia
Chestnut-sided Warbler
Dendroica pensylvanica
Magnolia Warbler
Dendroica magnolia
Cape May Warbler
Dendroica tigrina
Black-throated Blue Warbler
Dendroica caerulescens
Yellow-rumped Warbler*
Dendroica coronata
Black-throated Gray Warbler
Dendroica nigrescens
Townsend's Warbler
Dendroica townsendi
Hermit Warbler
Dendroica occidentalis
Black-throated Green Warbler
Dendroica virens
Golden-cheeked Warbler*
Dendroica chrysoparia
Blackburnian Warbler
Dendroica fusca
Yellow-throated Warbler*
Dendroica dominica
Grace's Warbler*
Dendroica graciae
Pine Warbler*
Dendroica pinus
Prairie Warbler*
Dendroica discolor

Palm Warbler
Dendroica palmarum
Bay-breasted Warbler
Dendroica castanea
Blackpoll Warbler
Dendroica striata
Cerulean Warbler*
Dendroica cerulea
Black-and-white Warbler*
Mniotilta varia
American Redstart*
Setophaga ruticilla
Prothonotary Warbler*
Protonotaria citrea
Worm-eating Warbler*
Helmitheros vermivorus
Swainson's Warbler*
Limnothlypis swainsonii
Ovenbird
Seiurus aurocapillus
Northern Waterthrush
Seiurus noveboracensis
Louisiana Waterthrush*
Seiurus motacilla
Kentucky Warbler*
Oporornis formosus
Connecticut Warbler (A)
Oporornis agilis
Mourning Warbler
Oporornis philadelphia
MacGillivray's Warbler
Oporornis tolmiei
Common Yellowthroat*
Geothlypis trichas
Gray-crowned Yellowthroat* (A)
Geothlypis poliocephala
Hooded Warbler*
Wilsonia citrina
Wilson's Warbler
Wilsonia pusilla

Canada Warbler
Wilsonia canadensis
Red-faced Warbler (A)
Cardellina rubrifrons
Painted Redstart*
Myioborus pictus
Golden-crowned Warbler (A)
Basileuterus culicivorus
Rufous-capped Warbler (A)
Basileuterus rufifrons
Yellow-breasted Chat*
Icteria virens

Family THRAUPIDAE: Tanagers

Tribe THRAUPINI: Typical Tanagers
Hepatic Tanager*
Piranga flava
Summer Tanager*
Piranga rubra
Scarlet Tanager
Piranga olivacea
Western Tanager*
Piranga ludoviciana
Flame-colored Tanager
Piranga bidentata

Family EMBERIZIDAE: Emberizines

White-collared Seedeater*
Sporophila torqueola
Yellow-faced Grassquit (A)
Tiaris olivacea
Olive Sparrow*
Arremonops refivirgatus
Green-tailed Towhee*
Pipilo chlorurus
Eastern Towhee
Pipilo erythrophthalmus
Spotted Towhee*
Pipilo maculatus
Canyon Towhee*
Pipilo fuscus

Bachman's Sparrow*
Aimophila aestivalis
Botteri's Sparrow*
Aimophila botterii
Cassin's Sparrow*
Aimophila cassinii
Rufous-crowned Sparrow*
Aimophila ruficeps
American Tree Sparrow
Spizella arborea
Chipping Sparrow*
Spizella passerina
Clay-colored Sparrow
Spizella pallida
Brewer's Sparrow**
Spizella breweri
Field Sparrow*
Spizella pusilla
Black-chinned Sparrow*
Spizella atrogularis
Vesper Sparrow**
Pooecetes gramineus
Lark Sparrow*
Chondestes grammacus
Black-throated Sparrow*
Amphispiza bilineata
Sage Sparrow
Amphispiza belli
Lark Bunting*
Calamospiza melanocorys
Savannah Sparrow
Passerculus sandwichensis
Baird's Sparrow (A)
Ammodramus bairdii
Grasshopper Sparrow*
Ammodramus savannarum
Henslow's Sparrow*
Ammodramus henslowii
LeConte's Sparrow
Ammodramus leconteii

Saltmarsh Sharp-tailed Sparrow
Ammodramus caudacutus

Nelson's Sharp-tailed Sparrow
Ammodramus nelsoni

Seaside Sparrow*
Ammodramus maritimus

Fox Sparrow*
Passerella iliaca

Song Sparrow
Melospiza melodia

Lincoln's Sparrow
Melospiza lincolnii

Swamp Sparrow
Melospiza georgiana

White-throated Sparrow
Zonotrichia albicollis

Harris' Sparrow
Zonotrichia querula

White-crowned Sparrow
Zonotrichia lencophrys

Golden-crowned Sparrow (A)
Zonotrichia atricapilla

Dark-eyed Junco*
Junco hyemalis

Yellow-eyed Junco (A)
Junco phaeonotus

McCown's Longspur
Calcarius mccownii

Lapland Longspur
Calcarius lapponicus

Smith's Longspur
Calcarius pictus

Chestnut-collared Longspur
Calcarius ornatus

Snow Bunting (A)
Plectrophenax nivalis

Family CARDINALIDAE: Cardinals, Grosbeaks and Allies

Crimson-collared Grosbeak (A)
Rhodothraupis celaeno

Northern Cardinal*
Cardinalis cardinalis
Pyrrhuloxia*
Cardinalis sinuatus
Rose-breasted Grosbeak
Pheucticus ludovicianus
Black-headed Grosbeak*
Pheucticus melanocephalus
Blue Bunting (A)
Cyanocompsa parellina
Blue Grosbeak*
Guiraca caerulea
Lazuli Bunting*
Passerina amoena
Indigo Bunting*
Passerina cyanea
Varied Bunting*
Passerina versicolor
Painted Bunting*
Passerina ciris
Dickcissel*
Spiza americana

Family ICTERIDAE: Icterines

Tribe DOLICHONYCHINI: Bobolinks

Bobolink
Dolichonyx oryzivorus

Tribe AGELAIINI: Blackbirds, Meadowlarks and Allies

Red-winged Blackbird*
Agelaius phoeniceus
Eastern Meadowlark*
Sturnella magna
Western Meadowlark*
Sturnella neglecta
Yellow-headed Blackbird*
Xanthocephalus xanthocephalus
Rusty Blackbird
Euphagus carolinus
Brewer's Blackbird*
Euphagus cyanocephalus

Common Grackle*
Quiscalus quiscula
Boat-tailed Grackle*
Quiscalus major
Great-tailed Grackle*
Quiscalus mexicanus
Shiny Cowbird (A)
Molothrus bonariensis
Bronzed Cowbird*
Molothrus aeneus
Brown-headed Cowbird*
Molothrus ater

Tribe ICTERINI: American Orioles and Allies

Black-vented Oriole (A)
Icterus wagleri
Orchard Oriole*
Icterus spurius
Hooded Oriole*
Icterus cucullatus
Altamira Oriole*
Icterus gularis
Audubon's Oriole*
Icterus graduacauda
Baltimore Oriole*
Icterus galbula
Bullock's Oriole*
Icterus bullockii
Scott's Oriole*
Icterus parisorum

Family FRINGILLIDAE: Fringilline and Cardueline Finches

Subfamily CARDUELINAE: Cardueline Finches

Pine Grosbeak (A)
Pinicola enucleator
Purple Finch
Carpodacus purpureus
Cassin's Finch
Carpodacus cassinii
House Finch*
Carpodacus mexicanus

Red Crossbill*
Loxia curvirostra
White-winged Crossbill (A)
Loxia leucoptera
Common Redpoll (A)
Carduelis flammea
Pine Siskin*
Carduelis pinus
Lesser Goldfinch*
Carduelis psaltria
Lawrence's Goldfinch (A)
Carduelis lawrencei
American Goldfinch*
Carduelis tristis
Evening Grosbeak
Coccothraustes vespertinus

Family PASSERIDAE: Old World Sparrows

House Sparrow* (I)
Passer domesticus

PRESUMPTIVE LIST

The following is the official TBRC list of species for which written descriptions of sight records have been accepted by the TBRC but the species has not yet met the requirements for full acceptance on the Texas list (specimen, photograph, or tape recording).

White-crowned Pigeon
Columba leucocephala
Berylline Hummingbird
Amazilia beryllina
Social Flycatcher
Myiozetetes similis
Crescent-chested Warbler
Parula superciliosa
Slate-throated Redstart
Myioborus miniatus

The following species have had records submitted to the TBRC that are currently pending. These will represent new species on the main Texas List if accepted.

Black-capped Petrel
Pterodroma hasitata

Roseate Tern
Sterna dougallii

Arctic Tern
Sterna paradisaea

Eurasian Collared-Dove
Streptopelia decaocto

Dark-billed Cuckoo
Coccyzus melacoryphus

Amazon Kingfisher
Chloroceryle amazona

Red-breasted Sapsucker
Sphyrapicus ruber

The following species have had reports submitted to the TBRC for evaluation. The documentation on these is variable and some or all may not be accepted. All are currently still pending. These will represent new species on the Presumptive List if accepted.

Black Swift
Cypseloides niger

2

Scientific Bird Collections in Texas

The following is a list of museums, institutions, and other locations of study skins, skeletons preserved in fluid, mounted birds, and egg set collections in Texas. These collections are maintained primarily for research by biologists; however, they are also very useful to persons interested in identification and variations within species. The collections are listed in alphabetical order by city.

Abilene

Abilene Christian University, Abilene, TX 79699. Fifty skins, 6 skeletons, 15 in fluid, 6 mounted. Collection available to interested persons by prearrangement. Contact Thomas E. Lee, Jr. Local area and Taylor County best represented, with 30 Texas species.

McMurry University, Abilene, TX 79697. 46 skins. Collection available to interested persons by prearrangement. Contact Dr. C. W. Beasley. Taylor County best represented with approximately 25 Texas species.

Austin

The University of Texas, Texas Natural History Collection, 10100 Burnet Road, PRC176E. R4000, Austin, TX 78758. 1,750 skins, 50 mounted, 500 egg sets. Collection available for research purposes (otherwise by exception). Contact Carol K. Malcolm. Southwest United States and Northern Mexico best represented with approximately 296 Texas species.

Big Bend

Big Bend National Park, TX 79834. 286 skins, 2 egg sets. Collection available to interested persons. Contact Raymond Skiles. Big Bend National Park best represented with 324 Texas species.

Canyon

West Texas A&M University, Dept. of Life, Earth & Environmental Sciences, Canyon, TX 79015. About 1,000 skins, 30 mounted birds. Collection available to interested persons by prearrangement. Contact Dr. Kathleen Blair.

College Station

Texas A&M University, Department of Wildlife and Fisheries Sciences, College Station TX, 77843. 12,101 skins, 738 skeletons, 272 in fluid, two mounted, about 300 egg sets. Collection available to interested persons by prearrangement. Contact Dr. K. A. Arnold [kaarnold@tamu.edu] or Dr. George D. Baumgardner, [g-baumgardner@tamu.edu], (409) 845-5777. Texas (7,983 specimens) and Mexico (3,263 specimens) best represented in collection, with majority of remainder from Southwestern United States and Central America.

Corpus Christi

Corpus Christi Museum, 1900 North Chaparral, Corpus Christi, TX 78401. 1,341 skins, 10 entire skeletons, 40 skulls only, five in fluid, 107 mounted, 3,301 egg sets, 703 nests. Collection available to interested persons by prearrangement. Contact Curator, Jane E. Deisler-Seno, (512) 883-2862, Tuesday-Saturday. The South and Central Coasts of Texas are best represented with approximately 220 Texas species.

Dallas

Dallas Museum of Natural History, P.O. Box 150349, Dallas, TX 75315. 7,000 skins, 1,000 mounted, 400 egg sets. Collection available to interested persons by prearrangement. Contact Collection Manager. Texas is best represented in the collection with approximately 525 Texas species.

El Paso

Centennial Museum, The University of Texas at El Paso, El Paso, TX 79968. 126 mounted skins, 662 study skins, 830 skeletons, 798 partial skeletons, 10 in alcohol, 693 egg sets. Collection available for study by appointment. Contact Scott Cutler, Curator of Collections and Exhibits, (915) 747-6668, e-mail: scutler@utep.edu; or Arthur H. Harris, Director, Laboratory for Environmental Biology,

(915) 747-6985 or 6835, e-mail aharris@utep.edu. Area represented is mainly Trans-Pecos Texas and southern New Mexico.

Fort Worth

Fort Worth Museum of Science and History, 1501 Montgomery Street, Fort Worth, TX 76107. 1,770 skins (100 African), 3 skeletons, 300 mounted, 150 egg sets, 30 nests, 150 teaching specimens in tubes, 50 mounted specimens on permanent public display. Collection available to interested persons by prearrangement. Contact William J. Voss, Curator. Texas and Southwest best represented with approximately 80 percent Texas species.

Huntsville

Sam Houston State University, Dept. of Biological Sciences, Huntsville, TX 77341. 1,300 skins, 10 skeletons, 65 mounted. Also, approximately 300 species of recorded birds in Sound Library. Collection available to interested persons by prearrangement. Contact Ralph R. Moldenhauer. East Texas best represented with approximately 300 Texas species.

Irving

University of Dallas, Department of Biology, Irving, TX 75062. About 500 skins. Collection available Monday–Friday to scientists or interested persons doing special studies (only when curator present). Contact Warren Pulich, (214) 721-5307. North Central Texas best represented.

Lubbock

Museum of Texas Tech University, Lubbock, TX 79409. 3,500 skins, 425 skeletons, 400 in fluid, 25 mounted, 30 egg sets. Collection available to interested persons by prearrangement. Contact Dr. Richard Monk. Northwest Texas best represented with approximately 290 Texas species.

Nacogdoches

Stephen F. Austin State University, Department of Biology, Box 3003, Nacogdoches, TX 75961. 3,150 skins, 15 mounted birds. Collection available to interested persons by prearrangement. Contact Brent Burt. East Texas best represented with approximately 375 Texas species.

Sinton

Welder Wildlife Foundation, Drawer 1400, Sinton, TX 78387. 2,500 skins, 4,000 egg sets. Collection available to interested persons by prearrangemment. Contact Selma Glasscock, Conservation Educator/Curator. South Texas well represented with approximately 500 Texas species.

Stephenville

Tarleton State College, Stephenville, TX 76402. 50 skins. Collection available to interested persons by prearrangement. Contact P. D. Sudman. North Central Texas best represented with 25 Texas species.

Waco

Baylor University, Strecker Museum, Waco, TX 76798. 1,581 skins, 40 skeletons, 269 mounted, 1,839 egg sets and nests. Collection available to interested persons by prearrangement. Contact Calvin B. Smith, Director, (817) 755-1110. Texas best represented with approximately 200 Texas species.

Wichita Falls

Midwestern State University, Department of Biology, Wichita Falls, TX 76308. 300 skins, 10 skeletons. Collection available to interested persons by prearrangement. Contact Dr. Frederick B. Stangl, Jr. North Central Texas best represented.

3

The Texas Cooperative Wildlife Collections

The Texas Cooperative Wildlife Collections are housed in the Department of Wildlife and Fisheries Sciences, Texas A&M University, College Station. Dr. Keith A. Arnold is Curator of Birds. The bird collection contains more than 13,300 specimens, mostly study skins. A large portion of the bird specimens added each year results from salvage efforts. Most of the other birds added are collected in relation to research efforts.

This collection not only includes a wide representation of Texas birds, but also significant holdings from Colorado, Mexico, and, to a lesser extent, other parts of the world. Most orders and a large number of families of birds are represented.

The collections are open to the public. However, to facilitate visits, the curator should be contacted in advance for arrangements. Since special permits are necessary to hold bird specimens, even salvaged birds, persons interested in donating such specimens to the collecton should arrange this with those persons holding the necessary permits or through local game wardens. Dr. Arnold will furnish names of such persons upon request. The Texas Photo-Record file, with over 1,300 entries, is maintained as part of the Texas Cooperative Wildlife Collections. The file contains photographs of rare and unusual bird records (usually distributional records) that are important to Texas ornithology. Such records may include first documentation for a multi-county area, a bird that is on the Rare Bird of Texas Master List of Review Species of the Texas Bird Records Committee, first breeding record for an area, etc. Persons wishing to submit a photograph should consult Oberholser's *The Bird Life of Texas* to establish the worthiness of the record and should then submit photographs and as many details as possible, such as locality, date, who discovered, who identified, who photographed, weather conditions, and any other pertinent details. If desired, the sender can also send the type of camera, film, f-stop and speed, and lens. In the instance of a very rare or unusual record, it would be best to submit a completed Texas Ornithological Society Verifying Document of an Unusual Record, a form available from Dr. Arnold.

Photographs may be submitted in color or black-and-white, as slides, prints or movies; prints should not exceed 8 × 10 inches. Copies of the current contents of the file may be obtained from Dr. Arnold for $10.00 to cover printing and mailing. Make checks payable to the Department of Wildlife and Fisheries Sciences, Texas A&M University, College Station, TX 77843, (409) 862-3285.

4

The Texas Bird Sound Library

The Texas Bird Sound Library was established in 1979 and is housed in the Dept. of Biological Sciences at Sam Houston State University, Huntsville, Texas. The purpose of the library is to provide a depository for recorded bird sounds available to researchers, educators and the general public. The collection contains over 1,000 recordings of individual bird songs, calls, and other sounds for about 300 species. The Sound Library is primarily a Texas library. Most of the recordings are of Texas birds and include eastern as well as western species. However, birds recorded in other states and Mexico are also represented.

The major objectives of the library are:

1. To establish a collection of Texas bird songs, calls and other sounds that, with adequate corresponding data, will be made available to research scientists, educators and other persons interested in bird acoustics.

2. To serve as a repository for recorded bird sounds resulting from completed individual research projects. The recordings are catalogued on computer and properly stored so that they will be available for future use.

3. To establish a Texas Bird Sound Record File for documentation of unusual species, state records or declining species.

4. To provide audiospectrographs or sonagrams of bird sounds for those who are in need of such information but do not have access to an audiospectrograph. A sonagram provides a three-dimensional picture of frequency, time and amplitude of the bird sound, which then can be analyzed qualitatively and quantitatively.

Research scientists, educators and other persons interested in bird acoustics are encouraged to use as well as contribute to the library.

For further information contact Ralph R. Moldenhauer, Ph.D., Dept. of Biological Sciences, Sam Houston State University, Huntsville, TX 77341 (409) 294-1548.

5

Selected References

Bull, John and John Farrand, Jr., *The Audubon Society Field Guide to North American Birds, Eastern Region*, New York, NY: Alfred A. Knopf, Inc., 1977.

Checklist of the Birds of Texas, Third Edition, Texas Ornithological Society, 1995.

Check-list of North American Birds, Sixth Edition, American Ornithologists' Union, Washington, 1983.

Davis, L. Irby, *A Field Guide to the Birds of Mexico and Central America,* Austin, TX: University of Texas Press, 1972.

Elwonger, Mark, *Finding Birds on the Central Texas Coast,* 1995.

Farrand, John, Jr., Editor, *The Audubon Society Master Guide to Birding,* New York, NY: Alfred A. Knopf, Inc., 1983. Three Volumes.

Holt, Harold R., *A Birder's Guide to the Rio Grande Valley of Texas,* Colorado Springs, CO: American Birding Association, 1992.

Kutac, Edward A. and S. Christopher Caran, *Birds and Other Wildlife of South Central Texas,* Austin, TX: University of Texas Press, 1994.

Lane, James A., John Tveten, Harold R. Holt, *A Birder's Guide to the Texas Coast,* Denver, CO: L & P Press, 1984.

National Geographic Society, *Field Guide to Birds of North America, Second Edition,* Washington, DC: National Geographic Society, 1987.

Oberholser, Harry C. and Edgar B. Kincaid, Jr., *The Bird Life of Texas,* Austin, TX: University of Texas Press, 1974.

Peterson, Roger Tory, *A Field Guide to the Birds of Texas and Adjacent States,* Boston, MA: Houghton Mifflin Co., 1963.

Peterson, Roger Tory, *A Field Guide to the Western Birds, Third Edition,* Boston, MA: Houghton Mifflin Co., 1990.

Peterson, Roger Tory, *A Field Guide to the Birds, Fourth Edition,* Boston, MA: Houghton Mifflin Co., 1980.

Peterson, Roger Tory and Chalif, Edward L., *A Field Guide to Mexican Birds,* Boston, MA: Houghton Mifflin Co., 1973.

Peterson, Roger Tory, et al., *A Field Guide to Bird Songs* (Phonograph records keyed by page number to *A Field Guide to the Birds [eastern], Second edition.* Also available on cassettes.), Boston, MA: Houghton Mifflin Co.

Peterson, Roger Tory, et al., *A Field Guide to Western Bird Songs* (Phonograph records keyed by page to *A Field Guide to Western Birds, Third revised edition*. Also available on cassettes.), Boston, MA: Houghton Mifflin Co.

Pulich, Warren M., *Birds of Tarrant County, 2nd edition, 1979*.

Pulich, Warren M., *The Birds of North Central Texas*, College Station, TX: Texas A&M University Press, 1988.

Rappole, John H. and Gene W. Blacklock, *Birds of the Texas Coastal Bend*, Abundance and Distribution, College Station, TX: Texas A&M University Press, 1985.

Rappole, John H. and Gene W. Blacklock, *A Field Guide, Birds of Texas*, College Station, TX: Texas A&M University Press, 1994.

Robbins, C., et al., *Birds of North America: A Guide to Field Identification*, revised edition, New York, NY: Golden Press, 1983.

Stokes, Donald and Lillian, *Stokes Field Guide to Birds, Eastern Region*, Boston, MA: Little, Brown and Company, 1996.

Stokes, Donald and Lillian, *Stokes Field Guide to Birds, Western Region*, Boston, MA: Little, Brown and Company, 1996.

Texas Parks and Wildlife Department, (Kelly Bryan, Tony Gallucci, Greg Lasley, Mark Lockwood, David H. Riskind), *A Checklist of Texas Birds, 4th Edition*, Technical Series No. 32, Austin, TX: Texas Parks and Wildlife Press.

Udvardy, Miklas D.F. *The Audubon Society Field Guide to North American Birds: Western Region*, New York, NY: Alfred A. Knopf, Inc., 1977.

Wauer, Roland H., *A Field Guide to Birds of the Big Bend, Second Edition*, Houston, TX: Gulf Publishing Company, 1996.

Unique Wildlife Ecosystems of Texas, U.S. Fish and Wildlife Service, 1979.

Index of Birds

Hooded, 23, 71, 75, 99, 124, 145,
219, 235, 318
Red-breasted, 48, 75, 82, 84, 100,
138, 148, 197, 219, 225, 228,
258, 260, 261, 318
Merlin, 14, 25, 26, 30, 48, 80, 150,
186, 289, 307, 320
Mockingbird
Northern, xvii, xviii, 149, 339
Moorhen
Common, 10, 52, 135, 146, 152,
171, 200, 220, 229, 237, 243,
244, 256, 262, 294, 305, 321
Night-Heron
Black-crowned, 73, 129, 131, 200,
216, 220, 229, 231, 232, 235,
239, 257, 314
Yellow-crowned, 73, 129, 145,
194, 203, 216, 220, 239, 276,
315
Nighthawk
Common, xvii, 21, 70, 117, 329
Lesser, 35, 38, 52, 59, 112, 117,
270, 273, 278, 287, 305, 329
Nightingale-Thrush
Orange-billed, 306, 338
Noddy
Black, 327
Brown, 326
Nutcracker
Clark's, 47, 335
Nuthatch
Brown-headed, 181, 183, 188, 192,
194, 200, 205, 206, 216, 337
Pygmy, 29, 50, 54, 337
Red-breasted, 9, 54, 88, 144, 153,
159, 175, 196, 275, 337
White-breasted, 9, 33, 44, 46, 54,
123, 159, 169, 181, 191, 194,
196, 205, 337
Oldsquaw, 21, 138, 183, 219, 228,
288, 317

Oriole
Altamira, 283, 293, 295, 300, 301,
347
Audubon's, 283, 285, 292, 293,
299, 300, 301, 347
Baltimore, 6, 7, 128, 129, 153,
158, 161, 166, 234, 306, 347
Black-vented, 36, 347
Bullock's, 7, 9, 14, 24, 35, 42, 52,
57, 61, 66, 71, 80, 83, 95,
158, 161, 164, 166, 274, 347
Hooded, 35, 42, 52, 109, 111, 117,
278, 285, 287, 290, 347
Orchard, 7, 12, 35, 80, 83, 100,
102, 110, 129, 149, 153, 158,
161, 164, 168, 192, 234, 237,
274, 347
Scott's, 35, 36, 38, 42, 50, 52, 55,
59, 109, 110, 111, 115, 347
Osprey, 16, 25, 58, 99, 100, 146, 149,
166, 167, 172, 173, 186, 222,
234, 278, 318
Ovenbird, 145, 230, 342
Owl
Barn, 21, 59, 168, 220, 242, 267,
295, 298, 328
Barred, 6, 82, 129, 145, 148, 153,
159, 163, 173, 175, 177, 178,
188, 205, 215, 216, 237, 239,
243, 249, 251, 329
Burrowing, 3, 10, 12, 14, 18, 24,
52, 57, 59, 80, 85, 230, 329
Elf, 35, 38, 76, 295, 298, 329
Flammulated, 29, 33, 50, 54, 56,
328
Great Horned, 21, 77, 86, 129,
132, 159, 163, 165, 168, 173,
242, 287, 328
Long-eared, 12, 14, 21, 80, 84, 329
Mottled, 329
Northern Saw-whet, 50, 56, 329
Short-eared, 21, 150, 156, 221,
242, 244, 329

Index of Locations